MINORITY AGING

Recent Titles in Contributions in Ethnic Studies
Series Editor: Leonard W. Doob

Nations Remembered: An Oral History of the Five Civilized Tribes, 1865–1907
Theda Perdue

Operation Wetback: The Mass Deportation of Mexican Undocumented Workers in 1954
Juan Ramon García

The Navajo Nation
Peter Iverson

An Unacknowledged Harmony: Philo-Semitism and the Survival of European Jewry
Alan Edelstein

America's Ethnic Politics
Joseph S. Roucek and Bernard Eisenberg, editors

Minorities and the Military: A Cross-National Study in World Perspective
Warren L. Young

The Emergence of Ethnicity: Cultural Groups and Social Conflict in Israel
Eliezer Ben-Rafael

MINORITY AGING

Sociological and Social Psychological Issues

Edited by Ron C. Manuel

CONTRIBUTIONS IN ETHNIC STUDIES, NUMBER 8

GREENWOOD PRESS
Westport, Connecticut • London, England

Library of Congress Cataloging in Publication Data
Main entry under title:

Minority aging.

(Contributions in ethnic studies, ISSN 0196-7088;
no. 8)
Bibliography: p.
Includes index.
1. Minority aged — United States — Addresses, essays,
lectures. 2. Minority aged — Services for — United States
— Addresses, essays, lectures. 3. Afro-American aged —
United States — Addresses, essays, lectures. 4. Ethnic
relations — Addresses, essays, lectures. I. Manuel,
Ron C. II. Series.
HQ1064.U5M55   305.26   82-930
ISBN 0-313-22541-9 (lib. bdg.)   AACR2

Library of Congress Catalog Card Number: 82-930
ISBN: 0-313-22541-9
ISSN: 0196-7088

First published in 1982

Greenwood Press
A division of Congressional Information Service, Inc.
88 Post Road West
Westport, Connecticut 06881

Printed in the United States of America

10 9 8 7 6 5 4 3 2 1

To
the successful aging of all Americans

CONTENTS

PERSONAL NEEDS AND SOCIAL POLICY

SERVICE DELIVERY AND UTILIZATION

**Part 5:   Theoretical Orientations and the Study of the
Minority Aged**

**Part 6:   Research Methodology and the Study of the
Minority Aged**

     and Potentials
     Linda Burton, Vern L. Bengtson   215

24. Measuring Age and Sociocultural Change: The Case of
     Race and Life Satisfaction
     K. Warner Schaie, Stan Orchowsky, Iris A. Parham   223

25. The Dimensions of Ethnic Minority Identification: An
     Exploratory Analysis Among Elderly Black Americans
     Ron C. Manuel   231

     References   249

     Index   273

     Contributing Authors   283

TABLES

SERIES FOREWORD

"Contributions in Ethnic Studies" focuses upon the problems that arise when peoples with different cultures and goals come together and interact productively or tragically. The modes of adjustment or conflict are various, but usually one group dominates or attempts to dominate the other. Eventually some accommodation is reached, but the process is likely to be long and, for the weaker group, painful. No one scholarly discipline monopolizes the research necessary to comprehend these intergroup relations. The emerging analysis, consequently, inevitably is of interest to historians, social scientists, psychologists, and psychiatrists.

Minority Aging is a significant contribution to our understanding of ethnic groups because it addresses in fact the following question: What is it like to be both an old person and a member of a minority in the United States? The analysis focuses upon the relatively neglected problem of the almost inevitable "double jeopardy" in which minorities find themselves during their later years. Perhaps they are in triple jeopardy: Misery comes not only from age and ethnicity, but also from their social class.

The book carefully examines the demographic status of minorities and nonminorities. The relative disadvantages of the minority elderly are studied, ranging from deteriorating health to diminished financial resources to inequities in the use of public services. Promising hypotheses are examined to account for differences within this country. Yes, for example, the life expectancy of nonwhites is generally less than that of whites, but why is there a "crossover" at advanced ages so that the expectancy of nonwhites of both sexes then exceeds that of whites? Most of the studies reviewed here concentrate upon blacks, but historical and contemporary data are also offered concerning Hispanics, Asians, American Indians, Irish, and Italians. To be sure, in the tradition of good scholarly works, a few popular stereotypes are punctured.

Minorities have severe personal and social problems. In spite of their disadvantaged positions in society, however, they remain resilient human beings who have evolved coping and support mechanisms, such as the church, that often but certainly not always make their existence more tolerable and sometimes even satisfactory. Pension plans and government services seek to. ease strains, but unquestionably they may penalize minorities. Beneficial changes were evident during the 1960s and 1970s, but the outlook in the 1980s, if an understatement is permitted, appears gloomy.

The editor has not been content to offer facts, a few case histories, and copious references to the contents of relevant research. He and his contributors have explicated the perplexities of the minority aging in the broad context of social science. Current theories of gerontology are examined and then modified as they are applied to minorities. A single illustration is sufficient: Is the hypothesis of disengagement adequate to describe their plight? The peculiar and distinctive methodological difficulties that arise in locating and interviewing older minorities are delineated in detail and, again, with copious illustrations.

The practical and conceptual challenges of this contribution to ethnic, as well as to aging, studies are stimulating, depressing, and will be—for better or worse—long enduring.

Leonard W. Doob

PREFACE

Minority Aging: Sociological and Social Psychological Issues is a collection of original, scholarly essays logically integrated around three predominant themes. First, the book emphasizes that the lifelong socialization represented by the minority experience in the United States is such that it would be unwise to assume that all older people automatically have the same needs and experience the same conditions of aging. Second, it is frequently concluded, or can be concluded, that the distinction of the minority aged is not so much a function of the *novel* conditions of their aging as it is the *direr* circumstances of their existence. That is, economic, health, and other quality-of-life indicators typically reflect the heterogeneous circumstances of aging within both elderly minority and nonminority groups. Conditions of poverty, poor health, and societal neglect, for example, characterize significant segments of both groups; these and other conditions, however, are found to be much more profound among the minority elderly. The third theme underscores the fact that, while relatively more disadvantaged because of the minority experience, the minority aged have often adopted distinguishable strategies for successfully coping with their problems. Several of these strategies, it is argued, may indeed serve as models on which to pattern programs for successful coping among *all* elderly persons.

Minority Aging is a pioneering effort inasmuch as it introduces the first systematic framework, or at least the most comprehensive framework to date, for examining the issues and concepts pertinent to the study of aging and minorities. The purposes of the volume are threefold: to provide a comprehensive review and integration of, and a contribution to, the major substantive, policy, theoretical, and research issues concerning minority aging; to encourage additional thinking with respect to what is, and is not, known about the minority aged; and to impress upon both the young and the old, whether minority or nonminority, the vulnerabilities and strengths of America's minority elderly. Ideally, it is expected that the book will help dispel many of the myths that currently pervade much of the current understanding of the minority aged.

The book is organized into six parts. Part 1, the introduction, provides an orientation to the topic of minority aging. The next three parts focus on the substantive and policy-related issues, while the two concluding sections consider theoretical and methodological concerns. Each part, except the introduction, begins with a probing overview of the issues to be reviewed.

The first chapter in part 1 introduces the topic of minority aging in the context of the historical development of gerontology. Following this historical treatment, chapter 2 considers the problem of defining a minority status. The assumption is that an appreciation of the perspective of the elderly minority can be broached most effectively through an examination of the historical and political forces shaping their lives.

Parts 2 and 3 discuss the consequences of being both an old person and a minority. The three chapters of part 2 review demographic indicators on the comparative status of the minority and nonminority elderly; the nine chapters in part 3 emphasize the psychosocial issues associated with economic and health status; familial and social integration; and retirement, death, and dying.

The five chapters of part 4 focus on planning for the minority elderly. The topics in these chapters follow logically from preceding chapters by emphasizing the policies or services portended by earlier discussion. The chapters are divided into two subsections: personal needs and social policy, and service delivery and utilization.

The emphasis changes in the concluding chapters. Rather than a preoccupation with practical and substantive issues, a study of the tools of the trade are discussed. Issues in theory development (part 5) and research methodology (part 6), which both shape and are shaped by the substantive issues, are considered.

Minority Aging is addressed to three specific audiences: students of social gerontology and students in the field of ethnic—particularly black—studies; scholarly investigators, again, in the fields of both aging and ethnic studies; and professional planners for, or practitioners with, the aged. The volume is especially beneficial for instructors of general introductory gerontology courses (undergraduate or graduate) inasmuch as it provides a much needed supplementary reading source for a largely neglected topic. Similarly, because the elderly are rarely discussed within general ethnic study courses, the book will also be useful as a supplementary text in such courses. Among instructors of minority aging courses, or short-term workshops and seminars, the book can serve as the major reading resource.

Both planners for the aged and specialists in aging research will find that the book has been designed not only to offer a review of what is currently known about aging minorities, but also to identify major research questions. The nationally reputable contributors to the twenty-five chapters in this volume have, without question, constructed their presentations in such a way that the excitement of the sociology of aging, generally, and of minority aging, particularly, is clearly evident.

Achieving these objectives has not been an easy task. Most likely the ideas in the writer's mind would yet be unformed conceptions if not for the contribu-

tors to this volume. Special gratitude is expressed to each of them. Acknowl-
edgment is also made to the students who have shared in my classes on aging
and minority aging during the last few years at Howard University. Their
inquiries were a continual source of new ideas and intriguing possibilities.

Many other persons, too numerous to mention, have also contributed
suggestions for the book. I am indebted to each one. I am particularly
indebted to the reviewers of early versions of various chapters. The input from
Wilbur H. Watson (Atlanta University), Richard Dodder (Oklahoma State
University), Doris Y. Wilkinson, Johnnie Daniel, Ralph C. Gomes, and
Wardell Payne (all of Howard University) is responsible for many of the
positive qualities of the book. A special note of gratitude is also in order for the
secretarial assistance rendered by Denise Thompkins and Flora Whaley, unquestionably among the elite of those possessing the virtue of patience. Finally,
I am grateful to the staff of Greenwood Press for making this book a reality.

Most importantly, I hope that the collective venture represented by this
volume will serve to encourage further dialogue about the minority aged.

Ron C. Manuel

Part 1

INTRODUCTION:
AN ORIENTATION TO THE STUDY
OF THE MINORITY AGED

THE STUDY OF THE MINORITY AGED IN HISTORICAL PERSPECTIVE

RON C. MANUEL

Interest in the aged is not new. Speculations on why people age have been proposed since the beginning of recorded history, and, correlatively, implications for intervening in the aging process have been forthcoming equally as long (Freeman, 1979). Thus, following the assumption that longevity is associated with upholding moral dictates, it was believed that a long life was dependent upon, say, feeding the poor or honoring one's parents. Or consider the idea of "hygientic prolongevitism." The hygientic prolongevitists emphasized the life-extending virtues of temperance, moderation—especially in diet—and a simple life (Gruman, 1977).[1]

While interest in the aged is not new, the scientific study of aging is a relatively recent phenomenon. Gerontology, the disciplined study of aging and the aged, was not introduced until 1903, and it was not until the 1930s in this country that explicit public attention was given to the aged. Since World War II, the literature on aging and the aged has expanded, seemingly, exponentially by decade. In addition to scholarly journals and treatises on the social, psychological, and biological mechanisms of aging, there have been numerous private and governmentally sponsored conferences documenting the specific problems of the aged (Calhoun, 1978).

The growth in interest and study of the aged is due, in large part, to the increasing number of aged persons in the population. When one considers the growth of the aged population, along with their relatively lower quality of life, especially in industrial societies and for significant proportions of the less fortunate elderly in all societies, it becomes quickly evident why there has been an increasing interest in the aged.[2] Specifically, aging draws attention as a social problem because of the increased visibility of the disadvantaged status of the elderly.

3

Interestingly, throughout the period from 1940 to 1970, during the time of considerable growth in both scholarly and political concern with the aged in the United States, little was written about the even more devastating conditions of aging among America's ethnic minorities.[3] While many of these conditions and the issues to which they give rise are reviewed in the chapters that follow in this book, it is pertinent at this juncture to ask why so little attention was given to the minority aged during the early years of scientific writing and government-sponsored conferences on aging. Additionally, this chapter shall review the forces that did eventually lead to a burgeoning interest and later scientific study of the minority aged. This discussion is divided into two sections, roughly corresponding to two epochally defined periods: the first, beginning in 1956, was initiated with the simple inquiry of whether the black aged were doubly disadvantaged by virtue of their race as well as age; the second period was initiated in 1971, with the fairly general recognition that the study of aged blacks and other minorities did in fact represent special topics in the gerontological enterprise.

First, why was so little attention given to the minority aged during the period 1940–1970? The reason given or implied by most of the recently accumulating literature on the minority aged suggests that there was a naive assumption that the aged were a homogeneous group; as such, there was no reason to study the minority aged separately. Jackson (1967), on the other hand, stresses that the assumption of differential intrinsic or extrinsic characteristics was equally important as a determining factor in the neglect of interest in the black aged. Unlike the assumption of homogeneity of the aged, the latter perspective emphasizes the extremely specialized topic represented by a concentration on the minority aged.

The early exclusion of the study of the black and minority aged has also been observed to be due to the general insensitivity shown by nonminority gerontologists to the social circumstances of the black and other minority aged. As late as 1971, during planning for the 1971 White House Conference on Aging, there remained outright hostility by nonminority gerontologists toward providing a focus on the black aged (Jackson, 1974). Accepting the latter perspective, the reason, then, for the original neglect of the minority aged must be traced to the racially and ethnically stratified larger society.

There is certainly enough evidence in the racial and ethnic minority literature to support this contention. Kutzik (1979), for example, argues that while the early English, the economically and politically dominant group in early American society, provided adequately for their aged, poor, and disabled, they failed miserably in providing for the welfare of the non-English poor and elderly.[4] English neglect, Kutzik continues, forced the development of two ethnically stratified institutional arrangements for the care of the poor and the elderly: one among the English and the other among the non-English.

The legacy of this dual system is important for appreciating the fact that despite the failure initially to recognize the special circumstances of the minority aged within mainstream humanitarian, as well as gerontological, efforts, concern and provision for the minority elderly have not been absent. As early as 1914, even before focused national concern for the nonminority elderly, Du Bois and Dill (1914), two early black social scientists, had described the informal, care-giving patterns among elderly blacks. Moreover, throughout the history of the United States, inaccessibility to public support has been a motive for black and other minorities to care for their own elderly and disabled members.[5] In their efforts to help themselves, black Americans, for example, formed numerous mutual aid societies that, either directly or indirectly, helped to sustain the elderly in their communities (Du Bois, 1909; Drake and Cayton, 1945). In fact, it shall be argued in this text that informal, help-giving networks—friends, kin, church, and neighbors—continue to provide a pivotal resource for responding to the needs of today's elderly minority community. Froland and his associates (1981) stress the necessity for professional care givers to use the informal network to augment formal service delivery. It is argued in this volume that the historical significance of the informal network for the care of the black and minority aged offers a useful model for exploiting this resource for all elderly Americans, minority and nonminority.

Other literary references on the nature of aging within the black community were also available in the early decades of this century. Davis's (1980) recent, comprehensive bibliography on the black aged reviews numerous citations, indicating that there was evidence available on the varying conditions of aging among black Americans, despite characteristic assumptions of the homogeneity of the aged within mainstream gerontological efforts.

THE EARLY YEARS: THE FIFTIES AND SIXTIES

The landmark question, beginning the cumulative—albeit slowly emergent— literature on the minority aged in the United States, was posed in 1956. Talley and Kaplan (1956) asked their readers a simple question: Are the black aged doubly jeopardized relative to their white counterparts? That is, do the factors of age-related, as well as racially or ethnically related, injustices make the circumstances of aging more problematic among blacks than whites? Although considerable time has passed since Talley's and Kaplan's inquiry, it is noteworthy that the question of multiple jeopardy continues to be a central issue in discussions about the minority aged. It shall become evident, with the unfolding of the issues in this book, that the concept of "double jeopardy" may consistently be invoked for its explanatory utility. This is true whether the effort is with documenting the greater needs of minority elderly, as in selected chapters in parts 2 and 3; or explaining the factors underlying the underutilization of social services (see part 4); or explaining the factors underlying the lower life expectancy of minorities (part 2).

Actually, the first systematic treatment of the topic of minority aging (in this case, black aging) was two years after Talley and Kaplan's inquiry. While Smith (1957) did not focus explicitly on the hypothesis of double jeopardy, he did supply data that helped to solidify the argument of the doubly disadvantaged position of the black elderly. Most importantly, Smith's demographic study of the changing number and distribution of the aged black population called attention to the black elderly as an exceptionally fast growing, but impoverished, segment of the population. Likewise, Beatty's (1960) early question of the relevance of conventional health care and income maintenance policies for elderly blacks, given their forced unemployment histories, was also later used to buttress the double jeopardy hypothesis.

The next frequently cited study, appearing in 1964, represented the first attempt explicitly to document the hypothesis of double jeopardy. The National Urban League study (1964), utilizing national data from a variety of governmental sources, reported lower percentages of elderly black, relative to white, Americans on a wide gamut of quality-of-life indicators: housing adequacy, living conditions, income, and health resources. Although the conclusions were suggestive, the study actually never tested the central idea: Do racial or ethnic injustices *compound* age injustices?

A less cited, but methodologically more correct, analysis of the double jeopardy hypothesis was reported by Orshansky, also in 1964. While initiating her discussion with the assumption of the doubly jeopardized status of the black elderly on income, she, nevertheless, produced analyses, using U.S. census data, that implied that the black aged may be economically better off—relative to their white counterparts—than blacks in general, relative to whites in general. Orshansky found, for example, that nonwhite median income in 1959 was 45 percent of white income among males between 55 to 64 years of age. The statistic rises to 51 percent among males over 65 years. Seemingly, to the extent that income maintenance supports replace earned income, as is increasingly the case for the aged, the less relative nonwhite/white disadvantage.[6] With this conclusion, although not emphasized by Orshanslay, the foundation was construed for debate which has continued intermittently, until the present day: Are the black and minority aged doubly jeopardized, and, if so, on which quality-of-life indicators?

Perhaps the most frequently cited study that appeared during the 1960s is Jackson's (1967) review of the literature on aging blacks. Jacquelyne Jackson, easily the most consistent contributor to the early literature on the minority aged, focused attention upon the methodological inadequacies of the burgeoning studies of the minority aged. She challenged investigators of the minority aged to produce more refined, scientific analyses of the hypotheses that were beginning to emerge. While stressing the need for comparative studies between the black and white aged, Jackson warned against using statistical portrayals of the nonminority aged as indicative of the ideal, normal pattern. Such an assumption, she stipulated, would undermine the subcultural differences that are present.

Few of the remaining published studies appearing during these early years are extensively cited in the current literature. More attention, however, should be given to several of these analyses. Petersen (1971), Demeny and Gingrich (1967), and Hill (1970), for instance, study differential longevity among Japanese, black, and native Americans, respectively. While Japanese life expectancies were found to exceed even the nonminority expectancies, black and native American life expectancies were substantially lower than the nonminority. The conclusions from these studies suggest that current investigators of "differential life expectancy" would do well to seek race- or ethnic-specific data in order to advance investigations beyond simple white/nonwhite comparisons.

Henderson's (1965) caveat that practitioners may need to seek out actively the less obvious needs of the black elderly is also a pertinent study from the early literature. Thus, his conclusion, that lifelong patterns of adjustment among blacks include the tendency to deny disadvantaged circumstances, is relevant for the currently puzzling question of why elderly minorities express relatively strong life satisfaction, even when their objectively viewed circumstances indicate abject poverty.

Finally, while rarely cited, Smith's (1967), Leonard's (1967), and Levy's (1967) papers, appearing in E. Grant Youman's analysis entitled *Older Rural Americans*, are exemplary of the range of factors apropos to demographic analysis of the minority aged. The studies focus, respectively, on the black, Hispanic, and native American. And each study considers the often neglected factor of rurality as an additional jeopardizing factor for the minority aged.

Leonard's and Levy's studies are among the first systematic, published analyses specifically focused on the elderly Hispanic and native American populations. While Leonard's study was closely followed by several studies on factors underlying the use of health services and public housing among Mexican Americans (see, for example, Carp, 1969, and Clark and Mendelson, 1969), studies of the elderly native Americans have been less numerous. Suzuki (1975), for example, located only four studies on elderly native Americans. A similar conclusion is in order for the early literature on Asian Americans.

Several additional, but rarely cited, studies on the black and Hispanic elderly were introduced during the 1960s. For these items, the reader is referred to several of the recent bibliographic reviews of the literature. (See Suzuki, 1975, for a review of the literature on Japanese, Chinese, black, Mexican, and native Americans; see Ragan and Simonin, 1977, for a review of elderly black and Mexican Americans; see Sherman, 1980, for selected, but topically organized bibliographies on elderly black, Hispanic, Pacific/Asian, and native Americans, respectively. Davis (1980) provides the most comprehensive—and annotated—bibliographic review to date on the black aged.)

The growing diversity of topics appearing during the latter part of the sixties prompted Jackson (1971b) to update her 1967 literature review. Summarizing the literature, she identified three major conceptual areas of study regarding the black aged. These areas included: (1) social patterns and resources; (2) health-related concerns; and (3) psychological well-being and attitudes. With this abstraction the first attempt at conceptualizing the growing minority aging literature took shape. As the initial decades of study, the 1950s and 1960s, drew to a close, the findings from research in each of the aforementioned study areas were seen by Jackson (1971b) as leaving a fertile ground for additional research: Are there significant intra-ethnic minority variations in aging patterns and adjustment? Or, what effect, if any, will changing racial attitudes, or economic resources, among minority youth have upon traditional, intergenerational, care-giving patterns? Or, regarding the hypothesis of double jeopardy, in what specific ways is it applicable to describing the needs of the minority aged? And, if the hypothesis is only applicable in certain sociocultural realms, why? Certainly the emerging literature, and the additional questions that it raised, represented a significant advancement beyond the limited, initial inquiry in 1956 on whether the situation of the black elderly was one of double jeopardy.

THE DECADE OF THE SEVENTIES

The construction of knowledge, scientific or otherwise, is socially based. That is, as knowledge evolves through the fallible social process of use, reuse, or disuse, it either becomes increasingly accepted or is rejected by the scientific community (Ravetz, 1973). The recognition of scientifically based data on the minority aged, while initially slow for most of scientific gerontology's existence, mushroomed during the 1970s.

The year 1971, more than any other year, epitomizes the turning point in the recognition of the minority aged as a special area of study within gerontology. Reminiscent of the early discussions on the nonminority elderly in the 1940s, several workshops and conferences on black and minority aging emerged in 1971. These meetings were sponsored by a variety of aging-related organizations, including the National Council on Aging, the United States Senate Special Committee on Aging, the University of Michigan, and the University of Southern California. It was also during 1971 that the first roundtable discussion sessions on minorities were held at the annual meetings of the Gerontological Society; moreover, during the same year, special issues of the *Gerontologist* and *Aging and Human Development*, two of the major journalistic forums for the dissemination of information about the aged, were focused entirely on presenting current information and motivating additional research on the minority aged. Special conferences and publications in other journals followed throughout the decade, including a special academic journal devoted to reporting research about the black and minority aged: *Black Aging*, later entitled, the *Journal of Minority Aging*.

The academic and research emphasis in 1971 was complemented by an equally viable policy orientation (see chapter 15 for a more detailed discussion). Hobart Jackson, a pioneering advocate for improving the conditions of life among the black aged, helped to form the National Caucus on the Black Aged in 1971. Feeling that all persons would benefit from efforts that removed inequities at the point of greatest inequality, Jackson stressed the virtues of justice, equity, and dignity among the aged. Jackson's philosophy provided the foundation for the caucus's instrumentality in organizing one of the seventeen special concerns sessions for the 1971 White House Conference on Aging (WHCOA). The session called "Aging and Aged Blacks" was deemed necessary because of the failure, during the planning stages of the conference, to consider the accumulating evidence on the differences between the needs of the black and white aged.[7]

The report of the session, like the reports about the special concerns sessions on the Hispanic (proposed by the League of United Latin American Citizens, among others), Asian (requested by the Japanese American Citizens League), and native American (requested by the National Congress of American Indians), sought to provide a perspective for policy development that would address the special problems of the minority aged (see WHCOA, 1971). Over ninety recommendations, for example, were proposed by the session on elderly blacks. Most importantly, each report from the elderly minority sessions emphasized a core of common problems, particularly the need of the respective populations for income and health-care supports, given evidence that relative to the white elderly, twice as many of the minority elderly were below the poverty level.

It is noteworthy that Congress in 1972 did in fact replace the ineffective, state-level, Old Age Assistance income support program with a federal-level, Supplemental Security Income (SSI) program. For individuals eligible among the aged (and also among the blind and the disabled), the SSI program established a national minimum income, thereby eliminating the wide, state-to-state, fluctuations in conditions of eligibility and amount of income support. The program, however, has never been funded sufficiently to permit the needy elderly, even with SSI payments and social security benefits, to live significantly beyond the poverty threshold. Manuel and Reid demonstrate in chapter 3, for example, that close to one-half of all the black elderly in 1979 were below 125 percent of the poverty level. As in 1971, representatives of the older minorities to the 1981 White House Conference on Aging will again, no doubt, push for greater income supports for the poorest of the elderly poor.

In addition to its advocacy role, the National Caucus on the Black Aged was also effective in obtaining federal funding, in 1973, for a National Center on the Black Aged, today called the National Center and Caucus on the Black Aged (NCCBA). The center was established to provide comprehensive service delivery (including housing, employment, and training) and research development on behalf of the aged. Since the early seventies, organizations representing other aged ethnic minorities have also evolved special advocacy and research agencies. In 1975, 1976, and 1979, respectively, the National Association for Spanish Speaking Elderly (sponsored by the National Chicano Planning Council), the National Indian Council on Aging (sponsored by the National Tribal Chairman's Association), and the National Pacific/Asian Resource Center on Aging (sponsored by the Pacific/Asian Coalition) were each, like NCCBA, funded by the Administration on Aging (United States Department of Health and Human Services). Through collaborative relationships with various civic, educational, governmental, and other aging organizations, these four aging minority groups function as advocacy groups and as research and academic development centers. For example, NCCBA, the most resourceful of the aging minority organizations, has played a pivotal role in fostering the continued development of literature on aging minorities. In addition to providing consultation for the development of gerontological training programs in both predominantly black and white institutions of higher learning, the center has produced several publications addressed to curriculum or research development in minority aging. Some of these publications include *Health and the Black Aged* (Watson and associates, 1977); *Research and Training in Minority Aged* (Sherman, 1978); *Curriculum Guidelines in Minority Aging* (Sherman, 1980); and *Curriculum Modules and the Black Aged* (Sherman, 1983).

While NCCBA and the other aging organizations have functioned to stimulate academic and research development on the minority aged, it has been within the major university research institutes and academic departments that the accumulation of data and information on the minority elderly has actually taken place. Throughout the last several years, major data bases have been established throughout the country. The Andrus Gerontology Center's (University of Southern California) study on the "socio-cultural contexts of aging," for example, has been the basis of numerous scholarly publications on minority/nonminority contrasts in the experience of aging (see, for example, Dowd and Bengtson's [1978] often cited analysis of the double jeopardy hypothesis). The Center on Aging at San Diego State University has complemented the Andrus Center's study by its comparative cross-cultural series on aging among Indian, black, Chinese, Guamanian, Latino, Philippine, and Samoan Americans (see, for example, Stanford, 1978; and Valle and Mendoza, 1978). And, of course, the annual Minority Aging Institutes of the San Diego Center on Aging are a continual source of new information about the minority aged (see, for example, Stanford, 1981).

Other major sources of data include the Duke Longitudinal Studies (see, for example, Jericho's [1977] analysis of the impact of religion in the lives of the black elderly) and the National Council on Aging's nationally representative analysis. Jackson and Walls (1978), utilizing data from the National Council on Aging research, conclude that there appears to be few differences in minority and nonminority aging. Jackson and Wood (1976), on the other hand, using the same source of data, had earlier found similarities as well as substantial differences in the aging of minorities and nonminorities. See chapter 6 for additional study of these contradictory conclusions.

The preceding, rather large data bases exclude, of course, the wide gamut of data available from smaller-scale studies. Consider, for example, Cuellar and Weeks's (1980) and Guttmann's (1980) studies on minority elderly utilization of social services, or Dancy's (1977) analysis of coping resources, or Watson's (1980a) examination of stress and adaptation. The Administration on Aging, alone, one of the primary funding agencies for research and demonstration projects in aging, has funded close to thirty minority focused projects since 1977 (Brown, 1981). Moreover, investigators have also begun the task of summarizing the existing knowledge on the ethnic and minority aging (see Gelfand and Kutzik, 1979; and Jackson, 1980).

This review is not meant to suggest that an extensive data base is in place on the minority aged; rather, the intent is to signify that data have become increasingly available throughout the decade of the seventies. Actually, it is easily true that little is known in the way of definitive conclusions about the minority aged.[8] What is emphasized is the slow, thoughtful, and steadily emergent process, characteristic of the scientific enterprise, by which knowledge is generated. Sound policy and programmatic decisions are dependent upon this process.[9]

In conclusion, it is evident that the decade of the seventies was a major turning point in recognition of the minority aged as a special area of study within gerontology. It is equally clear that the literature on the minority aged has progressed, conceptually, well beyond Jackson's (1971b) tripartite scheme: social patterns, psychological well-being, and health-related concerns. As an update to Jackson's early design, the organizational foundation for this book offers a theoretical framework that easily reflects the diversity of current issues in the field.[10]

It shall become clear that many of the concerns of the minority aged are also the concerns of the elderly in general, but with the added dimension of the relatively direr circumstances in the conditions affecting the minority elderly. There are, however, some unique social forces shaping the lives of the minority aged. The next chapter considers some of these forces.

NOTES

1. An excellent literature on the historical study of aging and the aged has developed within the last few years. In addition to Gruman's (1977) and Freeman's (1979) historical treatises on aging, see Fischer (1978) and Achenbaum (1978) for an overview of the study of the aged within early America. See Calhoun (1978) for a good discussion on recent historical developments in the study of aging within America.

2. See Watson and Maxwell (1977) for evidence on the inverse relationship between industrialization and the status of the aged. Fischer (1978), on the other hand, argues the existence of an ambivalent attitude toward the aged, even in preindustrialized societies.

3. It is sufficient at this point merely to identify the major ethnic minorities currently in the United States. They include Asian, Hispanic, black, and native Americans. The next chapter will

be explicitly concerned with providing a systematic conceptualization for whom, among the aged, shall be called minority.

4. During the earliest years of the United States, the non-English (all of whom were clearly among the country's minorities at that time) primarily consisted of the free blacks and the Irish, French, German, and, later, non–Northern European immigrants. Further discussion on who a minority is and how these definitions change with time is provided in chapter 2.

5. Several of the chapters in this book provide demographic (chapter 3), sociological, as well as historical (chapters 9–11) documentation of the centrality of informal support networks for the care of elderly minorities. Chapters 18 and 19 also present several of the programmatic implications suggested by these systems of care giving.

6. Consistent with usage in much of the pre-1980 literature, Orshansky (1964) uses the distinction black/white interchangeably with nonwhite/white. This usage is usually considered acceptable inasmuch as census figures have not been traditionally specified by race and ethnicity. Blacks, moreover, throughout the century have constituted the overwhelming majority of the nonwhite population. In 1970, for example, the black elderly constituted 91.1 percent of the nonwhite elderly population. The reader is referred to the discussion on the demography of the minority aged, chapter 3, for further discussion on the applicability of interchanging the black and nonwhite designations.

7. The White House Conference on Aging (WHCOA), since 1961, has been a major event every ten years for shaping national aging policy directions, from the grassroots or community level. The special concerns sessions of the 1971 conference were to provide a forum for in-depth discussions of the varying circumstances of the aging of specified groups, including ethnic minorities (WHCOA, 1971). While the special concerns sessions for minorities represented a last-minute effort to include minority representation in the 1971 WHCOA, it is noteworthy that the 1981 White House Conference on Aging sought, during the early planning efforts, to heighten the visibility of the special needs of the minority elderly through a series of mini–White House conferences. The concerns and recommendations from the mini-conferences were reviewed by all delegates to the national conference. Moreover, delegate selection to the national conference was designed to reflect accurately, among other things, the distribution of members of ethnic minorities in the population.

8. Not only has the quantity of studies remained limited, but the quality of the existing studies must also be considered. Jackson, in 1971a, in 1971b, and again in 1980, challenges investigators for more rigorous research.

9. The argument here is neither for nor against minority-specific legislation among the elderly. Instead, the important matter is that any programmatic decision be fairly weighed as to its consequences for a variety of potentially affected groups. The consequences for the minority aged will not be known unless a credible knowledge base is in place.

10. See Manuel (1980a) for an earlier endeavor to summarize the major issues in the study of the minority aged. Several of the topics considered in this book derive from and are responses to questions that were raised by this earlier analysis.

2

THE MINORITY AGED: PROVIDING A CONCEPTUAL PERSPECTIVE

RON C. MANUEL

The aged are not a homogeneous population. An appreciation of the sociocultural heterogeneity, historically, of the general population in the United States is sufficient to warrant this conclusion. Consider, for example, the recent estimate in *The Harvard Encyclopedia of American Ethnic Groups* (Thernstron, 1980) that over 100 different ethnic groups are currently distinguishable within the country. A major thesis underlying the discussion in the chapters of this book is that the distinct, lifelong socialization patterns represented by varying ethnic backgrounds, particularly ethnic minority backgrounds, are such that it would be a mistake to assume that all individuals, during their elderly years, automatically have the same needs or experience the same conditions of aging.

Recognition of this thesis, in conjunction with a growing sensitivity to the vulnerabilities of all people, has compelled the nation to focus increasing attention on its various elderly ethnic minority groups. The National Urban League (1964:1) eloquently concluded some years ago that "today's aged Negro is different from today's aged white. . . . For he [the Negro] has . . . been placed in double jeopardy: first by being Negro and second by being aged. Age merely compounded those hardships accrued to him as a result of being a Negro." More recently, the National Institute on Aging (1980) observed that elderly minority groups are less likely than their nonminority counterparts to have adequate education, money, housing, or health. They are more likely to experience discrimination, language barriers, and difficulty in obtaining needed social services.

It is within this context that the scientific study of elderly ethnic minorities assumes its greatest importance. For it is due to the substantially direr (rather than novel) nature of the problems facing elderly minorities, relative to their nonminority counterparts, that this subpopulation may be defined as one in need of special scholarly and policy-directed attention.

Before an analysis of the context of, and implications for, aging among ethnic minorities, it is appropriate in this chapter to devote some time to the question of what a minority is and who are to be considered in the stratum of the minority elderly. This chapter, in particular, emphasizes the conceptual dimensions that must be reflected by the experiences of any group that is to be considered a minority. The ultimate objective is to derive a clear definition of a minority such that current confusion in the use of the term can be lessened. The assumption here, as in the preceding chapter, is that an appreciation of the elderly minority can best be broached by providing a clear understanding of the historical forces that have shaped the lives of those in this population.

THE NATURE OF ETHNIC MINORITIES

It has been estimated that at least 80 percent of the population in the United States can be considered minority, when including such diverse groups as women, homosexuals, students, as well as the traditional ethnic minorities (African, Asian, Hispanic, and native Americans). From a theoretical perspective, the concept, when applied so broadly, loses its usefulness as a relevant construct. And, from a practical or political perspective, the indiscriminate application of the term, whether consciously or unconsciously, too easily serves subtle, ideological purposes, directing public, political, and humanitarian attention away from those groups who are most disadvantaged. Thus, the majority (the nonminority) is able to continue discriminatory practices toward, say, blacks by employing white women to meet affirmative action guidelines. Or social service resources for low-income, minority elderly may be diverted to groups more culturally similar to the majority.

To illustrate further, Binstock (1981) has observed that one-fourth of annual federal spending is on aging-related problems. Yet, he notes, poverty among the aged remains substantial. Recognizing that the income problems of the aged are primarily concentrated among the black and other minority elderly (see chapter 3), Binstock (1981:188) concludes: "Something is wrong because that money ($133 billion, annually spent for the aged) is not being targeted for the people most in need."

The indiscriminate use of the "minority" concept has led some to advocate substitute terminology when wanting to delimit only specified groups within the range of possible minorities. But, considering the rich sociological and gerontological tradition in the use of the concept, it seems more important to provide for the term's clear and explicit conceptualization, rather than abandoning it. The discussion in this chapter seeks to provide clarification of the concept. It is argued that to focus attention upon only one criterion of a multicriterion concept is to invite misapplication and confusion in the use of the term.

THE CONCEPTS OF RACE AND ETHNICITY

What is a minority? How do minority groups differ from ethnic groups? And, in what ways do racial designations differ from both minority and ethnic designations? Undoubtedly, ambiguity of terminology is a major factor underlying much of the current confusion in applications of the minority concept. Thus, the task of clarifying the definition of a minority begins with distinguishing between racial, ethnic, and minority status. First, how shall race be defined? Most scholars today see races as physically distinct aggregates that, while differing in the average incidence of specified genes, are capable of exchanging physical distinctions (Dunn and Dobzhansky, 1964). The emphasis clearly is on common biological descent. But, because races are not characterized by fixed, clear-cut physical differences, it is difficult to differentiate concisely between races; estimates of racial types vary from three (Caucasoid, Mongoloid, and Negroid) to more than 150 (Dunn and Dobzhansky, 1964). Given this complexity, it seems futile, for sociological purposes, to seek definitive racial classifications.

So who then is an Hispanic, a black, or a white American? The perspective seemingly resulting in the fewest pitfalls is realization that racially labelled groups are ultimately socially defined (Bahr, Chadwick, and Strauss, 1979). As Berreman (1972) stipulates, even racists define varying groups less on the basis of physical distinctions than the socially significant aspects of ancestry. In practice, moreover, most social scientists, when making racial references, have sociocultural distinctions in mind. Sociocultural variations, such as differences in languages, mannerisms, values, and religious practices, provide indicators of one's ethnic background. Because of the ultimate cultural definitions associated with racial distinctions, ethnicity, rather than race, would appear to be more accurate terminology when designating either traditionally specified racial or ethnic groups.[1] In this chapter ethnicity is used to designate ethnic, as well as racial, labels. Thus, black, white, or Hispanic Americans are ethnically distinct groups. This perspective, however, is not necessarily followed by other contributors to this volume.

Ethnic groups, defined, are relatively endogamous social aggregates consisting of those who subjectively classify themselves as similar, and are so classified by others, because of their common ancestry, historical experiences, or sociocultural similarities (Shibutani and Kwan, 1965; Schermerhorn, 1970; and Gordon, 1978). Ethnicity obviously has a multifarious base potentially subsuming religious, sexual, generational, national, as well as racial criteria. Gordon (1978) identifies the common social psychological core of these criteria when he speaks of ethnicity as indicative of a sense of peoplehood resulting from an awareness of the historical importance of one of the above criteria.

Again, ethnicity appears as a conceptually more generic term than race, easily and logically incorporating the racial dimension. This use, moreover, is consistent with evidence indicating that sociocultural distinctions are often accentuated by physical factors, thereby increasing the possibility for conflict between the differing groups. For example, the obvious physical distinctions of black Americans punctuate cultural distinctions inasmuch as the physical characteristics serve to make concrete the cultural variations. As a consequence, conflict between whites and blacks has been more intense and prolonged than between whites and, say, Japanese Americans.

ETHNICITY AND MINORITY STATUS

To the extent that conflict between ethnic groups becomes pronounced, chances are increased that one group will overpower the other. Thus, as one ethnic group is able to subordinate another to its dictates, distinctions arise between a dominant or majority ethnic collective in contrast to a subordinate or ethnic minority collective.

The concept of a minority, as originally conceived, referred to ethnically distinct, European nationality groups, whose existence and cultural independence were made subordinate to a conquering, more powerful national (ethnic) group (Yetman and Steele, 1971). Rose (1981) notes that the multifarious peoples of the Soviet Union represent such minorities. Since the original usage of the concept, however, it has been associated with a multiplicity of groups. Many of the applications, beginning with Young's (1932) substitution of the term for race and continuing in recent attempts to apply the term to such groups as women (Davis, 1978) and the aged (Palmore, 1969), have deviated substantially from the original conceptualization.

The primary reasons, underlying at least the recent, increasingly broad application of the term, reside in (1) the failure to apply a consistent conceptualization of the term and (2) the failure, correlatively, to provide an adequate operationalization of the conceptual criteria suggested by the term. The first of these concerns is addressed in the remaining sections of this chapter; the second problem, a methodological one, is treated in the concluding chapter of this book.

THE MINORITY ELDERLY: A DEFINITION

Wagley and Harris (1964) have identified several criteria that shape minority and nonminority relations. These criteria include prejudice, discrimination, distinctive physical and cultural characteristics, awareness of inequitable treatment, and marital endogamy. According to this conceptualization, any group, given possession of characteristics resented by a second group, can potentially be made subordinate to the whims of the second group. The victimized group, the minority, is denied opportunities by the discriminatory practices of the dominating group. Moreover, the awareness of common victimization creates a sense of isolation and shared consciousness among the minority, which in turn reinforces the group's tendency toward endogamous marital relations. Endogamy perpetuates the distinctive characteristics, which in turn perpetuate discrimination, and so forth.

While, as Wirth (1945) stipulated, the existence of a minority implies a majority or dominating group, Yetman and Steele (1971) maintain that conceptualizations, such as the one by Wagley and Harris, put too little emphasis on the power relations that distinguish minority and majority groups. That is, because no explicit mention is given to the relative power resources between ethnic groups, one is at a loss to understand how one group can be made subordinate to a second.

Although this is a noteworthy observation, Yetman and Steele—in their zest for emphasizing the idea of "differential power"—unfortunately neglect to treat the remaining criteria of a minority, as outlined by Wagley and Harris. One easily concludes, after reading Yetman and Steele, that the distinguishing factor of the minority group is its powerless, vulnerable position.

Failure to consider the totality of criteria that fashion a minority has also characterized other investigations of the minority concept. Consider, for example, Wirth's (1945:347) often cited definition:

> We may define a minority as a group of people who, because of their physical or cultural characteristics, are singled out from the others in the society in which they live for differential and unequal treatment and who therefore regard themselves as objects of collective discrimination.

One would not know it from this definition, but Wirth's essay, from which this definition was excerpted, goes to considerable length to emphasize the idea of the relative power disadvantage of the minority group. As is evident from the definition, Wirth also emphasized most of the additional criteria that have been associated with a minority status. He fails, however, to emphasize the important dimension of endogamy. And, inasmuch as Wirth's definition is often followed by contemporary investigators (see, for example, Davis, 1978, or Martin and Franklin, 1973), they too fail to view the minority in its total complexity.

It is contended here that confusion over what groups are to be considered minority, and particularly what groups constitute the minority elderly, rest in part with the failure to study the minority concept in its full complexity. When conceived from the total perspective represented by the theorists above, the following definition would seem warranted. Minorities, or the minority elderly for the purposes of this chapter, are social aggregates within a larger political stratum whose experiences, throughout life, have been largely shaped by virtue of their status in an ethnically distinct, predominantly endogamous, common ancestral line. On the basis of their status, these individuals are more or less systematically denied—by other, more socioeconomically and politically powerful aggregates—the opportunities that are normally expected within the society.

As is evident, unlike popular usage, the sociological understanding of a minority has nothing to do with relative numbers of specific groups within the population. Irrespective of whether blacks constitute 12 percent of the population, as in the United States, or from 50 to 95 percent, as in many of the former British colonies in the Caribbean, they remain minorities within their respective populations, given their common experience with an economically powerful white majority (Millette, 1971).

What is emphasized in the definition is the importance of insuring that each of the features of a minority are included in applications of the term. The remainder of this chapter is devoted to clarifying the major features in this definition. After a study of prejudice and discrimination, attention turns to the power relation. The chapter concludes with a consideration of the delimiting function played by a third, and most often neglected, criterion: the endogamous nature of social relations within a minority.

Prejudice and Discrimination

Practically all definitions of a minority give substantial weight to the impact of prejudice and discrimination, either as it is expressed by the dominant group or as it is experienced by the subordinate group.

Prejudice is the emotionally charged tendency to act toward another on the basis of limited information, in a typically unfavorable manner. The assumption, in part, is that limited information, and thus little to reason cognitively with, gives free play to emotional feelings, which in turn prompts the tendency toward discriminatory behavior. Discrimination refers to the actual act of expressing unfavorable treatment toward another. Prejudice is thus an attitude, and discrimination refers to actual behavior. While both ethnic minorities or nonminorities may hold prejudices, it is the nonminority, by virtue of its control of societal, economic, or political positions, that is able to discriminate systematically.

Prejudice Since humans first joined, collectively, in groups, the members of one group have been suspicious of those in other groups. A review of the history of the great wars and conflicts throughout history underscores the tendency of group members to scorn and downgrade members of other groups. And no less has been true within the United States. Why is it that groups express hostile and negative sentiments toward one another? Or stated differently: Why do prejudicial attitudes develop?

Many social psychologists contend that prejudice occurs because of limitations in human perceptual ability. Secord and Backman (1974) note that human beings would be overwhelmed by perceptual stimuli if they were unable to categorize some of the information concerning their physical and social environment. Stereotyping, or the tendency to perceive others solely in terms of a limited number of attributes that are then associated with a categorical label, thus often functions as a time-saving, psychological mechanism, reducing the need to attend to the minute details in the perceptual field. An older person, for instance, irrespective of individual qualities, may instantaneously appear feeble, or perhaps frugal, to those possessing stereotypes of older people. Stereotypes automatically result in inaccurate information and, as such, are conceived by some social psychologists as the primary psychological precursors of prejudicial attitudes.

Prejudices, of course, have sources other than in stereotypes. Prejudicial attitudes may be learned from prevailing normative patterns in a society. While explicit instruction probably plays an insignificant role today in the transmission of prejudicial attitudes against ethnic minorities in this country, it is likely that a substantial number of implicit cues are shared between members of the majority and their children, as well as other adults (Raab and Lipset, 1962). Weinstock's and Bennett's (1968) data, for instance, illustrate the implicit fashion by which prejudicial attitudes are typically reinforced today. Studying an interracial sample of nursing home residents with a primarily nonwhite nursing staff, but a white, top-level administration, Weinstock and Bennett note that significantly more of the white, relative to black, residents communicated their problems, except service-related needs, directly to the white administrative personnel, thus bypassing the nursing staff, the accepted channel of communication. The white patients were consciously or unconsciously attempting to structure the system in the nursing home in line with their prior experience in the community.

Prejudice also results from socioeconomic forces. Given the association between economic depression and resentment of minorities, prejudice may be used by the majority to defend its own perceived threatened economic position (Cox, 1948; Bonavich, 1972). According to this rationale, accusations of reverse racism, as expressed by nonminorities, regarding application of affirmative action guidelines in the delivery of services to the minority aged, should increase with decreases in general economic prosperity.

There are obviously other correlates of prejudice, including personality type (see, for example, Barron, 1977) and ideological forces, such as ethnocentrism and racism (see, for example, Sumner, 1906, and Wilson, 1978). Inasmuch as it is beyond the scope of this chapter to consider these correlates, in toto, or even to discuss adequately those introduced above, the reader is referred to the sociological literature.[2] It is sufficient here merely to sharpen the awareness that prejudice toward ethnic minorities is interpretable from realities occurring in the psychosocial world of individuals. These are realities that have helped to shape the perspective and circumstances of today's generation of elderly minorities.

Discrimination Discrimination, as previously noted, refers to actual behavior whereby members of the majority group express unfavorable treatment toward members of the minority. When discussed in relation to attitudes, discrimination is conceived as the overt expression of an attitudinal tendency. Thus, in times past, the policy of public segregation between blacks and whites was the overt expression of an attitude that suggested the inferiority of blacks.

But just as attitudes do not necessarily correspond with behavior, nor does prejudice necessarily find expression in discriminatory acts (Merton, 1949). Rather, situational factors interact with attitudinal or prejudicial variables to influence behavior uniquely. Consider the case of an all-Caucasian work force in a service delivery agency for the aged. While the personnel in the agency are conceivably attitudinally hostile toward, say, Mexican Americans, it is likely that they will act in compliance with federal laws prohibiting discriminatory treatment of clients. Rather than hostile or even indifferent attitudes, however, prejudicial attitudes are reflected perhaps more often by an insensitivity to subcultural differences.

On the other hand, an unprejudiced discriminator is also conceivable. Unlike the prejudiced nondiscriminator, considered in the preceding paragraph, the unprejudiced discriminator discriminates, if ever so subtly, whenever such behavior is called for. Thus white administrators of private retirement homes may deny any personal resentment against minorities. Yet, they may set exorbitant rental rates to lessen the number of minorities accepted because of their realization that the presence of too many minorities would lessen business relations with potential white residents. In the latter case, a situationally specific perspective outweighed the relatively nonprejudicial attitude.

The important point in this discussion is that although, historically, ethnic minorities in the United States have been victimized by restrictive public policies based on attitudinal hostility, prejudicial attitudes are not a necessary prerequisite for the often private forms of discrimination that exist today. Neither is overt discrimination a necessary consequence of obviously hostile or insensitive attitudes. In spite of federal statutes against discrimination, Schneider (1979) reports that prejudice remained a significant barrier, impeding the effectiveness of service delivery to the aged under the Title VII (Older Americans Act) nutrition program. Meal sites that were identified with particular racial neighborhoods, for example, stood as barriers because older persons of a different race were fearful to venture into the neighborhood to attend the meal.

DIFFERENTIAL POWER RESOURCES

Superior size, skills, and weaponry are a few of the resources important for the initial subordination of one ethnic group by another (Yetman and Steele, 1971). The minority persists as a subordinate group, however, because the nonminority has access to powerful political offices and economic positions through which it is able to exercise prejudice and discrimination. To discriminate in employing practices, for example, requires control over the distribution of occupational and educational resources.

Yetman and Steele (1971) maintain that the fundamental variable in the maintenance of a minority group is the relative power capabilities of the ethnic groups involved. One school of thought in sociology theorizes that differential sources of power derive ultimately from differential distributions in the ownership of property or economically valuable assets. Further, the unequal distribution of power invariably creates conflicts of interest between the holders of power (the majority or dominant group) and those who lack power, the minority (Dahrendorf, 1959). To maintain its favorable position and to aggrandize itself more, the majority exercises its power to exploit, coerce, discriminate, and so forth. Wilson (1978) asserts that "racial" oppression, for instance, has been deliberate and overt, ranging from slavery to segregation and from endeavors to exploit black labor to efforts to neutralize black competition. Consider, for example, the importance of a readily available pool of potential, low-wage laborers—the uneducated, unemployed, minority, young adult males in urban industrial areas.

Yetman and Steele (1971) note that a vicious cycle for maintaining the minority status of a group is strengthened when the consequences of discriminatory acts (for example, excessive poverty, relative to the majority, and its correlates: undernourishment, substandard housing, or low I.Q. scores) are used to justify the original prejudicial claims of minority inferiority. Sociologists have labelled the vicious cycle created by the interdependency between prejudicial attitudes and discriminatory behavior as the self-fulfilling prophecy.

This conceptualization suggests that to the extent that it is in the economic interests of the majority to discriminate against other groups, it will do so. Correlatively, when economic interest in the minority lessens, discrimination should also lessen. Wilson (1978) argues that as long as there was an abundance of low-wage, low-skilled jobs in this country, it was in the interest of the majority to have a ready pool of available labor. But with the expansion of the economy it is possible to foresee the declining significance of a pervasive minority status for black Americans. This is true, Wilson continues, at least for those who are able to grasp power resources such as the increasingly available occupational opportunities in the growing government and corporate sectors. These individuals, therefore, will be in position to compete in the marketplace. Wilson concludes that it will be increasingly difficult to justify continuing assumptions that traditional forms of oppression (white on black and other minorities) are operative, given the rapid economic improvements of at least segments of the black, minority population.

Contrary to Wilson, a major thesis in this book is that the long history of domination of ethnic minorities in this country has resulted in a legacy for the minority elderly—just as it has for the large pool of uneducated, unemployable black and minority males (the black underclass)—that is directly traceable to traditional forms of oppression in this country. Further, should all forms of discrimination and prejudice end today, the life experiences of the current generation (as well as future generations for several decades to come) of minority elderly is such that it would be mistaken to assume necessary similarities in the need patterns of these elderly with other older people. Due to their victimization by a lifetime experience with discrimination, the minority, relative to the majority, elderly can be expected to experience substantially different conditions of aging, including fewer economic resources, poorer nutrition, less adequate housing, and underuse of institutional services.

Concurrently, it is expected that the minority experience will also foster innovative strategies for coping with the disadvantaged position; for example, the minority, relative to the nonminority, aged more often utilize the naturally existing coping resources available in the community: family, friends, neighbors, and church. (See Stagner, 1981, and Slater, 1976, for informative discussions of the coping resources represented by such institutions as the family and church.) Thus the minority elderly are deserving of specialized study, not only because their problems are more profound than the problems of the elderly nonminorities, but also because their patterns of adjustment may serve as models on which to base programs for successful coping among all elderly persons.

THE ENDOGAMOUS NATURE OF SOCIAL RELATIONS

It has been concluded that the minority is denied opportunities by the discriminatory practices of the powerfully situated, majority group. But, beyond victimization through discrimination, a minority must be shown to be a predominantly endogamous group.

The sociological reference to endogamy typically has applied to norms of mate selection. Thus, a rule of endogamy prescribed that societal members choose mates from within the group, while a rule of exogamy stipulated that mates were to be selected from outside the group. In North India, for example, while mates must be selected outside of the patrilineal kin group (exogamy), they must be selected from within the caste (endogamy).

Rules of endogamy have traditionally been rigorously enforced in the United States by both the majority and minority. Formal laws of miscegenation in this country have now largely been repealed, however. Yet there are powerful informal expectations of marriage endogamy among ethnic minorities. Expectations for endogamous relations are also evident, although to a lesser extent, for extramarital social relations among minorities; severe informal sanctions are frequently invoked for their violation, including social disapproval or ostracism. Thus, while the use of the term *endogamy* in this chapter is meant to refer primarily to rules of mate selection, its use is applicable to a large number of social, especially primary, relations.

Obviously, restriction of a large proportion of one's social relations to the group, especially in mate selection, strengthens the sense of peoplehood, accentuates the distinctive characteristics, and generally reinforces the special ethnic qualities of the group.

At a nominal or attribute level of measurement, there are currently four sizeable statistical aggregates within the United States, among all groups that have been hypothesized to be minorities, whose characteristics squarely fit the endogamous criterion, as well as each of the other criteria of a minority. In each case, the recognition of a predominantly endogamous, more or less common ancestral line—along with victimization throughout life by a systematic and inclusive system of discrimination—is crucial in delimiting the applicability of the minority label. These four groups include Hispanic, African or black, Asian, and native Americans.[3] Utilizing this perspective, one may observe the reemergence of nationality identification, albeit via ancestral lineage, as a distinguishing attribute among these groups and between them and the dominant majority. (The reader will recall that a minority group, as originally defined, referred to a national group that had become subordinated to another nationality group.)

The majority in the United States has always had ancestral lines traceable to European origins. And, correlatively, the ancestral lines of the current groups of ethnic minorities derive, at least in large part for each group, from non-European nationalities. This notation is somewhat at variance with Rose (1981), who prefers to limit the ancestral line of the majority in the United States to nationalities represented by northern European origins. Rose, unlike the perspective here, considers the "white ethnics" as minorities.

Generally, the circumstances leading to the subordination of each of the four ethnic minorities is straightforward, beginning either through voluntary or involuntary migration, conquest, or annexation. Black Americans are the only group that initially, and in significant numbers, migrated to the United States involuntarily. Although the forced servitude of black Americans ended over 115 years ago, this group—along with the native Americans—has experienced the most consistent and systematic barriers in seeking a satisfying existence within the United States.

The subordination of the native American is also unique inasmuch as this is the only group that in significant numbers experienced conquest in their own land; hence, the designation native American. As a matter of fact, the history of the territorial expansion of the United States can be charted in terms of the frontier wars of conquest between early European settlers and various native North American Indian nations. Thus, today the numerous native American tribes cannot be properly defined as one culturally similar group. All, however, represent the legacy of exclusionary public policies of the past in which natives were forcefully removed from their homeland to federal reservations.

Like native Americans, the Hispanic population consists of several subgroups with diverse historical backgrounds. Hispanics, however, are ultimately linked, given the fact that each has ancestral lines that combine Spanish and various native American cultural heritages.[4] Although today's Hispanic population is voluntarily migrant to the United States, initially many of those having Mexican, Indian, and Spanish heritage (and living in what is now the southwestern United States) were annexed through the expansionist policies of early U.S. government administrations.

Unlike the Hispanos, as the latter group of Hispanics are sometimes called, the Asian Americans were initially voluntary immigrants. While discrimination against Asian Americans was at a peak during the late 1800s and early 1900s, hostility toward the groups composing the Asian American population (primarily Japanese and Chinese, but also including Pacific Asian groups such as Samoans and Guamanians) has continued, intermittently, throughout the twentieth century. The Chinese Exclusion Act of 1882 and its renewals and the Immigration Act of 1924, for example, restricted or denied immigration, respectively, to Chinese and Japanese for close to half of this century. And, of course, it was relatively recent history that Japanese Americans, by military decree during World War II, were housed in "security" camps in the name of national security.

While a detailed examination of these four groups is beyond the scope of this chapter, a study of the historical forces shaping the minority status of each group is preliminary to gaining an appreciation of the aged in these groups.[5] It is sufficient to conclude by noting that the experiences shaping the minority status of these elderly have consequences that remain psychologically and sociologically imprinted on the individual throughout life. The study in the remaining chapters seeks to document these consequences.

SUMMARY AND CONCLUSIONS

The emphasis in this chapter has focused on deriving a theoretically grounded definition of the minority aged. The assumption underlying this emphasis has been that an appreciation of the elderly minority can best be broached by providing a clear understanding of the historical forces that have shaped the lives of those in the population.

The chapter began by distinguishing between racial, ethnic, and minority status. A minority group was shown to be a special type of ethnic group, subsuming racial criteria and having several distinctive features, including victimization by prejudice and discrimination; differential power resources, relative to the implied majority; and a sense of consciousness, which, in turn, fosters marital and social endogamy. Four contemporary elderly groups in the United States were found to be characterized by these characteristics. They include Hispanic, African or black, Asian, and native Americans.

Defining a minority such that its full complexity is notable was seen as a step in the direction of salvaging the concept from the existing confusion surrounding its use. Too often, it was shown, theorists emphasize only one of the features of a minority to the exclusion of others. Thus, to emphasize only the dominant and subordinate power relation, as do Yetman and Steele (1971), or to fail to emphasize marital and social endogamy, as is true in the case of Wirth (1945) and the contemporary investigators who follow his definition, easily suggests that minorities include women (Blalock, 1967); the aged (Palmore, 1969); widows (Lopata, 1971); students (Davis, 1978); and conceivably even next year's rookies in the major baseball leagues. Applications such as the preceding would be unthinkable if theorists asked whether women, the aged, or widows are predominantly endogamous, or whether the groups are aware of their special ethnic status, or whether indeed they possess distinctive subcultural traits. Strieb (1965) asserts, for example, that the aged possess few distinctive subcultural traits and are themselves aware of still fewer.

As has been shown, once the conceptual morass surrounding the concept of a minority is cleared, it becomes relatively straightforward as to who the minority aged are and why they are considered minorities. The chapters that follow proceed from this conceptualization. In the next chapter, for example, some of the demographic consequences of a minority status among the aged are reviewed.

NOTES

1. For additional reading on the relative merits of the use of race and ethnic labels, see Montagu (1972). Montagu proposes that "race" be dropped from discussions of human affairs altogether, inasmuch as the term is artificial and lacks specificity.

2. See Allport (1958) for an exceptionally good, but dated analysis; for a succinct and more recent discussion, see Rose (1981).

3. It is not the intention to disparage the history of the minority status of the elderly southern European immigrants, today called the "white ethnics"; evidence clearly documents the fact that these early immigrants would be considered minorities. But it is also clear that a minority status is a social phenomenon and thus is neither static nor unchangeable. Greeley (1976) observed that there has been a general integration of white ethnics into the American economy. Jews, along with Italian and Polish American Catholics, have incomes higher than a substantial number of all other groups in the United States. Thus, while the "melting pot" may be an inappropriate description for American intergroup relations, as some have argued, it must be remembered that mere ethnic consciousness is not a sufficient basis for conceptualizing groups as minorities. Moreover, once integrated into the larger society, many of these earlier ethnic minorities have joined the ranks of the dominant majority, perpetuating injustices toward the four contemporary minority groups.

4. The Hispanic population includes all persons in the United States whose heritage combines Spanish and native American ancestry. The aggregate would include Mexican, Cuban, and Puerto Rican Americans, as well as inhabitants from the numerous other Central and South American cultures. While a simple white/nonwhite dichotomy is largely coterminous with the majority/minority distinction, and is so used in selected chapters in this book, it is not at all clear whether Hispanics are white or nonwhite. Thus, while over 90 percent of the Hispanics considered themselves white in the 1970 decennial census of the United States, only 56 percent did in 1980 (for additional discussion, see chapter 3). It is clear, however, given a general reading of history, that Hispanics, particularly Mexican Americans, in every fashion meet the criteria of a minority status. Moreover, their ancestral line is derivable, in part, from a non-European origin.

5. For additional reading regarding the forces shaping the life circumstances of members of each of the ethnic minorities, see the following selective references: Wilson (1978) for the black group; Wax (1971) for the native American group; Jaffe, Cullen, and Boswell (1976) for the Hispanic group; and Sue and Wagner (1973) for Asian Americans.

_____ Part 2

THE DEMOGRAPHY OF
THE MINORITY AGED

INTRODUCTION TO PART 2

"More Americans are living to be older." "Those over 75 years of age are the fastest-growing segment of the population." "The United States is an aging population."

These are but a few of the declarations that typically preface discussions of the demography of the aged. Dramatic introductions, such as the above, are designed to alert the citizenry to the changing age structure in the country and to the implications that this change portends for the care of a dependent or potentially dependent group.

The need for planning for the care of the elderly is dramatized further when one considers the demography of the minority aged. In chapter 3, Ron Manuel and John Reid report, for example, that while there was a 25.2 percent increase (between 1970 and 1980) in the white population, aged 65 years and over, there was a 40.3 percent increase in the population of elderly blacks, aged 65 years and over. Both figures are to be contrasted with the 11.5 percent increase in the total population.

It is not merely in terms of increases in relative population size that the conditions of the minority aged assume significance. Manuel and Reid consider a broad range of sociodemographic indicators of the comparative status of the minority and nonminority elderly. They demonstrate, for example, that the gap between the black and white elderly in the relative percentage of elderly living below poverty increased, not decreased, between 1976 and 1979. When juxtaposed with trends showing the faster growth rate of elderly black Americans, it is clear that projections for the future quality of life among the increasing numbers of black and other minorities are not encouraging.

Throughout the analyses of population growth and economic characteristics, and including other analyses for educational, familial, and health status, the authors illustrate the unique consequences of a minority status for the minority aged. Considering health, for example, the authors note that, next to economic resources, health is the most important context for describing the consequences of the minority experience among the aged. Manuel and Reid conclude that in addition to poorer relative health status, the minority, relative to nonminority, elderly are less likely to have access to medical care, even through the publicly subsidized Medicare program. In sum, the minority aged represent a fast-growing, but impoverished population. Manuel and Reid reason that this circumstance may, in time, threaten to overwhelm the familial and informal support systems that traditionally have played a crucial role in the care of the minority aged.

Two concepts, discussed by Manuel and Reid for generally describing the health of the minority aged, are considered in detail in chapters 4 and 5. These concepts are differential life expectancy and the crossover effect.

Helen Giles first discusses the factors impacting on differential life expectancy during the early and middle ages (chapter 4). The basic question is: "Why do nonwhites live longer than whites after the first roughly 65 years of life?" She finds that the answer to this question, while initially traceable to differential patterns of death, ultimately derives from socio-environmental experiences. Because minorities are more likely to be economically disadvantaged, they are, correlatively, less likely to receive adequate health care, but more likely to adapt to their stressful circumstances through self-destructive means, such as excessive drinking (and thus increased chances of death due to cirrhosis and accidents) or violence, turned either inward (suicide and hypertension) or outward (homicide).

Kenneth Manton extends Giles's analysis in the final chapter in part 2. He endeavors to uncover the basis for changes in the relation of white to nonwhite differential life expectancies throughout the life span: the crossover effect. Ruling out methodologically based, census enumeration errors (in which elderly nonwhites may be overenumerated) as a sufficient explanation for the effect, he entertains several alternative hypotheses. "Mortality selection" as an explanation, for example, suggests that those least able to cope, the minority, will die at a faster rate than the majority during the younger ages. "At advanced ages," Manton concludes, "this mortality differential will cause the disadvantaged population to be proportionately smaller and composed of a group . . . far more robust than the population experiencing lower early mortality rates."

In sum, the chapters in this section illustrate demography's emphasis on the study of the size, composition, and distribution of the population. It is through an understanding of these characteristics that one may come to appreciate the great diversity of the older population.

3

A COMPARATIVE DEMOGRAPHIC PROFILE OF THE MINORITY AND NONMINORITY AGED

RON C. MANUEL AND JOHN REID

Historical forces continually shape the status and character of the older population. Each age cohort is defined through its date of birth by a unique history of sociocultural events. Thus the circumstances of aging among the current population of elderly citizens is affected by the social climate of the first half of the century.

The elderly cohort (age 65 and over) examined in this chapter are "special survivors" in that many in this group experienced, during their formative years, some of the most traumatic events historically characterizing this country. During childhood, many in this cohort experienced and survived the Great Influenza Epidemic of 1918, and their late adolescence and early adulthood occurred during the period of the Great Depression. This was, by any criterion, an unfortunate period for one to pass through. The period was doubly disadvantageous for minorities, however. As minority group members, current cohorts of the minority aged spent their lives dealing with the realities of prejudice, discrimination, and a subordinate position in society. After having experienced conditions that reduced their life chances of becoming a senior citizen, these survivors now face the prejudice and discrimination associated with what an eminent gerontologist, Robert Butler, has labelled ageism.

The theoretical basis shaping the status of the minority elderly has been sufficiently described in the preceding chapter. In this chapter, the most current national data are consolidated in order to provide an overview of a select number of the demographic consequences of a minority status for the minority elderly. All of the data were compiled by the Bureau of the Census, the National Center for Health Statistics, or the United States Health Care Financing Administration. Because other chapters will present detailed, theoretical explanations and implications for several of the conclusions introduced in this chapter, the objective here will primarily focus upon highlighting the demographic facts.

THE SIZE AND COMPOSITION OF THE AGED POPULATION

THE GROWTH OF THE ELDERLY POPULATION

The elderly population of the United States has increased constantly throughout this century. From 1900, when slightly more than 3 million persons were aged 65 years and over, to 1940, the elderly population tripled to 9 million; and in 1980 it was more than 25 million. This eightfold gain in eighty years was far greater than that of the total population, which itself more than tripled from 76 million to 226 million over the same period. Several factors have contributed to this rapid expansion, but the most important factor has been the high fertility rate beginning before 1900 and continuing into the early part of the twentieth century. Large birth cohorts around the turn of the century resulted in large numbers of the elderly sixty-five to seventy-five years later. It will be crucial to keep this cohort effect in mind when interpreting the remaining data in this chapter.

The cohort experiences of blacks and other ethnic minorities, relative to the experiences of whites, the majority population, have been different during this period, however.[1] Prior to 1940, the percentage of population increase from the preceding decade was much larger among whites than among blacks. What is striking and demographically significant is the substantially greater increase among blacks since 1940. Thus, while the elderly black, and white, populations increased between 1920 and 1930 by 12.0 percent and 36.2 percent, respectively, the respective rates of increase between 1930 and 1940 were 65.2 percent and 33 percent (U.S. Bureau of the Census, 1975).[2] Because fertility at any one period of time is a determining factor for the size of the elderly population some sixty-five years later, it is reasonable that the rapid increase in the black aged population, beginning in the 1930s, is the result of birth events during and following the Civil War; however, a greater degree of certainty concerning this issue would require a reexamination of existing vital records for the period under question. Moreover, although black infant mortality has been and remains substantial when compared to the white rate, it is clear that progress in medicine and sanitation has helped to reduce black, like white, infant deaths, thereby sustaining the high relative fertility rate among blacks.

The greater relative rate of growth among elderly blacks continued between 1970 and 1980. In contrast to a 25.2 percent increase within the aged white population, the number of elderly blacks increased by 40.3 percent (see table

3.1). Both figures are substantial when compared to the 11.5 percent increase in the total population.[3]

Although the black aged population is growing at a faster rate than the general, as well as the white aged, population, the black population is not as aged as its nonminority counterpart.[4] Only 7.9 percent of the black population, for example, was over 65 years of age in 1980; a little over 12 percent of the white population was aged. When compared to the proportion of the population that was aged in 1900, these figures also illustrate the aging of the entire population. Thus in 1900, aged whites and blacks constituted only 4.2 and 2.9 percent of their respective populations (U.S. Bureau of the Census, 1975).

The percentage of the elderly also varied within specific ethnic minority groups. In 1980, while 7.9 percent of the black population was over 65 years of age, only 4.9 percent of Hispanics and 5.3 of native Americans were over 65. Slightly over 6 percent of the Asian population was aged.

The United States, for the future, can expect a continuing increase in the number of both minority and nonminority elderly, at least through the year 2020. As table 3.1 shows, the white elderly population is expected to increase by 22.7 percent by the year 2000. On the other hand, the black aged will increase by 45.6 percent, over 20 percentage points more than the nonminority population. In the year 2000, elderly whites will represent 12.9 percent (relative to the 12.2 percent in 1980) of the total white population, and the black aged proportion of the total black population will rise from 7.9 to 9.3 percent. A little over 7 percent of the nonblack minority population will be over 65 in the year 2000.

Contrary to popular opinion, it is important to note that even with below-replacement fertility assumptions (1.7 children per woman), it is unlikely that the older population will be much greater than 13 percent in the year 2000. Demographers, as a matter of fact, note a drop in the growth rate, expected to begin around 1990 and to last about two decades. This decline in growth rate reflects the small cohorts resulting from the low birth rate during the 1930 depression and up to World War II. When the present "baby boom" cohort (born from 1945–1957) begins reaching age 65 around the year 2010, however, the elderly population will increase dramatically until about 2020, suggesting corresponding dramatization of many of the current unresolved problems for society and government.

THE AGE AND SEX COMPOSITION OF THE ELDERLY POPULATION

Table 3.2 extends the discussion by a detailed analysis of 1980 census data on the age, sex, and ethnic composition of the elderly population. The 1980 sex ratios (the number of males for every 100 females) evidence a distinct female advantage (more women than men) throughout the analysis, by ethnicity. Moreover, the female advantage increases by age within each ethnic category. Thus, for the general population there were 80.0 males for every 100 females

TABLE 3.1

Population of the United States by Ethnicity and Age: 1970 and 1980, with Projections to the Year 2000 (Numbers are in thousands)

Ethnicity[a]	Total Population					Projection[b]
	Number		Percentage of Total			
	1970	1980	1970	1980		2000
Total Population	203,212	226,505	100.0	100.0		260,378
White	177,749	188,341	87.5	83.2		218,913
Black	22,580	26,488	11.1	11.7		32,838
Native	827	1,418	0.4	0.6		
Asian and Pacific Islander	1,539	3,501	0.8	1.5		
Other	517	6,757[c]	0.2	3.0		8,627[d]
(Spanish Origin or Hispanic)	(9,073)	(14,606)	(4.5)	(6.4)		

(Table 3.1 continued)

| Ethnicity[a] | Number | | Population Aged 65 and Over | | | | |
| | | | Percentage of Total Population: Aged 65 and Over | | Projection[b] Numbers (Percentage) | Percentage Increase in Population | |
	1970	1980	1970	1980	2000	1970–1980	1980–2000
Total Population (Aged 65 and Older)	19,971	25,545	9.8	11.3	31,822 (12.2)	27.9	24.5
White	18,330	22,944	10.3	12.2	28,155 (12.9)	25.2	22.7
Black	1,487	2,086	6.6	7.9	3,037 (9.3)	40.3	45.6
Native	44	75	5.3	5.3			
Asian and Pacific Islander	101	212	6.6	6.1			
Other	9	228[c]	1.7	3.4	620[d] (7.3)		
(Spanish Origin or Hispanic)	(382)	(709)	(4.2)	(4.9)			

SOURCES: United States Bureau of the Census, 1970, 1977, 1981a.

[a]Population counts by ethnicity for the 1980 decennial census are provisional at this writing. Moreover, the 1970 and 1980 data are not directly comparable. See text notes 1, 2, and 3 for additional commentary.

[b]All projections are based on a low fertility assumption (2.1 children per woman), with a constant annual net immigration of 400,000.

[c]The substantial increase (1970 to 1980) in the population classified as Other is due in large part to changes in the manner of coding the Hispanic population. In 1970, persons who ethnically identified themselves as Other, but who indicated Spanish ancestry (for example, Mexican), were classified as white; in 1980, such persons were not recorded as white, but were left in the Other category. See text note 2 for additional commentary.

[d]Projections for the Other category include all nonwhite persons, except blacks.

TABLE 3.2

Population of the United States Aged 65 and Over by Ethnicity, Age, and Sex: 1970 and 1980

Ethnicity[a] and Age	1970			1980		
	Male	Female	Sex Ratio	Male	Female	Sex Ratio
Total[b]						
65-69	3,122,084	3,869,541	80.7	3,902,083	4,878,761	80.0
85 and Over	542,379	968,522	56.0	681,428	1,558,293	43.7
White						
65-69	2,807,924	3,491,080	80.4	3,481,097	4,329,974	80.4
85 and Over	486,957	899,855	54.1	614,309	1,430,396	42.9
Black						
65-69	277,117	349,800	79.1	331,484	445,113	73.4
85 and Over	45,998	71,386	64.4	52,980	105,881	50.0
Native						
65-69	8,349	8,993	92.8	12,781	15,475	82.6
85 and Over	1,655	2,056	80.5	2,295	3,557	64.5
Hispanic						
65-69	77,746	81,901	94.9	115,542	148,156	78.4
85 and Over	10,840	15,103	71.8	18,557	30,273	61.3
Asian						
65-69	22,537	15,983	141.0	39,180	40,543	96.6
85 and Over	4,065	3,441	118.1	5,203	8,651	60.1

SOURCES: United States Bureau of the Census, 1970, 1981a.

[a]Counts for the 1980 population data by ethnicity are provisional (see text notes 1, 2, and 3 for additional commentary).

[b]Population counts cumulated over the ethnic categories by age are not constructed such that they sum to the total; Hispanics may be white, black, native, or Asian.

aged 65 to 69; among those over 85 years of age there were 43.7 males for every 100 females. The female advantage, of course, reflects the effect of higher male, relative to female, mortality, on the leading causes of death (Waldron and Johnston, 1976).

Clearly the advanced old-aged (85 years and over) are mostly females. While the female advantage for this age group among the ethnic minorities is pronounced, it is not as substantial as among the nonminority population. Thus, while the sex ratio among the nonminority was 42.9, it was 50.0 among blacks; among Asians, Hispanics, and natives it was 60.1, 61.3, and 64.5, respectively. The relative favorability of the advanced old-age sex ratios for males among the ethnic minorities reflects the fact that the mortality differentials between the sexes become less pronounced during the advanced years among the ethnic minorities relative to the nonminority. Following the "mortality selection thesis" of the "crossover effect" (see chapter 5), it is reasonable to suggest (at least for blacks) that the hearty, robust population of blacks who manage to survive into advanced old age consist of a survivor population of both males and females. While males among this population—like in the younger black, as well as in the younger white, population—are more susceptible to death than their female counterparts, they are at less of a disadvantage than the white advanced old-aged males relative to their female counterparts. The black (relative to white) advanced old-aged male, following the mortality selection thesis, is simply an effective survivor of, or coper with, life stresses.

While the advanced old-age sex ratios for minority groups are consistently greater than the nonminority ratio, the ratios, by ethnicity, are less simply related among those 65–69 years of age. For example, the sex ratio among Asians is 96.6 (relative to 80.4 among whites); among blacks, on the other hand, it is 73.4. The higher ratio (relative to the nonminority) among Asians reflects, in part, the continuing influence of the excessive male immigration during the early part of the century;[5] the lower relative ratio of blacks mirrors the excessively greater risk to mortality by black males throughout the younger and middle years.

For context, table 3.2 also presents 1970 data on the elderly sex, age, and ethnic composition. The reader, however, is cautioned on the comparability of the 1970 and 1980 data as it currently exists (see note 2).

ECONOMIC RESOURCES

With retirement, there is a precipitous decline in income. It has been estimated that in order to maintain a level of living comparable to preretirement levels, an older couple (with no children) would need to replace 75 percent of preretirement income (Henle, 1972). But, it is common for income to be slashed by as much as one-half upon retirement (Hendricks and Hendricks, 1981). What does this reduction mean for the elderly? Are they significantly more likely, as a group, to encounter need?

One of the popular approaches for determining need, and who the needy are, is the poverty index. (See Manuel, 1982b for an indepth discussion of numerous approaches for documenting the extent of relative need among elderly blacks and whites.) The poverty index is the level of income considered necessary to maintain a minimum acceptable standard of living for families with specified sets of characteristics.[6] The value establishing the poverty level varies by year; in 1979, for example, it was $3,472 for elderly persons living alone and $4,364 for elderly couples (U.S. Bureau of the Census, 1980c). As can be observed in table 3.3, 8.9 percent of all white persons in 1979 were below poverty threshold, whereas 30.9 and 21.6 percent, respectively, of all blacks and Hispanic persons were so characterized. Among the elderly the respective proportions were even higher. Relative to 13.2 percent of the white elderly, 35.5 percent of aged blacks and 26.7 percent of their

TABLE 3.3

Persons Below and Near the Poverty Level by Ethnicity and Age: 1970, 1976, and 1979

(in percentages)

Ethnicity[a] and Year	Persons Below Poverty			Persons Near Poverty (125% of the Poverty Level)
	All Ages	Aged 65 Years and Over	White/Minority Poverty Gap	Aged 65 Years and Over
All Groups				
1979	11.6	15.1		24.7
1976	11.8	15.0		
1970	12.5	24.5		
White				
1979	8.9	13.2		22.3
1976	9.1	13.2		
1970	10.1	22.5		
Black				
1979	30.9	35.5	22.3	49.1
1976	31.3	34.8	21.6	
1970	33.4	48.0	25.5	
Hispanic				
1979	21.6	26.7	13.5	38.8
1976	24.9	27.7	14.5	
1970	26.6	—[b]	—	

SOURCE: United States Bureau of the Census, 1980c.

[a]Hispanics may be black or white.
[b]Not available.

Hispanic counterparts were below poverty. Clearly, the majority of the aged in each of the ethnic groups is above the poverty level, thus dispelling the myth that most elderly persons are poor or that all elderly minority persons are poorer than all nonminority elderly.

On the other hand, some would stress, as is shown in table 3.3, that conditions have improved for the minority aged since 1970, just as conditions have improved for the majority group aged. It is also a fact, however, that the difference between the percentages of elderly blacks and whites below the poverty threshold — the poverty gap — has remained relatively unchanged over the last ten years, and if anything, the short-term trend is toward an increasing gap. Thus 25.5 percent more of the black, relative to the white, aged were below poverty in 1970; and while this figure was down to 21.1 percent in 1976, it increased to 22.3 percent in 1979.

Even more alarming are statistics for the near-poor (persons living below

125 percent of the poverty level) elderly. Here, just about one-half of today's elderly black population are close to or below the poverty threshold. Nearly 39 percent of elderly Hispanics are near or below poverty, but only 22 percent of the nonminority aged are so characterized. Clearly a substantial number of the minority elderly are, if not living in poverty, near the poverty threshold. With the loss of public income supports, the proportion of the minority elderly below poverty undoubtedly would easily and significantly increase (see chapter 16 for a detailed analysis of the impact of changes in public income supports on elderly minorities).

Table 3.4 extends the analysis of the resources of the elderly. The table presents comparative data, over time, on the education of the elderly. Education is an important indicator of the relative status of the minority elderly, given the association between education and ability to adapt needs to the bureaucratized service-delivery system for the aged. Moreover, while there is a direct correlation between income and education, it does not follow that the relation is perfect or the same for all groups.[7] Thus when examining data on education, one should not assume a necessary causal relation between income and education. This is especially the case for the current cohort of elderly blacks. In other words, those in poverty are not there totally because of educational disadvantage. Minority elderly, because of their minority status, were often denied jobs commensurate with their education during their working years, and among those who had jobs they frequently were paid less than their white counterpart. Furthermore, even assuming that minority/nonminority variation in poverty status is due, in part, to education, it remains true for the current aged cohort of minority elderly that education was differentially accessible by ethnicity.

It is evident from table 3.4 that the educational level of both the minority and nonminority elderly has improved since 1970. For example, almost 60 percent of the elderly did not have high school educations in 1979; in 1970 close to 72 percent were without high school educations. But in 1979 substantially greater percentages of both the Hispanic (84.6 percent) and black (83.0 percent) elderly populations, relative to the nonminority elderly population (57.7 percent), had less than a high school education. Again, the gulf between the minority (for example, black) and nonminority populations is instructive. As is calculable from table 3.4, the black/white percentage gap actually widened (1970–1979) by almost 5 percentage points (20.9 to 25.3) among those with less than a high school education.

To conclude, considering that 27.6 percent more blacks (aged 45 to 54 in 1979) than whites had less than a high school education, the black/white education gap for the aged in the foreseeable future will remain unchanged.

FAMILIAL INTEGRATION

Contrary to popular belief, most older persons, whether minority or nonminority, live in communities and in families. While the family is frequently

TABLE 3.4
Educational Attainment by Ethnicity and Age: 1970 and 1979
(in percentages)

Ethnicity by Year	Aged 25 to 34		Aged 45 to 54		Aged 65 and Over	
	Less Than High School	Four or More Years College	Less Than High School	Four or More Years College	Less Than High School	Four or More Years College
1970						
All Ethnic Groups[a]	26.2	15.8	41.8	10.0	71.7	6.3
White	23.9	16.6	38.8	10.6	70.1	6.7
Black	46.7	6.1	70.9	3.8	91.0	2.0
Hispanic	—[b]	—	—	—	—	—
1979						
All Ethnic Groups	15.3	23.8	32.5	15.0	59.9	8.5
White	13.9	24.9	29.7	15.8	57.7	9.0
Black	26.6	12.8	57.3	7.2	83.0	2.5
Hispanic	45.7	7.8	63.4	5.5	84.6	3.5

SOURCE: United States Bureau of the Census, 1980b.

[a] Hispanics may be black or white.
[b] Not available.

one that has dwindled to an older couple with no children or other relatives, there are important variations by population group (sex by ethnicity, as well as by age). For example, fewer women continue to live in a family setting during their old age. Thus, at ages 75 and over, 77.8 percent of nonminority men are in families, but only 46.8 percent of their female counterparts are in familial settings (see table 3.5). While a similar conclusion holds for black males and females of the same age, roughly equal proportions of similarly aged Hispanic males and females are in families.

The data in table 3.5 show that in addition to sex variations there are also important ethnic differences. Thus, over 75 percent of Hispanic females are in families after age 75, relative to 46.8 percent of their white counterparts. To illustrate further, elderly black women, aged 65 to 74, are much more likely to maintain families (19.0 percent) than similarly aged white females (7.4 percent). And there is a trend across age cohorts for more white (than Hispanic) females to live alone or with nonrelatives. As a matter of fact, Hispanic females, aged 75 and over, are slightly less likely than their younger cohorts to live as primary individuals.

And, as is evident in table 3.6, greater percentages of the white (5.8 percent) relative to nonwhite (3.0 percent) elderly live in nursing homes. Besides greater familial dependence (Hill, 1978), elderly other factors that impact the relative number of minorities in nursing homes include discrimination in referrals (Bozak and Gjullin, 1979), geographical distribution of nursing homes, as well as shorter life spans (Scanlon and associates, 1979).

The fact that relatively greater percentages of the minority elderly (75 years and over) are in familial settings does not, however, suggest that these individuals are automatically and overwhelmingly surrounded by kin. Manuel (1980b), studying a large random sample of elderly respondents in southern California, for example, has noted that while 16 percent of the elderly white respondents were in extended familial settings, 40 percent (less than one-half) of the black and Mexican American respondents were so situated. Thus, although the minority elderly were relatively more often in extended families, neither the minority nor the nonminority elderly were typically in extended settings.

In conclusion, the section ends as it began: While the minority elderly are more familially integrated, neither minority nor nonminority elderly are abandoned by, or abandon, their families. Even among nursing home residents, a predominantly white population, most are there because they have no family or because the family has been overwhelmed by the extreme burdens of the infirm elderly relative.

TABLE 3.5
Familial Status of Persons Aged 65 and Older by Ethnicity, Age, and Sex: 1979

| Ethnicity, Sex, and Age | Familial Status[a] as % of Total Population | | | | Total Population (in thousands) |
| | In Primary Family | | Primary Individual | Secondary Individual | |
	Total	Primary Family Head			
White					
Male					
65–74	86.1	81.7	12.5	1.4	5,726
75 and Over	77.8	71.7	21.0	1.1	2,872
Female					
65–74	62.2	7.4	36.7	1.1	7,557
75 and Over	46.8	8.5	52.3	0.9	4,795
Black					
Male					
65–74	71.3	65.3	21.6	7.1	558
75 and Over	71.2	48.1	23.5	5.3	254
Female					
65–74	59.9	19.0	37.8	2.0	757
75 and Over	54.6	17.9	42.2	2.8	385

(TABLE 3.5 Continued)
Familial Status of Persons Aged 65 and Older by Ethnicity, Age, and Sex: 1979

| Ethnicity, Sex, and Age | Familial Status[a] as % of Total Population | | | | Total Population (in thousands) |
| | In Primary Family | | Primary Individual | Secondary Individual | |
	Total	Primary Family Head			
Hispanic[b]					
Male					
65–74	82.8	77.8	16.7	0.6	157
75 and Over	76.7	60.6	17.7	3.5	93
Female					
65–74	73.3	14.5	25.2	0.5	192
75 and Over	76.1	6.4	22.0	1.9	97

SOURCE: United States Bureau of the Census, 1980a.

[a]A primary family includes the person who maintains the household. A subfamily is a unit of a primary family, excluding but related to the household head, consisting of a married couple (with or without children) or one parent with single children (under 18 years). While a primary individual maintains a household and lives either alone or with nonrelatives, a secondary individual lives in a household or group quarters with nonrelatives.
[b]Hispanics may be either black or white.

TABLE 3.6
Health Status by Age and Ethnicity: 1976 and 1977

Age and Ethnicity	Self-Perceived Health Status: 1977			Number of Restricted Activity Days per Person by Economic Status: 1976[a]		Number of Bed Disability Days per Person by Income: 1977		Nursing and Personal Care Home Residents, Aged 65 and Over: 1977	
	Population (in thousands)	Excellent %	Poor %	Poor[a]	Nonpoor	Poor	Nonpoor	Number	% per Group
All Ages	211,400	48.6	2.8	28.8	14.7	–c	–c		
White	160,129	51.5	2.5	29.6	14.6	11.7	5.3		
Black	23,066	35.3	4.3						
Hispanic	11,913	44.1	2.7						
Nonwhite[b]									
Aged 17 to 44	85,666	52.5	1.4	26.0	15.1	11.5	6.1		
White	64,281	56.2	1.1	19.9	12.7	–c	–c		
Black	9,374	36.7	2.5	19.1	12.3	7.6	4.5		
Hispanic	4,957	44.3	2.0						
Nonwhite[b]									
Aged 65 and Over	22,033	29.3	8.7	22.4	16.2	12.0	6.1		
White	18,109	30.9	7.4	46.6	31.2	–c	–c	1,126,000	5.1
Black	1,807	20.3	16.7	45.1	30.7	15.7	11.9	1,059,900	5.8
Hispanic	505	24.4	11.4						
Nonwhite[b]				57.8	39.8	22.4	12.3	66,100	3.0

SOURCES: U.S. Department of Health and Human Services, 1980; National Center for Health Statistics, 1980b.

[a] A poor economic status is defined as family income under $7,000.
[b] Nonwhite includes all groups other than white.
[c] Not available.

HEALTH INDICATORS

HEALTH STATUS

Health, according to the World Health Organization (1959), is not merely the absence of disease, as traditionally assumed by the biomedical perspective; it is a state of physical and psychosocial well-being. Health, then, cannot be described merely in terms of the objective, clinical assessment of the presence or absence of disease. Subjective evaluations of health, therefore, appear to be of at least some importance.

Self-assessment of health has been identified as the most important determinant of satisfaction among the aged (Palmore and Luikart, 1972). Moreover, Maddox and Douglass (1972) aver that there is a positive congruence between self and physical ratings of health. They note, however, that self-assessments cannot serve as a substitute for epidemiologic diagnoses.

As table 3.6 shows, the aged are more likely than the young and middle-aged to perceive their health as poor, and the minority aged are even more likely to report poor health. For example, 16.7 percent and 11.4 percent, respectively, of the black and Hispanic populations assessed their health as poor in 1977; only 7.4 percent of their white counterparts perceived likewise. Correlatively, a smaller proportion of the minority aged perceived their health as excellent.

To merely note that older (relative to younger) people or minority (relative to nonminority) elderly perceive more health problems is rather simplistic. What about the nature of the conditions shaping relative health assessments? Some illnesses are acute, while others are chronic. Chronic diseases refer to long-term or permanent health disabilities, such as rheumatism or high blood pressure (hypertension); on the other hand, acute diseases are short-term conditions, such as certain infectious diseases or injuries.

With age, acute conditions decrease and chronic conditions increase. Because the chronic diseases play such a prominent role in the relative causes of death among the aged, little more need be explicitly noted regarding them in this chapter; chapter 4 will consider the topic in detail.

It is noteworthy at this point, however, to look at the impact of disability, whether acutely or chronically based, on functional ability or the ability to function routinely. Table 3.6 shows that subjective assessments of poor health, by age, correspond to age-related differences in activity limitations. Whereas activity among the poor and nonpoor elderly, respectively, was restricted on 46.6 and 31.2 days (per person) in 1976, the corresponding rates among the young and middle aged were 19.9 and 12.7. Thus, the more prevalent chronic conditions of the elderly are more restricting of functional ability. These conditions are even more restricting among the minority elderly. Elderly poor minorities experienced 57.8 activity-restricted days in 1976 in contrast to 45.1 days for their white counterparts.

Similarly, the minority (relative to nonminority) elderly were more likely to experience bed-restricted disabilities. In 1977, for instance, minorities (with family incomes below $7,000) experienced 22.4 bed-restricted days; the nonminority elderly experienced 15.7 days. Interestingly, this disparity, unlike the case for the measure on restricted-activity days, almost disappears among the higher-income elderly. While the nonminority experienced 11.9 bed-restricted days, the minority experienced 12.3 days. Apparently, better economic conditions serve to lessen the minority-related impact, at least for the bed-restricted activity measure.

An ultimate, but crude, indicator of disability among the elderly is nursing home utilization. Only 5.1 percent of the elderly generally were in nursing homes in 1977 (see table 3.6). Thus, unlike popular conceptions, most aged are not in nursing homes, although at advanced ages the percentage of the elderly in nursing homes is more pronounced. For example, in 1977, 449,900 persons over 85 years of age were nursing home residents, representing 20.6 percent of this population.

Obviously, an isomorphic relation does not exist between nursing home utilization and disability. If so, one would expect higher proportions of minority elderly as nursing home residents. Inequity by ethnicity in the use of nursing homes thus reflects other processes. These factors need not be recalled here inasmuch as several of them were reviewed in the preceding section.

To conclude the thesis that a minority status does impact on health status, one can mention the most general indicator for summarizing the differential health status of minorities and nonminorities: differential life expectancy. Differential life expectancy is an excellent measure of differential health status because life expectancies are calculated from death rates; and differences in death rates from various causes, between groups, reflect differences in health status. Differential life expectancy, defined, refers to subcultural and time variations in the average number of remaining years of life for individuals who have survived to a specified age.

While it is beyond the scope of this chapter to describe or consider the explanation of differences in life expectancies (see chapters 4 and 5 for in-depth discussions), it is clear that there are minority and nonminority differences. Reflective of the poor health of minorities, data from 1978 show that minority females, at birth, could expect to live roughly three years less than nonminority females and minority males could expect to live roughly five years less than their nonminority counterpart (NCHS, 1980c). Interestingly, by age 85 this conclusion is reversed. That is, at age 85, minority females and males can expect to outlive, respectively, nonminority females and males. In other words, life expectancies of respective "sex by ethnic" populations, over time, cross each other (see chapter 5 for a detailed analysis of this crossover phenomenon).

In sum, the minority experience does uniquely impact on the health of the minority aged, just as it does on the economic and other sociodemographic factors that have been examined in this chapter.

TABLE 3.7
Medicare Utilization and Reimbursement Among the Population Aged 65 Years and Over by Ethnicity: 1978

Service Type	Use Rate and Ethnicity per 1,000 Enrolled			Average Reimbursement per enrollee[b]		
	White	Ethnic Minority	White/Minority Ratio[a]	White	Ethnic Minority	White/Minority Ratio
Hospital Insurance and/or Supplementary Medical Insurance	600	536	1.12	$869	$846	1.03
Hospital Insurance	235	204	1.15	625	641	0.98
Inpatient	233	201	1.16	603	615	0.98
Skilled Nursing	12	8	1.50	13	10	1.30
Home Health	22	26	0.85	12	16	0.75
Supplemental Medical Insurance	612	562	1.09	259	248	1.04
Physician and Other Services	597	521	1.15	223	181	1.23
Outpatient	229	260	0.88	32	60	0.53
Home Health	10	14	0.71	4	7	0.57
Total Enrolled	22,803,000	2,248,000				
Total Served	12,948,000	1,138,000				
Total Reimbursement				18,744,000	1,796,000	

SOURCE: United States Health Care Financing Administration (n.d., prepublished data for 1978).

NOTE: The data in this table are preliminary (prepublished).
[a]Ratios are formed by dividing the use rate for whites by the rate for minorities.
[b]Values are formed by multiplying the "reimbursement per person served" (not shown) by the use rate, multiplied by .001.

HEALTH CARE COST

In view of the high cost of being ill, the final question concerns accessibility to health care. Health care cost in 1979 was $212.2 billion for the nation, an average of $943 per person. This amount represented an increase of 12.5 percent from the preceding year, consistent with the 12.2 percent average annual increase since 1965. Fueled by inflationary cost (for example, cost of labor, fuel, and supplies), increasing utilization, and ever changing medical advances (National Center for Health Statistics [NCHS], 1980b), increases of such magnitude have long prompted concern that health care cost will eventually overwhelm the individual citizen.

The high cost of illness is of particular concern for the elderly, and the concern is of even greater significance for the minority elderly, given their higher relative illness risks.

Sources of payment for the nation's $188.5-billion personal health care bill in 1979 included direct payment, 31.8 percent; private insurance, 26.7 percent; and federal, state, and local government, 40.3 percent (NCHS, 1980b).

Government spending clearly is a major payment source. Two-thirds of all public spending for personal health care was accounted for by Medicare and Medicaid. Both were primarily introduced in order to reduce the inaccessibility to health care for the elderly and the needy. Medicare, the major program for the elderly, was authorized in 1965 (Title XVIII of the 1965 Amendments to the Social Security Act). As is evident in table 3.7, it consists of two basic components, a compulsory hospital insurance program and a voluntary program of supplemental medical insurance (for example, for physicians' bills). Generally, persons aged 65 years and over, if eligible, do not pay premiums for the hospital insurance (HI); it is financed by employer-employee contributions, from federal taxes on the earnings of the currently employed. On the other hand, the supplemental insurance component (SMI) requires a premium, per enrollee, along with matching funds from the federal government.

Medicare is thus a national health insurance, albeit of modified form, providing free hospital insurance for those entitled to Social Security. Reflecting the American cultural tradition of individual responsibility for well-being, the program, however, was not designed with the purpose of providing a comprehensive system of protection against the cost of illness. Consequently, despite Medicare, the elderly, especially the low-income minority elderly, continue to be burdened with substantial annual out-of-pocket health expenses. As shown in table 3.8, for example, the average 1977 out-of-pocket health expense, when excluding health insurance premiums, was $563 for blacks, aged 65 and over. On the other hand, the corresponding expense for whites, aged 65 and over, was $438, an amount that was 77 percent of the elderly black expense. Out-of-pocket health-related costs primarily reflect the deductibles and noncovered services of Medicare (for instance, prescription drugs outside of the hospital).[8]

TABLE 3.8
Average Annual Out-of-Pocket Health Expenses
for Persons with Expense by Age and Ethnicity: 1977

Age and Ethnicity	Average Expense (Dollars)	
	Including Health Insurance Premiums	Excluding Health Insurance Premiums
All Ages	336.00	276.00
White	342.00	275.00
Black	270.00	286.00
Aged: 17–44	298.00	250.00
White	302.00	251.00
Black	251.00	236.00
Aged: 65 and over	539.00	447.00
White	555.00	438.00
Black	349.00	563.00

SOURCE: Unpublished data from the National Health Interview Survey, National Center for Health Statistics, U.S. Department of Health and Human Services.

In addition to this type of concern, the crucial question for consideration in this section remains: Has Medicare been effective in increasing the accessibility of the minority aged to high-cost medical services? Table 3.7 provides an answer, in part, to this inquiry. Two measures are provided as indicators of access to the Medicare program. First, use rates, or the number of people served, are studied in relation to types of services offered through Medicare. This measure represents the differential extent to which major health services are available to the minority (relative to the nonminority) elderly. On the other hand, following Ruther and Dobson (1981), a second measure, average reimbursement per Medicare enrollee, was used to represent a measure of "equity in the use of Medicare benefits"; it combines the joint impact of the access to utilization and the amount of reimbursement. Table 3.7 shows the nonminority to minority ratios for service utilization. Generally, 1.12 times more whites, per 1,000 enrolled, used HI or SMI services than did nonminorities. The pattern for specific service rates reflects this general conclusion. For example, the ratios for inpatient hospital services and for physician services, major sources for health care expense, were 1.16 and 1.15, respectively (a ratio of 1.00 represents equity in accessibility). Thus, although Ruther and Dobson have found significant decreases in the ratio since 1969, when the two previous ratios were 1.23 and 1.58, respectively, there remain minority-related differentials in accessibility to medical care.

Equity between minorities and nonminorities in the "use of Medicare benefits," however, is reflected in the data. The overall ratio, 1.03, is down from 1.53 in 1967. Only the ratio of benefit from physician services, 1.23, indicates substantive nonminority disadvantage.

To conclude, inasmuch as elderly minorities have been shown to be less healthy than their nonminority counterparts, it can be assumed that they should use services relatively more often and should receive higher reimbursements. The data, however, support this assumption only in part. That is, fewer of those eligible for Medicare actually use the service; but for those who do utilize the service, their reimbursement is generally comparable to that of the nonminority, except for physician services.

CONCLUSION

This chapter has introduced the most recently available demographic data on the elderly in the United States. While the chapter has only touched the surface of the rich array of data available, it has presented a representative sampling of conclusions derivable from existing information. Most important for the current context, it has been concluded that (1) the minority aged are growing, and will continue to grow in the near future, at a faster rate than the nonminority aged; (2) the minority (relative to the nonminority) aged are more disadvantaged with respect to income, education, and health resources; and (3) while the extended familial household is typical of neither the minority nor the nonminority elderly, substantively more of the minority elderly do live in extended households.

In the final analysis, the minority elderly—a growing, but impoverished population that conceivably, in time, could threaten to overwhelm the traditional familial-based, care-giving system—constitute a special segment of the elderly population. As postulated in the preceding chapter, a minority status does have uniquely defining qualities for the target populations. These qualities, as indicated by the demographic indicators studied in this chapter, confirm this simple conclusion.

NOTES

1. Consistent with the rationale introduced in the preceding chapter, the term *ethnic* is used to subsume racial, as well as ethnic-related, divisions. Ethnic groups, it was argued, are distinguishable by their minority or nonminority (majority) status. Ethnic minorities in the United States currently include Hispanic, native, black, and Asian Americans. While white Americans represent a variety of ethnics, the various white subgroups are similar in that they (excluding Hispanics if the latter are considered white) have historically, or at least for the recent past, dominated, politically or economically, the ethnic minorities. Although this chapter, along with several of the remaining chapters in this book, uses the terms *white* and *nonwhite* interchangeably with *nonminority* and *minority*, respectively, this usage is not entirely clear-cut. It is not at all clear whether Hispanics consider themselves white or nonwhite (see chapter 2).

Thus while the variables studied in this chapter include separate analyses for Hispanics, counts for the Hispanic population are also reflected within counts for the white, as well as the black and other ethnic minority, populations. This actually is of little practical significance, at least for the conclusions of this chapter. For example, only 4.3 percent of the 1980 total white population count consisted of Hispanics, reflecting 56 percent of the total Hispanic count. Forty percent of the Hispanic population was classified as "other" in the 1980 population count (U.S. Bureau of the

Census, 1981a). Thus the proportion of Hispanics among the nonwhite groups is even smaller than among white groups. See notes 2 and 3 for additional detail.

2. Several of the analyses in this chapter are limited to the black and white elderly, representing, respectively, the minority and nonminority populations. Census data on elderly minorities other than blacks are limited prior to 1970 inasmuch as data on specific groups were coded only *white* or *nonwhite*. In this chapter, when data are available for minorities other than black, they are presented.

The failure of U.S. census publications to present ethnic-specific data for the elderly has constituted few problems in the past because the nonwhite population was overwhelmingly black. In 1900 and 1970, 96.6 and 91.1 percent, respectively, of the nonwhite elderly population was black. Provisional estimates from the 1980 population show that roughly 87.9 percent of the nonwhite elderly population is black.

Since 1970, census data are increasingly available on more specific ethnic designations. Data on ethnicity, or as the census bureau prefers "race," are generally provided on whites, blacks, and others. Data are also separately available on Hispanics. As noted earlier, when examining only the racial designations, data on Hispanics are confounded with each of the racial categories.

3. A number of factors must be considered when examining the provisional population totals, by ethnicity, from the 1980 census. Several of these factors lessen the accuracy of straightforward comparisons between 1970 and 1980. But, while these limitations must be identified, they are not of a magnitude to negate general or trend comparisons between the 1970 and 1980 data.

First, the 1980 (relative to 1970) population was more accurately studied. The 1980 count for the black population, for example, indicates that the undercount rate is down from 7.7 percent in 1970 to about 5.0 percent in 1980. The success in accounting for the population represents a more significant factor for comparative studies of the Hispanic population. Hispanics increased by 61 percent, between 1970 and 1980. The effective public relations campaign, without question, resulted in the inclusion of a substantial, but unknown number of Hispanics of questionable legal status.

Reports also indicate, as noted earlier, a significant change in the way the Hispanic population is reported. Forty percent of Hispanics did not report a specific racial designation, while 56 percent reported white. In 1970 about 93 percent of all Hispanics reported their race as white. In part, because of Hispanic inconsistencies in reporting ethnicity (race), the 1970 and 1980 data are not directly comparable without adjustments to the general population counts. At this writing, the weights for making adjustments for the elderly populations by ethnicity are not available. As previously indicated, this limitation does not constitute an extreme problem inasmuch as the Hispanic counts for each ethnic (racial) group are so small. Data, moreover, are observable in separate analyses for the Hispanic group. Only the "other" category is extremely affected by the change in coding of the Hispanic population. In this chapter, comparisons using this category are neglected.

There are other limitations in the data that plague straightforward interpretations of the data. Thus, part of the increase (1970–1980) in the Asian population also reflects changes in census coding procedures. The categories for Asians were expanded in 1980 to include Asian Indians, Vietnamese, Guamanians, and Samoans; Asian Indians were coded as white in 1970. And among native American Indians a substantial part of the 1980 population increase is reportedly due to changes in the likelihood of persons to identify themselves as Indian (U.S. Bureau of the Census, 1981a).

4. An aging population is one whose total population count, over time, is characterized by increasingly greater proportions of persons over 65 years of age.

5. The higher sex ratio of Asian Americans, reflecting the effect of excessive male immigration during the early part of the century, is clearly seen in the 1970 data. There is a distinct male advantage.

6. See Walther (1976) for a brief, but good, discussion of the limitations of the poverty index.

7. See Althauser and associates (1975) for an informative examination of the relation between

ethnicity (race), education, income, and occupational position.

8. Because of space limitations, this chapter is limited to an analysis of Medicare. Medicaid (Title XIX of the 1965 Amendments to the Social Security Act) is a second public health program that has been particularly beneficial for the elderly. Medicaid requires states to provide hospital and physician services, skilled nursing home care, and home health services to low-income needy families with aged, blind, disabled, and dependent children.

Inasmuch as the program is state-administered, with federal matching funds tailored to each state, its impact varies greatly by state, depending on the willingness of state governments to bear the financial burden. But as Feder and Holahan (1979) conclude, the coverage can be extremely important in facilitating assess to medical services for the minority elderly. Persons eligible for Medicaid, for example, do not pay required Medicare deductibles or copayments. See Harris (1975) for an informative discussion of Medicaid.

4

DIFFERENTIAL LIFE EXPECTANCY AMONG WHITE AND NONWHITE AMERICANS: SOME EXPLANATIONS DURING YOUTH AND MIDDLE AGE

HELEN FOSTER GILES

The preceding chapter introduced the concept of differential life expectancy. It was shown that life expectancies vary, depending upon the population group. When sex by race groups are compared for 1978, from data collected by the National Center for Health Statistics (NCHS, 1980a), the differential life expectancies at birth are as follows: white female, 77.8 years; nonwhite female, 73.6 years; white male, 70.2 years; and nonwhite male, 65.0 years. These data suggest that sex is a greater contributor to the overall differential in life expectancy than is race. However, the data also indicate a substantial racial difference in life expectancy.

The primary purpose of this chapter is to establish those variables that contribute to the differential life expectancies by race (nonwhites and whites) in the United States during the first 65 years of life. Inasmuch as blacks constituted 89 percent of the nonwhite population during the 1970 decennial census enumeration (Klebba, 1975), the basic question is "Why do whites generally live longer than blacks?" or, in the context of this discussion, "Why do whites, as the majority group, live longer than minorities?" In approaching this question, however, one ought to bear in mind that the effects of sex tend to confound the effects of race and ethnicity.

The expectation of life is calculated from race-specific mortality rates. Thus, it is appropriate to look at variations in mortality rates in order to study differential life expectancy. As table 4.1 shows, the death rate for all ages of

TABLE 4.1
Death Rates by Age and Race: 1960, 1969, and 1975
(U.S. rates per 1,000 population)

Age	Race					
	White			Nonwhite		
	1960	1969	1975	1960	1969	1975
All Ages	9.5	9.5	9.0	10.1	9.6	8.3
Under 1 Year	23.6	19.2	14.1	46.3	32.0	27.7
1–4 Years	1.0	0.8	0.6	1.9	1.3	1.0
5–14 Years	0.4	0.4	0.3	0.6	0.6	0.5
15–24 Years	1.0	1.2	1.1	1.6	2.1	1.6
25–34 Years	1.2	1.3	1.2	3.2	3.7	3.0
35–44 Years	2.6	2.7	2.3	6.3	7.1	5.3
45–54 Years	6.9	6.6	6.0	13.4	13.2	10.8
55–64 Years	16.3	15.8	14.2	27.7	26.2	21.8
65–74 Years	37.4	35.8	31.0	47.8	55.6	39.7
75–84 Years	88.3	79.8	73.8	76.3	69.3	70.8
Over 84 Years	203.5	202.2	157.1	139.1	99.6	101.0

SOURCE: National Center for Health Statistics, 1978b.

whites combined was 9.5 per 1,000 in 1960 and 1969. The total death rate for nonwhites decreased from 10.1 per 1,000 in 1960 to 9.6 per 1,000 in 1969. The substantial decline in the number of deaths of nonwhites who were younger than 1 year and older than 75, however, masked the increased mortality rates of nonwhites of other ages during this decade.

In order to establish the factors that contributed to the higher mortality rates of the nonwhite, racial differences in death rates will be analyzed for each of the following specific age groups: the neonatal and infancy period; ages 1 to 14 years; ages 15 to 44 years; and ages 45 to 64 years.

THE NEONATAL–INFANCY YEAR

Since 1959 the life expectancy at birth has increased more rapidly for nonwhites than for whites (Metropolitan Life Insurance Company, 1977). The leading contributor to this trend has been the drastic reduction in nonwhite infant mortality rates due to prenatal asphyxia and immaturity (Manniello and Farrell, 1977) and accidents, influenza, and pneumonia (see table 4.2). These decreases, in turn, have resulted from improved nutritional, prenatal, and family planning education for the poor mother. Improved obstetric procedures and more readily available prenatal care are also important factors (Manniello and Farrell, 1977, and Wallace, 1979).

TABLE 4.2
Death Rates by Selected Causes, Age, and Race: 1960, 1969, and 1975
(U.S. rates per 100,000 population)

Age	Race[a]	Cause of Death								
		Influenza and Pneumonia			Suicide			Accidents Other than Motor Vehicle Accidents		
		1960	1969	1975	1960	1969	1975	1960	1969	1975
All Ages	N	62.0	43.2	24.6	4.5	5.3	6.8	44.1	40.1	33.1
	W	34.1	32.6	26.4	11.4	11.9	13.6	29.4	28.6	25.9
Under 1 Year	N	650.6	433.5	152.4				181.2	106.6	70.3
	W	166.8	154.6	55.1				68.2	48.4	28.0
1–4 Years	N	38.8	16.7	7.0				44.5	32.2	26.0
	W	12.4	6.4	3.5				17.7	17.1	16.2
5–14 Years	N	4.6	2.5	1.4	0.1	0.2	0.1	20.9	16.4	13.7
	W	2.3	1.7	0.9	0.3	0.3	0.5	9.9	8.9	8.5
15–24 Years	N	5.7	4.3	2.5	3.4	6.9	9.1	27.6	33.8	26.7
	W	2.6	2.3	1.6	5.4	8.1	12.3	16.7	19.2	20.2
25–34 Years	N	4.4	12.4	6.5	7.9	11.6	14.8	32.1	36.9	31.6
	W	3.5	2.9	1.9	10.3	13.1	16.6	16.9	18.6	18.3
35–44 Years	N	31.2	28.4	14.9	8.3	9.8	9.9	41.5	41.9	37.6
	W	6.7	6.5	4.0	14.9	17.5	18.4	19.3	21.3	18.6
45–54 Years	N	56.1	45.2	27.0	7.9	7.6	8.4	49.7	47.7	41.8
	W	15.7	15.0	9.2	22.1	20.7	21.5	26.1	25.7	22.8
55–64 Years	N	107.8	80.6	50.1	10.1	6.2	7.5	58.7	59.3	49.5
	W	36.8	35.2	24.6	25.0	22.8	21.4	31.5	34.7	28.7

SOURCE: National Center for Health Statistics, 1978b.

[a]N = Nonwhite; W = White.

As table 4.1 shows, however, the rate of infant deaths for nonwhites in 1975 (27.7 per 1,000) continued to outnumber that for whites (14.1 per 1,000). There are several reasons that nonwhite infants continue to have an increased risk of death compared to white infants. First, for the period of 1968–1974, 13 percent of nonwhite newborns weighed less than 2,500 grams, compared to 6 percent of white infants (Manniello and Farrell, 1977); neonatal weights of less than 2,500 grams are associated with a higher risk of death. Low birth weight, moreover, has been shown to be indicative of poor nutritional habits of the mother, with the highest proportion of low-birth-weight babies born to mothers who are less than 25 years old (Wallace, 1979). The percentage of nonwhite mothers in this category is higher than the percentage for whites (Zackler, Andelman, and Bauer, 1969; NCHS, 1973a).

Other reasons for the higher death risk of nonwhite infants are also related to characteristics of the mother. For example, in 1973, infants born to unmarried mothers less than 20 years or more than 35 years of age had higher mortality rates; proportionately, more nonwhite infants are in these categories than white infants (NCHS, 1973b; NCHS, 1973c). Additionally, women with low incomes (below $5,000 per year) and with minimal education (less than 12 years of schooling) experience higher infant mortality than women with more education and income. Again, nonwhite women are more often poorly educated with low income (NCHS, 1973d).

AGES ONE TO 14 YEARS

In the first place, it is clear from table 4.1 that the age category of 1 to 4 reflects a larger contribution to racial differences in longevity than ages 5 to 14, reflecting in part the continuing operation of factors such as those discussed in the last section. In 1960, for example, nonwhite children aged 1 to 4 had an age-adjusted mortality rate of 1.9; the rate of their white cohorts was 1.0 (see table 4.1). By 1975 both nonwhite and white death rates for this age group declined to 1.0 and 0.6, respectively.

During these early childhood years, other factors also begin to play a role. Thus the primary causes of death responsible for the difference in the mortality rates of white and nonwhite children are (1) motor vehicle accidents; (2) "other accidents," that is, accidents other than those due to motor vehicles; and (3) influenza and pneumonia (see tables 4.2, 4.3, and 4.4). The data also show changes, with time, in rates of death. The decrease in the overall death rates for children aged 1 to 14 years has been attributed in part to a decline in mortality by influenza (Metropolitan Life Insurance Company, 1978) and to increased access to medical care (Wallace, 1979), although this is yet unequal for the poor. Bullough (1972) additionally points to differential patterns in physician visits with an associated possibility for preventive care.

Mortality by other accidents is a major contributor to death for the entire 1-to-14-year age range (see table 4.2). The death rates from other accidents for

TABLE 4.3
Death Rates by Selected Causes, Age, and Race: 1960, 1969, and 1975
(U.S. rates per 100,000 population)

Age	Race[a]	Cause of Death								
		Motor Vehicle Accidents			Cirrhosis of Liver			Malignant Neoplasms		
		1960	1969	1975	1960	1969	1975	1960	1969	1975
All Ages	N	31.9	30.1	21.4	10.2	19.0	19.0	121.6	134.4	144.0
	W	21.2	27.3	21.5	11.5	14.2	14.2	152.8	163.5	175.8
Under 1 Year	N	7.7	8.7	8.7	1.3	0.8	1.0	6.5	2.4	3.3
	W	8.1	11.0	8.2	0.7	1.3	1.2	7.4	5.2	4.4
1–4 Years	N	11.2	14.4	13.8	0.2	0.2	0.1	7.6	5.0	4.9
	W	9.8	11.3	9.6	0.2	0.2	0.1	11.4	7.8	5.7
5–14 Years	N	8.3	12.1	9.8	0.1	0.1		4.8	4.8	4.4
	W	7.9	9.4	8.5	0.1	0.1		7.1	6.3	4.9
15–24 Years	N	30.3	42.6	24.3	0.6	6.1	1.0	7.9	6.9	6.0
	W	39.0	52.3	41.7	0.2	0.4	0.3	8.4	8.1	6.9
25–34 Years	N	29.5	42.3	29.3	9.1	17.4	14.5	24.3	21.4	15.9
	W	23.6	31.0	24.3	2.1	2.5	2.3	18.8	16.3	14.7
35–44 Years	N	26.2	38.2	24.9	2.1	51.8	42.8	85.7	87.2	72.7
	W	18.5	24.2	18.0	10.8	14.8	13.0	56.7	58.0	50.2
45–54 Years	N	30.5	38.1	25.5	30.9	59.5	61.9	241.7	255.0	250.0
	W	20.4	23.8	16.2	27.2	33.9	33.8	170.0	170.4	173.4
55–64 Years	N	30.7	42.0	27.5	29.1	54.0	62.6	487.8	550.1	558.0
	W	24.5	27.0	17.1	33.1	47.1	47.8	387.9	406.7	417.2

SOURCE: National Center for Health Statistics, 1978b.

[a]N = Nonwhite; W = White.

TABLE 4.4
Death Rates by Selected Causes, Age, and Race: 1960, 1969, and 1975
(U.S. rates per 100,000 population)

Age	Race[a]	Cause of Death								
		Hypertensive Heart			Heart Disease (All Causes)			Homicide		
		1960	1969[b]	1975	1960	1969[b]	1975	1960	1969	1975
All Ages	N	69.9	8.5	5.4	287.1	280.1	244.1	21.9	34.1	37.1
	W	32.7	3.9	2.8	379.6	378.2	350.0	2.5	4.0	5.9
Under 1 Year	N	0.2			12.4	16.9	33.3	11.6	8.0	13.1
	W			0.1	5.6	9.7	17.7	3.7	3.5	4.3
1–4 Years	N				3.3	2.3	3.0	1.7	3.2	6.8
	W				0.9	1.2	1.5	0.6	1.3	1.6
5–14 Years	N				3.0	2.0	1.4	1.2	1.9	2.2
	W				1.0	0.8	0.8	0.4	0.5	0.8
15–24 Years	N	0.9	0.2	0.1	9.1	7.1	5.4	27.0	51.1	49.7
	W	0.1			3.2	2.4	2.1	3.0	5.0	7.6
25–34 Years	N	7.5	1.6	0.8	36.7	32.0	20.1	51.6	79.5	78.0
	W	0.4	0.1	0.1	12.8	8.7	7.0	4.1	7.4	9.8
35–44 Years	N	39.1	6.8	2.9	137.4	135.6	95.8	44.6	68.9	62.2
	W	2.6	0.5	0.3	67.2	61.0	47.9	3.8	6.3	9.2
45–54 Years	N	11.6	13.4	7.5	415.3	377.9	290.8	31.4	46.3	49.5
	W	13.0	1.8	1.3	256.2	227.2	194.5	3.5	4.6	7.0
55–64 Years	N	268.4	29.5	17.3	1,040.1	919.5	727.6	17.7	28.8	32.1
	W	47.6	5.6	3.9	708.2	642.4	547.3	2.9	4.2	5.4

SOURCE: National Center for Health Statistics, 1978b.

[a]N = Nonwhite; W = White.
[b]The rather drastic decline in death rates between 1960 and 1969 reflects, in part, the revision in causes of death by category.

nonwhites (1 to 4 years) was 44.5 in 1960 and declined to 26.0 in 1975. Death rates by this same cause was 17.7 in 1960 and 16.2 in 1975 for their white cohorts. In 1960, nonwhite children (5 to 14 years of age) had mortality rates of 20.9 for other accidents, compared to the rate of 9.9 for white children of the same ages. By 1975 the death rate for other accidents declined to 13.7 and 8.5 for the nonwhite and white children, respectively. Both nonwhite and white death rates by other accidents tend to decrease after the first year of life.

Although not shown in the tables, evidence on accidents due to fire and explosion are also instructive in this analysis. Iskrant and Joliet (1968) report black-to-white mortality ratios of five to one for children aged 1 to 10 and of three to one for children aged 11 to 14. Deaths by fire and explosion among the young (or very old) usually (80 percent) occur in the home during the winter months. Continuing, these investigators observe that poverty, inadequate stoves, poor knowledge of electricity, and poor safety habits are factors associated with these deaths.

AGES 15 TO 44 YEARS

Between 1960 and 1969 the total age-adjusted death rates for 15- to 24-year-olds increased by 22.1 percent, and the mortality rates for 25- to 44-year-olds increased by 6.0 percent (NCHS, 1973e). The total age-adjusted death rates of nonwhites for each ten-year category were higher than their white cohorts' rates (see table 4.1). The major causes of death that contributed to the increase in mortality during the sixties include homicide, motor vehicle accidents, other accidents, and suicide (see tables 4.2, 4.3, and 4.4). Because of the dramatic rise in mortality rates by causes of death that have been labelled as "sociopathological" (Dennis, 1977), the relationship between cause of death and race will be examined in some detail for the 15- to 44-year age group.

SUICIDES

Suicide rates for whites have been consistently higher than those for nonwhites (see table 4.2), and the rates for both have increased during the period from 1960 to 1975. The age group, however, at which the suicide rates are highest differs for the races. While suicide rates tend, generally, to increase with age among whites, peaking at age 75, among nonwhites no definite age-related patterns appeared until 1975. At this time dramatic increases in suicide rates are seen for the ages 15 to 34, with the peak rate between the ages of 25 and 34. Although not shown in table 4.2, nonwhites aged 65 and older show a decline in death rates due to suicide. This decline diminished the impact of the higher ratios among the younger cohorts on the overall death rates due to suicide. Dennis (1977) and Waldron and Eyer (1975) have shown that suicides are associated with alcohol use, broken families, lack of trust, and societal instability.

ACCIDENTS

The nonwhite death rates for all accidents are generally higher than those for whites (see tables 4.2 and 4.3). The only age group at which accident rates (motor vehicle accidents) was higher for whites than nonwhites was the 15- to 24-year range. However, the nonwhites of these ages show a greater increase (41.5 percent) in death rates due to motor vehicle accidents (from 1960–1969) than their white cohorts. For nonwhites aged 25 to 44 years, death rates due to motor vehicle accidents are higher than white rates throughout the observation period, 1960–1975. Here again the percentage increase in mortality rates is higher for nonwhites than for whites of the same age. One contribution to the higher death rates by motor vehicle accidents has been the increase in the distances travelled by motorists during the sixties, although it is difficult to hypothesize about the relationship of this factor with race. It has been established, however, that a large proportion of the individuals killed in motor vehicle accidents have consumed alcohol prior to death (Waldron and Eyer, 1975).

THE INFLUENCE OF ALCOHOL ON LIFE EXPECTANCY

Alcohol consumption has been suggested as a contributor to the risk of death by suicide and by accidents (Zackler, Andelman, and Bauer, 1969; Rushforth and associates, 1977; Weiss, 1976). It is also related to the incidence of homicide, to be considered in the next section. The direct effect of alcohol on life expectancy can be assessed by analyzing the number of deaths attributed to the alcoholic disorders: cirrhosis of the liver, alcoholic psychosis, and alcoholism. For the period extending from 1958 to 1969, both nonwhite and white groups at ages over 20 years experienced an increase in the proportion of alcohol-related deaths (Metropolitan Life Insurance Company, 1974). The rate for nonwhites (26.3) was much higher than that for whites (9.8) in 1969. Moreover, there was a substantial racial differential in the increase of alcohol-related deaths between 1958 and 1969: an 11.8 percent increase for nonwhites and a 6.9 percent increase among whites. In 1969 this continued rise in alcohol-related deaths was reflected in higher nonwhite (relative to white) deaths from cirrhosis (see table 4.3). This trend continued for nonwhites in 1975.

Data gathered between 1964 and 1965 from a sample that approximated the population of the United States indicated different reasons for drinking by race. Nonwhites were more likely to drink for reasons of "escape," loneliness, and despair of their situation. Escape drinkers were found to possess a high degree of alienation and low socioeconomic status; they also drank under stressful conditions. Because young low-status men may tend to dramatize their expressions of tension and maladjustment, they increase their risk of fatal consequences (Cahalan, Cisin, and Crossley, 1969).

HOMICIDES

The nonwhite rates for all ages for deaths due to homicide was 6.6 times larger than that of the white rate in 1976 (NCHS, 1978a). Deaths due to homicide have been declining for nonwhites and increasing for whites between the ages of 15 and 44 since 1969 (see table 4.4). Several factors have been shown to be associated with deaths due to homicide, including gun accessibility, alcohol consumption, and relatedness or prior acquaintance (Klebba, 1975; Weiss, 1976). During the sixties, three times as many guns were available in the United States as had previously been the case, due in part to an increase in their importation and manufacture (Weiss, 1976). Rushforth and his associates (1977) have determined that nonwhite male homicides by firearms accounted for the greatest proportion of murder (85.9 percent) during the period from 1958 to 1974 in the metropolitan area of Cleveland. In the final analysis, if all of the factors that are thought to increase the risk of death by homicide are combined, the largest number of nonwhite homicides would occur within the cities as a result of drinking situations with family or acquaintances when a gun is available.

AGES 45 TO 65

The causes of death for this age group also show substantially higher rates for nonwhites than whites. The causes include malignant neoplasms of the lymph and hematopoietic tissues, cirrhosis of the liver, nephritis and nephrosis, hypertensive heart disease, hypertension, accidents, and homicide (Metropolitan Life Insurance Company, 1977). The impact of minority status is suggested by these data inasmuch as it has been noted, for example, that the quality of the social conditions reflected in the level of income, education, and marriage affect the blood pressure through higher levels of stress (Elling and Martin, 1974; James and Kleinbaum, 1976). Because these causes of death affect such a large segment of the nonwhite, middle-aged population, they tend to obscure the effects of other causes of death that are important for the younger segment of the nonwhite population.

SUMMARY

When considering the issue of racial differences in longevity, several factors make it clear that minority status plays a major role. First, nonwhite deaths due to such behaviors as lower frequency of physician visits, as well as less prenatal care and nutrition, have contributed to racial differences; these differences are now beginning to diminish for the nonwhite because of attainable medical care and education (Elling and Martin, 1974). Second, rates of accidental deaths by fire and explosion, which are higher for nonwhites, have been associated with low education/low income and substandard housing. Third, alcohol consumption—implicated in deaths due to cirrhosis, accidents, homicide, and suicide—has been shown to be related to social conditions. Finally, deaths due to hypertension have been associated with the stress that accompanies inadequate housing, little money, and poor education. It appears that whites live longer than blacks, at least in part, because the majority are economically more advantaged and more likely to obtain, or able to obtain, medical care for themselves and their young; they are also more likely to possess fewer economic reasons to exhibit behaviors (for example, escape drinking) that can be considered potentially self-destructive.

5

DIFFERENTIAL LIFE EXPECTANCY: POSSIBLE EXPLANATIONS DURING THE LATER AGES

KENNETH G. MANTON

There has been recent interest in white/nonwhite mortality differentials in the United States because of the inconsistent observation of a phenomenon that has been called the white/black mortality crossover. While the concept was introduced in chapter 3, in this chapter it is considered in detail. As a special feature of differential life expectancies, as discussed in the preceding chapter, the crossover phenomenon is a feature of the pattern of the age-specific probabilities of death for white and nonwhite populations. Discussion of the crossover effect necessitates consideration of the complete life span, however, rather than a limited focus of attention to the incidence of death during the early and middle years, as in the previous chapter. Specifically, for each sex, it is noted that nonwhite probabilities of death, after reaching a peak differential in middle ages, converge with the probabilities of death for whites until about age 75, when the nonwhite probabilities of death actually fall below the probabilities of death for whites. This observation has led to controversy, with many people maintaining that the crossover is due to error in the age reporting on death certificates and census records, resulting in an overenumeration of the nonwhite elderly. Even when the denominator of the nonwhite mortality rates is adjusted, however, to reflect estimates of the hypothesized overenumeration of nonwhites, the white/nonwhite mortality crossover is observed—though at more advanced ages. In addition, a number of other phenomena seem consistent with a white/nonwhite mortality crossover. For example, human mortality crossovers have been observed in many international comparisons (Nam and Ockay, 1977), for cohort mortality data in the United States (NCHS, 1972),

and in certain types of epidemiologic studies. As a result, serious consideration has been given to the white/nonwhite mortality crossover and its implications.

The purpose in the remainder of this chapter is to illustrate and examine the
magnitude of the white/nonwhite mortality crossover in official period life
tables in the United States. Discussion shall also be given to various demographic
and social phenomena that might contribute to a mortality crossover or
convergence.

THE WHITE/NONWHITE MORTALITY CROSSOVER
IN U.S. LIFE TABLES: 1969–1971

In order to examine the white/nonwhite mortality crossover, three different
types of age-specific life table functions, from official U.S. complete period life
tables for 1969–1971 (NCHS, 1975), will be examined. The first type of
function examined is the age-specific probability of dying during a single year.
The second is the probability of surviving from birth to some given age. The
third is the average number of years of life expectancy remaining for persons
who have survived to a given age. Each of these functions describes a different
feature of population survival. The probability of death represents the average
mortality risk at a point in time. The proportion surviving to a given age
reflects the cumulative effect of past mortality risks. Life expectancy represents
future potential for survival.

To illustrate the white/nonwhite crossover, consider table 5.1. It contains the three types of life table statistics for selected ages for U.S. white
and nonwhite males and females estimated from 1969–1971 mortality data.

Table 5.1 shows that though both nonwhite males and females start out with
a considerable mortality disadvantage on all three indices, at advanced ages
they become advantaged; that is, their age-specific probabilities of death are
lower, while their life expectancy and the proportion surviving is greater. A
cross-sex comparison shows that females, within race, are advantaged with
respect to males on all three life table functions. The relative magnitude of
these differences is presented in table 5.2.

In table 5.2 it is evident that the probability of death for nonwhite males
reaches levels at least twice that for white males. Between ages 75 and 80,
however, the nonwhite mortality rates cross over, so that by age 80, nonwhite
rates are 12 percent lower than those for whites. This decline continues out to
age 100. The ratios of the life expectancies show that nonwhite males at birth
have a 10 percent lower life expectancy than white males. The crossover in life
expectancy occurs earlier than that for the probability of death, nonwhite life
expectancy rising beyond white life expectancy at about age 65. The probability of survival to age X shows that at age 75 there are 31 percent fewer survivors
from the nonwhite male birth cohort than the white male birth cohort. The
crossover in these statistics, which represent the cumulative mortality differen-

TABLE 5.1
Age-Specific Survival Characteristics of U.S. White and Nonwhite Males and Females: 1969–1971

Age	White Males			Nonwhite Males		
	Probability of Death at Age X	Life Expectancy at Age X	Probability of Survival to Age X	Probability of Death at Age X	Life Expectancy at Age X	Probability of Death to Age X
0	.020	67.9	1.000	.034	61.0	1.000
45	.006	27.5	0.907	.012	24.6	0.802
55	.015	19.5	0.830	.023	18.4	0.678
65	.034	13.0	0.663	.042	12.9	0.496
70	.049	10.4	0.541	.057	10.7	0.390
75	.072	8.1	0.403	.076	9.0	0.278
80	.105	6.2	0.259	.092	7.6	0.180
85	.150	4.6	0.135	.113	6.0	0.108
90	.213	3.5	0.051	.157	4.8	0.054
95	.290	2.7	0.013	.213	3.9	0.020
100	.355	2.2	0.002	.235	3.6	0.006

Age	White Females			Nonwhite Females		
	Probability of Death at Age X	Life Expectancy at Age X	Probability of Survival to Age X	Probability of Death at Age X	Life Expectancy at Age X	Probability of Death to Age X
0	.015	75.5	1.000	.028	69.1	1.000
45	.003	33.5	0.946	.007	29.8	0.886
55	.007	24.9	0.904	.014	22.4	0.802
65	.016	16.9	0.816	.027	16.0	0.661
70	.025	13.4	0.741	.039	13.3	0.564
75	.043	10.2	0.633	.052	11.1	0.448
80	.071	7.6	0.482	.067	9.0	0.334
85	.115	5.5	0.305	.087	7.1	0.228
90	.176	4.1	0.144	.134	5.4	0.132
95	.253	3.0	0.045	.182	4.6	0.057
100	.317	2.5	0.009	.204	4.2	0.020

SOURCE: National Center for Health Statistics, 1975.

TABLE 5.2

Age-Specific Ratios of Nonwhite/White Life-Table Functions by Sex: 1969–1971

Age	Ratios per Life-Table Function					
	Probability of Death at Age X		Life Expectancy at Age X		Probability of Survival to Age X	
	Males	Females	Males	Females	Males	Females
0	1.70	1.87	.90	0.92	1.00	1.00
45	2.00	2.33	.89	0.89	0.88	0.94
55	1.53	2.00	.94	0.90	0.82	0.89
65	1.24	1.69	.99	0.95	0.75	0.81
70	1.16	1.56	1.03	0.99	0.72	0.76
75	1.06	1.21	1.11	1.09	0.69	0.71
80	0.88	0.94	1.23	1.18	0.69	0.69
85	0.75	0.76	1.30	1.29	0.80	0.75
90	0.74	0.76	1.37	1.32	1.06	0.92
95	0.73	0.72	1.44	1.53	1.54	1.27
100	0.66	0.64	1.64	1.68	3.00	2.22

SOURCE: National Center for Health Statistics, 1975.

tial, shows that the nonwhite population is disadvantaged until some point between age 85 and 90.

Though both white and nonwhite females have markedly better survival than males, the age pattern of the ratios of each of the three life table functions for females is similar to the ratios observed for males. The crossover to a lower probability of death for nonwhite females occurs about the same age as it did for nonwhite males—that is, between ages 75 and 80. The ratio of nonwhite female to white female life expectancy is quite similar to the ratios observed for males except that the crossover occurs between ages 70 and 75 for females as opposed to 65 to 70 for males. The ratio of the probability of surviving to age X crosses over earlier for females than for males—that is, between ages 85 to 90, as compared to 90 to 95 for males.

POSSIBLE EXPLANATIONS OF THE WHITE/NONWHITE CROSSOVER

Several explanations have been proposed to explain the observation of white/nonwhite mortality crossover. One explanation is that the social, economic, and family status of the nonwhite elderly improves with age to a position relatively superior to that of the white elderly population at about age 75. Though some argue that there may be a decrease in differentials at advanced ages due to the loss of status among the white elderly population, it seems unlikely that there occurs a crossover in social, economic, and family status parallel to the mortality crossover. Thus, an alternate explanation must be sought. The alternate explanations of the crossover have important implications for our perception of the relative health status of the black elderly population and its requirements for governmental and health services. These explanations, along with their implications, shall be briefly considered.

Thus, another explanation of crossover is that it is due to census enumeration error: specifically, that the black elderly population is overenumerated. Though overenumeration exists, estimates indicate that it is insufficient to eliminate the crossover of the age-specific probability of death. The crossover of the probability of surviving to age X, however, might be eliminated by adjustments for enumeration error, because it does not occur until very advanced ages. Eliminating the crossover in the survival probability is significant since it is a measure of the cumulative mortality experience of a population. Consequently, if this type of crossover were eliminated, the conclusion would be that a cumulative mortality disadvantage for nonwhites exists over the total age span.

If enumeration errors for the black elderly were sufficient to eliminate the crossover in the age-specific probability of death, there would be a variety of important implications. First, it would suggest that our knowledge of white and nonwhite mortality differentials is deficient. This would imply that serious deficiencies exist in the collection of population and mortality data, indicating a need for research into the collection of information on vital events for minority populations and the implementation of new census and vital statistic procedures. If enumeration error explained the crossover, another implication would be that federal programs targeted to the nonwhite elderly would be based on faulty population estimates. Consequently, arguing that the mortality crossover in the age-specific probabilities of death is a data artifact has serious implications.

In addition to the factors described above, the mortality crossover could be due to certain population and individual dynamics. For example, the mortality crossover could be a function of "mortality selection" (Spiegelman, 1968). For mortality selection to operate, several conditions must exist. First, individuals in the populations must have different susceptibilities to different diseases so that individuals are heterogeneous in their potential for longevity. This individual variation in longevity could be due either to intrinsic factors or to environmental influences such as prenatal medical care. In addition to populations being heterogeneous in longevity potential, the mortality selection model requires that one of the populations be "disadvantaged," so that the mortality rates of that population, at the younger ages, are higher than those of the "advantaged" population. The higher mortality rates of the disadvantaged population mean that the most susceptible persons in that population are being selected (dying) at a faster rate than in the advantaged populations. At advanced ages this mortality differential will cause the disadvantaged population to be proportionately smaller and composed of a group that, on average, would be far more robust than the population experiencing lower early mortality rates.

This higher average robustness in the disadvantaged population at advanced ages implies that the mortality rates will rise less rapidly at those ages. Multiple-cause mortality data, data for which more than a single medical condition is assigned to each death (Manton, 1980), for example, show that certain chronic degenerative diseases occur at earlier ages and, as the underlying cause of death, more frequently for nonwhites than for whites. For whites these diseases occur more frequently at advanced ages and as conditions that are only contributing to death. This implies that the medical management of chronic disease is less adequate for nonwhites and that nonwhites with those diseases do not survive as long as whites with the same disease, though these diseases eventually take their toll indirectly on whites at advanced ages.

As we have observed, not only do the probabilities of death cross over, but the proportion surviving to any given age does as well. The mortality selection model can explain a crossover in the age-specific probabilities of death, but it cannot explain a crossover in the probabilities of surviving to a given age. Thus, if adjustments for enumeration error do not eliminate the crossover in this latter statistic, there is evidence of mechanisms other than mortality selection underlying the crossover.

One such mechanism could be that nonwhite and white populations have different rates of aging; in other words, it could be that the risk of death increases more rapidly for nonwhites at early ages and more rapidly for whites at later ages. An example of basic disease processes with this race-specific pattern are hypertension and generalized atherosclerosis. Specifically, nonwhites are at a greater risk of hypertension than whites—a disease process that begins at fairly early ages. On the other hand, generalized atherosclerosis seems to be a more significant chronic degenerative disease process for whites, but it is one that does not have a major impact until advanced ages (Manton, Poss, and Wing, 1979). Note that different rates of aging could be produced by environmental factors. For example, though poor nutrition early in life may increase early mortality risks, it may have a beneficial impact on the risk of circulatory disease at advanced ages. However, the differential rate of aging concept does imply that if the rate of aging is altered by environmental factors, the alteration is permanent.

The above material suggests that the relative health status of U.S. whites and nonwhites is not well understood. There is considerable debate even over the most basic age patterns of mortality risks. There seems to be less epidemiologic evidence on nonwhites than whites, so that morbidity statistics cannot resolve the debate. It is also clear that whatever explanation is made of the observed mortality patterns, there are important implications. For example, if the mortality selection or differential rate of aging concepts have any validity, then to understand the mortality of nonwhites at advanced ages, one must understand the health status and mortality experience of the nonwhite population at younger ages. The consequence of these observations is that there is a need for further research and increased understanding of the factors and mechanisms contributing to the age pattern of the relative health status of whites and nonwhites.

Part 3

EXPERIENCING LATER LIFE: THE SOCIAL AND SOCIAL PSYCHOLOGICAL CIRCUMSTANCES

INTRODUCTION TO PART 3

Aging is a complex, emergent process, involving biological, psychological, and sociological changes. Although aging can represent a period of increasing freedom from restricting role demands, and thus a time for creativity, it more often means increased susceptibility to economic loss, chronic health problems, mental depression, social isolation, and, eventually, death and dying. Concurrently, these stressful changes have sometimes prompted novel, or at least accentuated, strategies for successfully coping with the resultant conditions and with life in general.

Stressful age-related life events, and the modes of adaptation to which they often give rise, have been shown to be exacerbated among the minority elderly. Thus, in addition to the demographic indicators examined in the previous section, a second gauge of the consequences associated with a minority aged status is the psychosocial circumstances. The objective in this section is to outline a representative number of the circumstances characterizing the minority aged. The section is divided into three subparts, each focusing attention on a series of interrelated issues: economic and health status; familial and social integration; and patterns in social disengagement: retirement, death, and dying.

When considered as a whole, the chapters of this section illustrate each of the underlying themes of the book. Through their use of the concept of double jeopardy, Maurice Jackson and his associates document the differential needs and direr relative circumstances of the minority aged. While the concept of the doubly disadvantaged position of the minority elderly has been alluded to in preceding chapters, Jackson and his associates, writing in chapter 6, are the first to review the issues raised by the concept. These investigators find empirical support for the double jeopardy thesis among their national sample of aged blacks in both the economic and the perceived physical health realms. Finding support for the thesis also among their mental health indicators leads the authors to express their surprise inasmuch as a substantial literature suggests that the black (relative to white) elderly are more satisfied with life, despite their dire economic circumstances. Because Jackson and his associates perceive their measures of life satisfaction as closer approximations to quality-of-life indicators than other measures of mental health, they conclude that while elderly blacks may have positive self-conceptions, it does not follow that they are satisfied with the circumstances surrounding their lives.

Wilbur Watson furnishes additional perspective to the conclusions by Jackson and his associates. Mental health, Watson finds, is influenced by more than mere economic circumstance. There are important social-psychological variables that act in concert with socioeconomic factors. For example, to the extent that individuals believe that their lives are controlled by forces beyond their influence, stressful events may be accepted as facts of life. Watson's analysis suggests that when endeavoring to understand the seemingly anomalous relation of economic disadvantage and good mental health among the black aged, one is obliged to consider the total world view and condition of the elderly. Thus, in addition to economic factors, one must study psychological factors, as well as indicators of religious commitment and evaluations of health and functioning.

The discussion on mental health continues in the chapter by James Carter. The author, however, limits his analysis to one aspect of mental health: mental illness. Utilizing case vignettes drawn from his experience as a practicing psychiatrist, Carter provides a welcomed caveat for social workers, service providers, and others who work with the black aged relative to the diagnosis of mental competence. Carter reasons that while victimization by racism is, without question, a major factor in the emotional disabilities of some black aged, the diagnosis of paranoia—without careful scrutiny of the basis of the supposed problem, say, suspiciousness—may be unwarranted. Too often, as Carter implies, what is defined as dysfunctional behavior may in fact serve the individual as an effective coping device.

Susan Taylor extends the discussion of coping with an analysis of coping styles among a sample of elderly black women. She describes two major coping resources: one incorporating the perceived operation of an informal social support network, including family, friends, and community, and the second incorporating a mind set or value orientation toward self-help and independence. Both tactics are associated with effective coping inasmuch as the chance of coping is increased with the perceived availability of both a system of internal (for example, a certain psychological orientation) and a system of external (for example, family) coping resources. Stagner (1981) argues that such coping resources increase (1) the frequency of efforts to cope and (2) the probability of successful coping. Taylor observes that, indeed, cognitive perceptions and value orientations permit many of the women in her sample to define aging as "no big thing." It is expected, she concludes, that all people draw upon available, culturally based coping resources.

The case of the black elderly women in Taylor's sample illustrates the culturally based, naturally existing resources that, although perhaps varying in form among other elderly groups, might be exploited in all groups in the societywide search for an efficient system for caring for the elderly.

For Taylor, real or perceived religious and familial resources are identified as major informal coping supports. In the three chapters following Taylor's study, attention turns to detailed analyses of these coping resources of the minority elderly: the church and the family. The ultimate emphasis is on the adaptive, survival functions—represented by each of these institutions—for helping the minority elderly respond to their hostile environs. This series begins with Allen Carter's examination of the historical role that the church has played in serving the psychosocial needs of blacks throughout their lives. Carter reasons that because of the oppressed conditions of daily living, along with feelings of uncertainty and the threat of death, blacks have historically found a need for a source of strength beyond the material world. Religion, he notes, figures prominently in each of the role transits throughout the life of black Americans, including entry and adjustment to old age.

Forthcoming chapters stress the significance of Carter's observations on the centrality of religion, when suggesting the use of naturally existing institutions (for example, the church) in the lives of elderly persons for delivering needed social services (see chapter 19, for example).

While Carter's emphasis is on religion, Gari Lesnoff-Caravaglia's focus is on the family. Analyzing the roles of the black American "granny" and the Soviet "babushka," Lesnoff-Caravaglia delineates the various similarities between the two. Among both sets of grandmothers, she observes the powerful impact of an ubiquitous authority structure (the white-dominated authority structure in the United States and the government in Soviet society); she also observes, among other contrasts, the positive, functional role played by the grandmother in both groups. The nurturant role and the resultant positive self-image—as well as the command of familial respect—may well serve as a model for all elderly grandmothers, including nonminority grandmothers. What is needed, as Hill and Shackleford (1975) conclude, are policies and programs that build on, not weaken, the strengths of the extended, and potentially extended, families of grandmothers.

Some of the conclusions from studies of immigrant families to the United States, however, have implications for the study of the family and the aged that significantly vary from the preceding reasoning. The conclusions from the latter studies suggest that the assumption of a necessary direct covariation between familial integration and a positive self-image may be too simplistic. Bertram Cohler's analysis indicates that strain—rather than satisfaction—may result when older women, just freed from their own child-care responsibilities, are expected to assist in the care of various other kin. Cohler's study is timely on at least two counts. First, his conclusions imply, to those studying the relation of the minority aged to their family, that there are contexts in which the familial network may not represent the coping resource that is often assumed. Correlatively, this implication suggests the importance of further studying the hypothesis among the minority elderly.

The emphasis in the two concluding chapters in this section is on the phenomenon of withdrawal from societal networks. Although recognizing sociopsychological consequences of retirement, Lodis Rhodes contends that retirement is better conceived as an economic concept. Retirement, he notes, is one of the key factors for manipulating the size and profile of the labor force.

This fact is at the heart of decisions about policy issues such as mandatory retirement. Race-specific proposals, advocating a reduction in the age for retirement for selected groups, he concludes, fly in the face of trends in government to ensure the economic solvency of income maintenance programs for the elderly.

It has been said that "we all grow old and we all die." But just as aging is not a homogeneous phenomenon, neither is dying, as Bernice Harper argues in the concluding chapter of part 3. Because of perceived helplessness in controlling the frequent incidence of death within minority populations, dying and the adjustment to dying have often taken varying subculturally specific forms. Harper provides a series of brief, snapshot views of these patterns. Consider, for example, the relatively elaborate hallucinogenic rituals of native Americans. As Harper notes, failing to recognize the function of these culturally specific rituals in the adjustment process to the loss of loved ones could easily lead an outsider—say, a psychiatric worker in a nursing home—to a false diagnosis of psychosis.

When considered in toto, the chapters in this section illustrate, in complementary fashion, the major themes in this volume. Namely, due to lifelong victimization, the minority elderly experience a greater prevalence of both personal and social problems, but in this experience they have also adapted several functional and efficient strategies for coping with their position. These strategies may well serve as models on which to base programs of successful coping among all elderly persons.

ECONOMIC AND HEALTH ISSUES

6

TO BE OLD AND BLACK: THE CASE FOR DOUBLE JEOPARDY ON INCOME AND HEALTH

MAURICE JACKSON, BOHDAN KOLODY,

AND JAMES L. WOOD

This study addresses the most important theoretical and practical questions asked about the black aged. What is it like to be old and black? Is the situation of older blacks better explained by focusing on age (the gerontological approach) or by emphasizing race (the race and ethnic approach)? In straightforward terms, is age or race the more important variable in characterizing the lives of older blacks? The answer to this question should be sought in analyses that permit the determination of the relative contributions of age and race. There has been a tendency, however, for researchers to conduct another type of analysis, namely, the determination of racial effects after socioeconomic controls are introduced (Bell, Kasschau, and Zellman, 1976a; Jackson and Walls, 1978). This turns out to be an answer to the question of the relative importance of class and race rather than age and race.

While it is important to know which of several factors produce given social conditions, the logic of inquiry may not adequately represent the social situations at hand. Thus, it may be important to know that socioeconomic factors explain more about the situation of older blacks than do racial factors, but these factors probably have a combined impact rather than an independent one. The finding that one variable is more important than another does not exclude the analysis of the combined impact of multiple variables.

The situation of older blacks and the idea of "double jeopardy" provide the major focus of this study. The hypothesis of double jeopardy proposes that the situation of older blacks is best characterized as one resulting from the combined effects of age and race. So, while both the black aged and the white aged are handicapped by their age, the black aged are also handicapped by their race.

This is not saying that all aged blacks are equally at risk or are more disadvantaged than all aged whites. Instead, it is a hypothesis of comparative average disadvantage of the black aged. The specific analyses in this chapter focus on the hypothesis of double jeopardy with respect to income and health; aspects of both physical and mental health will be considered. These are key concerns of older blacks. Do they have sufficient money for living the lives they desire? Is their health condition adequate? And, utilizing a measure of life satisfaction as an indicator of mental health, are they satisfied with their lives? The central question is whether age and race affect the lives of the elderly in these areas.

OVERVIEW OF THE LITERATURE

Applying the idea of jeopardy or risk to the black aged is relatively recent. Following Talley's and Kaplan's (1956) question of whether the black aged were in double jeopardy, the National Urban League (1964) expressed the concept most explicitly and thereby generated interest in it. The Urban League report notes: "For he has, indeed, been placed in double jeopardy: first by being Negro and second by being aged."

Ample studies have documented the risks or disadvantages of both older people and black people. It seems reasonable to think that the black aged would be exposed to risks based upon both age and race simultaneously.

Other conceptualizations of the circumstances among the black aged have also been developed. It has been described as one of triple jeopardy (National Council on Aging, 1971), whereby age, race, and social class simultaneously impact on the circumstances of the aged, and one of multiple jeopardy (Lindsay, 1971), where in addition to the triple jeopardy factors, other factors such as sex may create an even more disadvantaged position. Thus elderly, poor, black females are hypothesized to experience more devastating conditions than elderly, poor, black males. In contrast, middle-class, black, elderly males may be in a more advantaged position than either the male or female, poorer counterpart. Certainly, the jeopardy approach has distinct advantages over approaches that simply state "the facts" about the lives of older blacks or minorities. The approach specifies the heterogeneity within the black aged population, thereby providing a way of organizing facts, and may be a step toward the development of a theory of black or minority aging and of aging in general.

After Lindsay's and the National Council on Aging's studies in the early seventies, it was a period of time before further research was conducted on the hypothesis of double jeopardy among older blacks. Jackson and Wood (1976), in an analysis of data from the national Harris survey (Harris, 1974) sponsored by the National Council on Aging (NCOA), tested the double jeopardy hypothesis and found that being old and black did generate some special disadvantages, but fewer than predicted. Compared to other groups—such as younger whites (18 to 64 years old), older whites (65 years of age and older), and younger blacks (18 to 64)—the black aged (65 years and over) rarely emerged superior in terms of their income, occupation, or housing. In short, the black aged tended to be doubly disadvantaged in the material conditions of existence. However, in contrast to material difficulties, older blacks were not especially disadvantaged in many other areas. They had friends and were not especially depressed, though a significant number said they were lonely. Still they had very positive self-images and similar positive images of older people in general.

Jackson and Wood also identified other types of jeopardies: the single jeopardy of age, the single jeopardy of race, the absence of jeopardy, and reverse jeopardy. This classification of jeopardies can be used to determine relative strengths as well as disadvantages for various groups.

In another analysis of the data from the NCOA-Harris study, Jackson and Walls (1978) found few significant racial differences between age and race groups. A number of problems plagued their research, not the least of which is their basing the findings upon incorrect sample and subsample numerical bases. For instance, they studied 51 aged blacks instead of 479 aged blacks interviewed in the NCOA-Harris study.

In another study Dowd and Bengtson (1978) tested the double jeopardy hypothesis against the competing hypothesis of age levelling on a probability sample of residents of Los Angeles County. They compared groups aged 45 to 54, 55 to 64, and 65 to 74. While the double jeopardy hypothesis proposes that age compounds or adds to the burdens of race, the age-leveller hypothesis suggests that age levels, or reduces, racial differences among the older age cohort. These researchers found both hypotheses to be supported on several variables. Older blacks were found to suffer from double jeopardy with respect to income and self-assessed health, but not on familial contact and life satisfaction factors of tranquility and optimism.

In conclusion, the studies of double jeopardy seem to indicate that older blacks are doubly disadvantaged in income and physical health, but not in terms of mental health. While Jackson and Wood interpreted the latter finding as a reflection of differences between difficulties in the material and nonmaterial conditions of life, Dowd and Bengtson assumed a levelling effect of aging upon racial differences. This study seeks to add further support to these conclusions. The research hypothesis is that the black aged will be in a state of double jeopardy with respect to income and health, but not to mental well-being, that is, mental well-being as reflected by life satisfaction.

METHOD

The data for this study were collected and interpreted in part by Louis Harris and associates (1974) for the National Council on Aging. A number of monographs have been developed from this data, including the study by Jackson and Wood mentioned above. The NCOA-Harris survey was the most comprehensive study conducted of attitudes toward the aged and aging. It was based upon an approach that is relatively rare in the social sciences. Leading gerontologists throughout the nation were brought together with Harris staff by NCOA to develop the survey instrument. After the initial meeting in which areas of study and questions were suggested for consideration, the Harris staff constructed an interview schedule. A second meeting was held to refine the interview items. The final schedule was then completed and administered to a national sample. To insure a representative sample of older blacks, an additional cross section of blacks aged 65 years and over was included. The final sample comprised 4,254 individuals, of whom 2,797 were 65 years of age and over and 1,457 were 18–64 years of age. The white subsample included 3,466 individuals, of whom 2,244 were 65 years of age and over; and the black subsample consisted of 619 individuals, of whom 479 were 65 years of age and over.

A different strategy for determining double jeopardy was employed in the present study than in the earlier study by Jackson and Wood. Rather than emphasizing that the black aged will be more disadvantaged than any other race by age groups, as in the earlier study, double jeopardy in this study is defined as differences between older blacks (65 years and over) and younger whites (18–39). If double jeopardy exists, it should be most apparent in comparisons between these two groups. Race jeopardy is defined here as differences between older (65 years and over) blacks and whites and age jeopardy as differences between older (65 years and over) and younger (18–39) blacks.

FINDINGS

While there are elderly black Americans with sufficient income and with good mental and physical health, double jeopardy, as a phenomenon describing the condition of older blacks, was found in each of the variables: income, health, and life satisfaction. Income has been found to be consistently lower for older blacks than for other age and race groups. These conclusions are supported in this study (see table 6.1). Nearly twenty times as high a proportion of older blacks than younger whites had low incomes (57.2 versus 2.9 percent), indicating a high degree of double jeopardy. Race jeopardy was also present: More than twice the proportion of older blacks than older whites had low incomes. Finally, older blacks were additionally jeopardized by age: More than twice the proportion of them than younger blacks had low incomes. Still, double jeopardy is the striking finding for these income data.

In terms of overall material assets, double jeopardy may even be greater. It is probably magnified by further disadvantages older blacks experience in other aspects of wealth such as stocks, pensions, and property.

The health situation of the black aged was indicated by responses to two questions regarding serious health problems. Respondents were asked about

TABLE 6.1

Income and Selected Measures of Physical and Mental Health by Age and Race (in percentages)

Indicators of Income, Physical and Mental Health	Race			
	Black		White	
	18–39	65 and Over	18–39	65 and Over
Income				
Under $3,000	21.1	57.2	2.9	25.4
Above $3,000	78.9	42.8	97.1	74.6
Number	(76)	(460)	(483)	(2,119)
Physical Health				
Serious Problem	34.2	71.1	11.2	50.3
Other than a				
Serious Problem	65.8	28.9	88.8	49.7
Number	(76)	(460)	(480)	(2,118)
Medical Care				
Serious Problem	31.6	47.8	14.6	22.0
Other than a				
Serious Problem	68.4	52.2	85.4	78.0
Number	(76)	(458)	(479)	(2,107)
Life Satisfaction				
High	21.3	11.5	37.9	24.0
Low	78.7	88.5	62.1	76.0
Number	(75)	(460)	(486)	(2,123)

SOURCE: Harris and associates, 1974.

difficulties with poor health and not enough medical care. Responses in the categories "a very serious problem" and "a somewhat serious problem" were combined and analyzed for this study. Referring again to table 6.1, double jeopardy was evident in self-reported health. Over six times the proportion of older blacks than younger whites saw poor health as a serious problem (71.1 versus 11.2 percent). Race and age jeopardy were also present, with age jeopardy being greater. Over twice the proportion of older blacks than younger blacks regarded poor health as a serious problem, with a smaller difference between older blacks and older whites. Again, double jeopardy stands out as the chief finding for perceptions of serious health problems.

Answers to the question about the adequacy of medical care give further indications about the quality of health. Older blacks also experienced double jeopardy in this regard. As is clear in table 6.1, over three times the proportion of older blacks than younger whites claimed that not enough medical care was a problem (47.8 versus 14.6 percent). Race jeopardy and age jeopardy were somewhat less important. Twice the proportion of older blacks than older whites saw medical care as a problem, while there was even less difference between blacks of varying ages. Once more, double jeopardy stands out.

Life satisfaction was indicated by a composite index of eighteen statements that expressed assessment about the quality of life. For example, one statement read, "As I grow older, things seem better than I thought they would be." (See the Harris study for a list of the life satisfaction statements.) The percentage of responses that reflected the most agreement (those in the upper third of the scale) was defined as high life satisfaction. Unexpectedly, as shown by table 6.1, older blacks showed double jeopardy on life satisfaction. Over three times the proportion of younger whites than older blacks were satisfied with their lives by this measure (37.9 versus 11.5 percent). Race jeopardy and, less so, age jeopardy were also present. Contrary to our initial hypothesis, double jeopardy existed with regard to mental well-being or life satisfaction as well as income and health.

CONCLUSION

In conclusion, the hypothesis of double jeopardy of older blacks was supported in the areas of income, health, and—contrary to our expectations—life satisfaction. It appears that older blacks are affected by age and race in nonmaterial as well as material spheres of life and that age did not act to level out the effects of race. This suggests that the combined effects of age and race penetrate deeply into the lives of older blacks. Thus, while it may be that older blacks have positive self-images and self-conceptions, as indicated in previous studies, it does not follow that they are satisfied with their life situations; a positive self-conception may be a practical orientation.

7

MENTAL HEALTH OF
THE MINORITY AGED:
SELECTED CORRELATES

WILBUR H. WATSON

In recent years social gerontologists have been much concerned with the concept of mental health (Stones and Kozma, 1980). Major efforts have been devoted to the conceptualization and measurement of "happiness" (Schonfield, 1973), "life satisfaction" (Neugarten, Havighurst, and Tobin, 1961), and morale (Lawton, 1972).

Another line of inquiry has focused on the mental health of the elderly as signified by their adaptations to stressful events in everyday life (Selye, 1974; Watson, 1980a). As conceived by Watson (1982), health is a state of well-being in biological, psychological, and social functioning that results from successful coping or withstanding stressors that impinge upon the individual in daily living. This conception is consistent with several current theories of positive coping in response to crises in everyday life (Dudley and Welke, 1977). It is also consistent with the findings of an earlier review of the literature by Jahoda (1950) that derived three general criteria for a working definition of mental health. According to Jahoda:

A mentally healthy individual (a) actively adjusts to, or attempts to master his environment, as distinct from both his inability to adjust and his indiscriminate adjustment through passive acceptance of environmental conditions; (b) shows a unity of his personality, for example through the maintenance of internal integration of self imagery which remains intact notwithstanding the flexibility in behavior required by active adjustment to changing environments; and (c) an ability to perceive correctly, the world and himself in it.

Unlike Jahoda, Clausen (1956) maintains that a positive definition of mental health must be based on a knowledge of the conditions that give rise to illness; the individual's ability to resist illness associated with stress is emphasized.

In each of the mental health criteria listed by Jahoda, clues are given about the nature of unhealthy behavior. If it is assumed that there is a continuum of wellness or well-being that ranges from healthy to unhealthy behavior or illness, then it can be inferred from Jahoda that unhealthy mental behavior or poor mental health is manifest by the following: inability to adjust, or indiscriminate adjustment to environmental conditions (for example, passive acceptance of conditions that are stressful and antithetical to personal integration); disunity of personality (for example, a lack of flexibility in adjustments to the environment); and inability to perceive correctly the world and oneself. In this chapter these derivations from Jahoda provide a point of departure for studying indicators of mental health and illness or of high and low mental health status among older members of minority ethnic groups. It will be shown that mental health is influenced by more than the immediate perception of surrounding circumstances. Research suggests that older minorities have developed psychologically based, coping resources that function to sustain successful adjustment to surrounding environmental circumstances (see Hill, 1972, for example).

AGE AND PSYCHOPHYSICAL CORRELATES

A number of recent studies have shown that there is no relationship between chronological age of older blacks and self-image in the later years (Watson, 1980b; Beard, 1977). This is surprising in light of the emphasis put in other research (Garvin and Burger, 1968; Wax and Thomas, 1961) on the youth-oriented character of American society. It seems reasonable to expect that elderly people who had incorporated into their own identity the presumed value of youthful appearances, vigor, and so on would show increasingly negative self-imagery in relation to their own aging. However, it is just as likely that older persons who do not share these values or expect them of elders will show no remorse or negative self-imagery merely because of their aging. The following excerpt from an interview with an 87-year-old black man illustrates a positive psychological adjustment to aging and mentally healthy behavior:

> I'm wearing the world as a loose garment. About being old, I enjoy life at my age. I look back; I see so many things that were mysteries at one age, but they have been revealed by study, years of experience, and seeing how they turned out. I approached life with the idea that I wouldn't always be young. If I live long, it won't worry me. If I would not be able to do what I want, I say well, tomorrow is going to be better; that's natural (Watson, 1980a).

To some extent, this kind of outlook and self-image may be explained by a deep sense of religiosity and, contrary to Peterson (1977), an external rather than an internal locus of control (Watson, 1980a). In other words, to the extent that a person or group sees life and character as outcomes that are determined and controlled by, for example, religious forces outside of self and neither seeks nor expects self-control, then changes in personal and environmental events that are not a consequence of personal volition may be less disturbing than they would be for the person who emphasized and expected a personal or internal locus of control. Other studies have also shown that change in physical health, especially a declining ability to toilet, feed, dress, and ambulate unaided, are far more significant than increasing age among the correlates of mental health status in the later years of life.

In previous research by Lowenthal (1964) on pathways of persons to mental hospitals, it was found that deterioration in physical health usually precedes in time the deterioration of mental health of the person. If it is assumed, for example, that a measure of activities of daily living (such as an ability to dress, feed, and toilet) is an indicator of physical health, then one should expect to find an inverse relationship between aging and activities of daily living and a positive correlation between activities of daily living and mental health status among the elderly. On the other hand, the relationship between age and mental health may be negative and may be weak so far as their correlation is concerned. In addition to Lowenthal's research, these patterns were recently confirmed by Watson (1980b) in a study of older blacks in the rural southern United States.

Watson's research identified a number of indicators of mental health that were significantly related to activities of daily living (ADL), but had no significant relationship to age. As measured by the Philadelphia Geriatric Center Morale Scale, these factors included morale, the older person's attitude toward his or her own aging, loneliness, and agitation. With decreasing levels of ADL, there was (1) a declining level of overall morale ($r = .25, p < .001$); (2) an increasingly negative attitude toward one's aging ($r = .21, p < .001$); (3) higher levels of expressed life dissatisfaction ($r = .21, p < .001$); and (4) a sense of agitation ($r = .17, p < .001$). Moreover, as expected, there were significant increases in self-reported need for nursing care with decreasing ability to function in activities of daily living ($r = .36, p < .001$). Further, while there was a positive correlation between increasing age and reported needs for nursing care ($r = .16, p < .04$), that relationship was weak and minor by comparison to the association between declining physical self-maintenance ability or ADL and the need for nursing care.

Finally, Watson studied selected factors to determine their association with the older person's self-reported need for mental health services. The aim was to identify correlates that might serve as useful indicators of unhealthy mental behavior and the older person's need for mental health services. There was not a strong relationship between the need for mental health services and any of the other social-psychological factors studied. Only the total morale scale score

$(r = 16, p < .02)$, attitude toward one's own aging $(r = -.21, p < .003)$, and agitation $(r = -.17, p < .01)$ had significant, but weak relationships to needs for mental health services. There was also a weak association between ADL and self-reported needs for mental health services $(r = -.15, p < .02)$. These factors showed that as ADL, morale, and self-attitudes declined, and as the personal sense of agitation increased, there was an increasing need for mental health services. Finally, contrary to expectations it was found that a decreasing ability to perform activities of daily living, rather than advancing age, was most consistently and significantly related to poor mental health in the later years.

SOCIOECONOMIC AND PSYCHOSOCIAL FACTORS

Following closely the conclusions of Jackson, Kolody, and Wood in the preceding chapter, it has also been shown that a relation exists between low socioeconomic class and poor mental health (Faris and Dunham, 1967; Hollingshead and Redlich, 1958). If one assumes that measures of life satisfaction are valid indicators of mental health, it seems reasonable to expect that low socioeconomic class (and, by definition, a minority status) will also be associated with low life satisfaction. Unlike the conclusions of Jackson, Kolody, and Wood, however, most research has shown that this conclusion does not necessarily hold for older poor blacks (Beard, 1977). For example, in spite of the fact that large numbers of older blacks are poorly educated, with extremely poor housing and low income, many show greater life satisfaction than their elderly white counterparts who live under comparatively better socioeconomic conditions (Adams, 1971; Bild and Havighurst, 1976).

According to Beard, the higher life satisfaction scores among older blacks may, in part, be accounted for by a deep sense of religiosity among them and by protracted years of poverty and economic uncertainty, which have conditioned many to expect less than their elderly nonminority counterparts.

Other research has suggested that the ability to sustain personal control and self-esteem is an important determinant of life satisfaction among elderly blacks and whites (Peterson, 1977). The extended family has also been studied as a major source of social and psychological support for older blacks in maintaining their self-esteem and sense of life satisfaction (Wylie, 1971; Watson, 1980a).

Among middle-class older blacks, working and employment have also been found positively associated with higher life satisfaction scores (Beard, 1977). Moreover, although Beard's sample was composed entirely of 100 blacks, aged 50 and over, who were well educated, felt economically secure, and had professional and working-class occupational backgrounds, 74 percent showed only moderate to low levels of life satisfaction. This finding corroborates the findings of Adams (1971) and Bild and Havighurst (1976) that variations in socioeconomic class alone are insufficient to account for life satisfaction and, perhaps, other indicators of mental health among older blacks.

In summary, it is clear that although prejudice, discrimination, and personal loss and economic poverty resulting from age changes, as well as racial and ethnic discrimination, have had negative effects on the mental health of older blacks, these effects have in no sense been consistent. Moreover, some of these elderly have shown relatively high levels of life satisfaction in spite of these and other socioenvironmental hazards. The mental health of older minorities is an area of study, training, and policy formulation that obviously warrants and hopefully will receive much more attention than it has heretofore attracted.

8

THE SIGNIFICANCE OF RACISM IN THE MENTAL ILLNESSES OF ELDERLY MINORITIES

JAMES H. CARTER

For more than a decade black mental health professionals have argued that the adaptive and behavioral patterns of black Americans are reflections of the chronic and persistent debilitating effects of racism. The defensive mechanisms observed in black patients regardless of age are contrived to minimize emotional conflicts peculiar to black citizens (Carter, 1974). Clearly, blacks are similar to other racial and/or ethnic groups to the extent that blacks suffer the full range of psychiatric disorders. Unfortunately, the dynamics of the psychopathology of blacks are often misunderstood by scholars unfamiliar with black values, culture, and life styles. Consequently, blacks have been overly diagnosed in some categories of mental disorders and underdiagnosed in others. A major controversial issue is whether suspiciousness, which seems common to blacks, is a cultural phenomena necessary for survival and is rampant among the black elderly.

This writer contends that aging is experienced differently across cultural lines, reflecting an accumulation of emotional and physical stress. Racism and a minority status, impacting the lives of black Americans, is a catalyst for the unique behavior that is baffling for those who have had limited personal experiences and insufficient training with black subjects (Bernard, 1972). Suffice it to say, the majority of black elderly citizens have had too many negative experiences that would preclude their trusting outsiders and the outside world. Blacks and other minorities are indeed victims of an incredible amount of social neglect including unemployment, poor housing, and inadequate health care. Yet, generalizations and oversimplification about black behavior must be discouraged. Aged black citizens, far from being homogeneous, make up heterogeneous groupings (Carter, 1972; Jackson, 1970). This fact carries drastic implications for program planners who must take into account such things as the differences in educational achievement, urban/rural variables, and levels of social achievement.

The discussion in this chapter illustrates the simple fact that psychological, defensive maneuvers are not always necessarily unhealthy. The life cycle history of the individual, irrespective of whether the individual is minority or nonminority, must be given due consideration in the diagnosis of mental competence. The following vignettes are descriptive of the experiences common to the black elderly and attempt to explain the utility of suspiciousness or paranoid defensive mechanisms. The vignettes illustrate the functionality of some typical coping tactics among the minority elderly. As shall become evident, these tactics are not always based on unconscious, dysfunctional efforts to reduce or avoid stress, but are often conscious, reasoned strategies for modifying the stressful circumstance (see Stagner, 1981).

For clarity, paranoia has been described by the American Psychiatric Association (1980:195–198) as "the manifestation of social isolation, seclusiveness or eccentricities of behavior. Suspiciousness, either generalized or focused on certain individuals, is common; complaints about various injustices and instigation of legal actions are frequent." From this definition, the following elderly black patients could be diagnosed as paranoid. Nevertheless, when consideration is given to the circumstances of their lives, values, and culture, the application of the diagnosis of paranoia is much too severe (Leighton, 1972).

THE CASE OF MR. JONES

Mr. Jones, a 68-year-old widowed black male, had been living alone for the past year in a home purchased just prior to his wife's death. When initially purchased, this property was located in the rural county, but with the growth of the city and annexations, the property was recently taken into the city limits. These changes had caused an increase in property value with a concomitant increase in taxes, creating financial difficulties for Mr. Jones, who was living on a fixed income. Further, Mr. Jones had noted that gradually his neighborhood had moved from approximately 60 percent white to 80 percent black. In spite of the increased conveniences of water and of fire and police protection, gained from being located within the city, Mr. Jones felt his tax increase was unjustified. Compounding the problem was a recent notification that an expressway was planned through the community and would ultimately force Mr. Jones to relocate. Mr. Jones retained an attorney, feeling that this was a racially motivated plot to obtain his property. In fact, he believed that the flight of his white neighbors was due to their having had prior knowledge of the planned expressway.

Subsequently, Mr. Jones became quite irritable and withdrawn and, at the insistence of his family, agreed to seek help from his mental health center. He was screened at the mental health center by an obviously well trained white female social worker with excellent professional credentials. After thoroughly evaluating Mr. Jones, it was her recommendation that the family seek involuntary commitment, feeling that he was paranoid and capable of inflicting bodily harm to anyone he believed to be interested in obtaining his property. Faced with this serious decision, the family referred Mr. Jones to the writer for a second opinion.

The recommendation for hospitalization created enormous psychological unrest for Mr. Jones, for now he believed that there was a conspiracy by the state to gain his material possessions unlawfully. He surmised that the social worker was in collusion with the state and was therefore attempting to have him declared incompetent and ultimately to obtain his property. My assessment of this situation was that Mr. Jones was indeed suspicious, but with justification. My professional opinion was that a set of circumstances common in the lives of many blacks had occurred, arousing the familiar defensive mechanisms of suspiciousness. Predicting his dangerousness was not a major concern of mine, for it is a fact that psychiatrists and other mental health professionals have a poor record of successfully predicting dangerousness.

To have completely ignored racism as a major contributing factor to this patient's symptoms would have been counterproductive, signalling an unwillingness to accept the realities of the black person's existence in the United States. Depression, contrary to earlier misconceptions about the happy-go-lucky black, was also an important feature of Mr. Jones' mental picture. Perhaps most perplexing to the social worker was the determination by the patient to hold on aggressively to his possessions. Unfortunately, healthy aggression in black men too frequently gets misinterpreted as mental illness. Had this same set of symptoms been seen in an individual from the dominant culture, perhaps they would have been interpreted as healthy male aggression, reflecting the American fighting spirit.

THE CASE OF MRS. BLUE

Mrs. Blue is a 69-year-old widowed black female who was placed in a black rest home because of her inability to cope alone successfully. This is a very petite black lady who had lived a rather successful life, giving birth to three children, all of whom are now happily married with stable lives. Because she displayed signs of depression, dissatisfaction, and annoying suspiciousness, she was referred for psychiatric evaluation. Although not emphatically stated, an additional reason for referral was to have Mrs. Blue sedated to facilitate "management."

Developing a rapport with Mrs. Blue was rather easy. She welcomed the opportunity to discuss privately her personal difficulties with her new environment, her disgust about being abandoned, and the happiness she had once shared with her family. She was indeed permitted to ventilate her feelings about being removed from her home and having to sacrifice her autonomy in a rest home. She confided that she was mistreated by the staff, but seemed frightened to state why. However, after several appointments she ostensibly grew comfortable enough to say that her dark skin had caused her such suffering and pain. In fact, she had grown to believe that it was because of her dark complexion that she was not afforded equal treatment with the residents. She stated that on several occasions she had observed that her roommate, who was of a lighter hue, had been shown preferential treatment, particularly by their male peers. Mrs. Blue made it clear that she did not feel comfortable openly discussing these feelings, fearing reprisal and a loss of friendship. In fact, she had attempted to discuss this matter with one of her daughters, who became angry and reprimanded Mrs. Blue for entertaining thoughts about discriminatory practices at the home.

Obviously, the concerns of Mrs. Blue are important and serious, especially given that she grew up in an era when black was not considered beautiful. She has had far too many past personal experiences both at home and with the outside world to reinforce the belief that her black skin made her unacceptable. Mrs. Blue recalled how her own father had shown preferential treatment for Mrs. Blue's niece, who came to live with them at an early age. The niece was described as being "light with long beautiful hair." Seemingly, the niece and Mrs. Blue were of the same age and size at a particular time when toys and clothes were scarce. She was the first of her siblings to awaken early one Christmas morning to find that her niece had received all of the most highly valued toys. Her father's explanation was that the niece was an orphan, having lost both her parents early in life, and thus was deserving of the gifts. Further, the niece was often made much of by family members and relatives, with references frequently being made to skin and hair. This gave Mrs. Blue sufficient reason to tell me that she was not "imagining things."

My opinion is that Mrs. Blue was able to cope with her feelings about being black during youthful years, but time had taken its toll. Her personality was not as pliable and her defenses not as operable, resulting in glimpses of the chronic stress she had previously mastered. Without supporting her beliefs or feelings about her current situation, it is inappropriate to attack her concept of her reality. Rather, the task became one of having her realize that if pursued, her accusations—real or imagined—could conceivably create further alienation. Mrs. Blue was to be reassured that she had access to an ear that not only listened, but was empathetic to all that she said and felt.

To cope with the perils of a bigoted society, blacks, regardless of age, must possess a high degree of individual ruggedness. Depressions and despair observed in blacks may in fact begin from birth and continue throughout life. Coping styles in the elderly have antecedents in early life. Clearly, as will become evident in the next chapter, there is much to learn from the black elderly regarding coping mechanisms. There is obviously a real need to continue to examine black experiences from a scientific base. Unfortunately, the literature has been filled with descriptions of mental illness among elderly minorities with little attention to etiologies, most specifically racism. This writer is convinced that the conditions of life stemming from racism and a minority status contribute significantly to emotional problems of minorities.

SUMMARY

For black Americans, racism is a major cause of emotional disabilities. Misunderstanding cultural differences has contributed to problems of misdiagnosing blacks as paranoid and extremely ill when the same set of symptoms seen in others may be characterized as normal. The impact of racism upon the health of black Americans is severe and should become the subject of greater research. However, far too many studies that deal with the black elderly are not really concerned with black life at all; the concern is with abnormal behavior and perversions. My experience indicates that a significant number of blacks do achieve a depth of satisfaction with age. Many black elderly citizens grow old gracefully; others resist and, with physical limitations, regress. With a reduction in racial- and ethnic-related bigotry, the number of emotional casualties among the black elderly will precipitously decline.

9

MENTAL HEALTH AND SUCCESSFUL COPING AMONG AGED BLACK WOMEN

SUE PERKINS TAYLOR

Little is known currently about ethnic and minority aging in the United States, and even less is known specifically about aging in black women. Members of different ethnic or minority groups are subjected to varying problems as they grow older. Women experience different kinds of problems than men. Consequently, both ethnic minority persons and women may be expected to use different strategies of adjustment to aging. In order to add clarification, in part, to this inquiry, this chapter focuses on some of the prevalent adjustment patterns of a sample of elderly black women in a metropolitan New England community. The discussion is based on data collected during a 1976–1977 ethnographic study of the lifeways and coping strategies of eighty-three women between the ages of 59 and 97. The field work was conducted over a period of thirteen months.

In the first phase of the study, a preliminary door-to-door survey was conducted to obtain a general profile of the demographic and socioeconomic characteristics of the older women in the area. The names and addresses of women aged 59 and older were obtained from the *1976 List of Men and Women*, which is compiled annually by the community's Office of Voter Registration. To insure the confidentiality of the participants in the study, the name of the city, as well as other pertinent information, has been deleted. Equal numbers of women were selected from three contiguous city wards. The second phase of the study involved the selection of eighteen informants from the original

Partial support for this research was provided by the National Institute of Mental Health (#1 F31 MH05546—01 CUAN) and is hereby gratefully acknowledged.

eighty-three women for in-depth interviews. Traditional anthropological methods of participant observing, informal interviewing, and recording of life histories on eighteen women were the primary methods of collecting, and sources for, the data. The latter informants were selected with a view toward sampling varied backgrounds, experiences, and living situations. The sample crosscut socioeconomic levels and included women with varied patterns of activity.

THE CONCEPT OF BICULTURATION

Several factors are important in providing a conceptual framework for this study. First, the women are viewed in terms of the situational factors impacting on them throughout their lives, including their responses to the processes of aging. Butler and Lewis (1977:24) state, "People are shaped not only by their own personal history, family environment, and inherent personality character- istics but also by the larger world around them." And Lindsay (1975:91) adds, "For any man or woman now 65 or older, the attitudes, behavior, and life expectations reflect the circumstances and conditions prevailing in the United States during his or her formative years."

Second, the concept of biculturation is utilized in this study to characterize the experience of black Americans. While blacks share all those traits that identify one as being an American, situational factors have also contributed to the creation of a rich and viable culture that is partially distinct from the culture of the dominant group (see Blauner, 1970; Cole, 1971; and Valentine, 1972). In situations where some subgroups are denied some of the rights and privileges of the dominant group in the society, the members of the subgroup learn to "manipulate the dominant culture as best they can and yet maintain their own distinctive patterns as well in order to survive" (Valentine, 1972:33). This becomes clear in the life histories of the women in the study. In order to survive, they developed coping strategies that allowed them to solve problems as they arose. Even though the women represent a heterogeneous group with differences in social class, North-South origins, and rural-urban backgrounds, there are definite similarities in their attitudes toward aging and in the ways in which they deal with problems.

These similar patterns of behavior can be attributed to cultural commonalities in personal experiences. It is contended that the ethnohistorical and bicultural experiences of black women have helped them to formulate their coping strategies. Prior life experiences shape individual attitudes about aging. In turn, such attitudes and expectations, continued from earlier years, influence the way people perceive problems and the choices they make in dealing with them. Individuals fall back on coping mechanisms that were used in the past; and they return consistently to strategies that have a cultural base (for exam- ple, the family and religion).

ATTITUDES ABOUT AGING AND PERCEIVED PROBLEMS

Aging, among the sample, was not viewed as a problem. Growing old was accepted as a natural process of life. Where age-related physical changes and personal problems were identified, they were taken in stride. One woman aptly stated, "getting old's no big thing—just one more thing to cope with." In spite of the positiveness that was expressed, specific problems stemming from insufficient income were identified for some. The primary source of income for seventy-five (90 percent) of the women was Social Security, SSI (Supplemental Security Income), or private pensions. Only eight (10 percent) of the women were employed at full- or part-time jobs outside the home. Problems related to living accommodations, household maintenance costs, and a decline in social and recreational outlets were described most often by women in financial need. Conversely, women who described their situation as financially secure generally managed to meet their needs and enjoy social outings as well.

Women with incomes drastically lower than they had maintained during their middle years found the greatest problems to be associated with their inability to meet their expectations in this period of their lives. Most had expected to be financially secure and enjoying retirement. On the other hand, women who had been poor all their lives found very little difference in their situation. Inadequate health care, insufficient food, poor housing, and no luxuries were just a continuation of a lifelong condition. These circumstances were not perceived as a special problem in old age.

TWO KINDS OF COPING STRATEGIES

In the analysis of the data, two basic kinds of coping strategies were identified. The first consisted of those things that were readily observable in the daily behavior of the women in the study. For the most part, these strategies incorporated the operation of a viable support network made up of kin and friends. Other strategies fell categorically within the realm of the mind set of the individual as part of a cognitive process of adaptation initiated in response to situational factors. These were based on individual perceptions of problems, values, and beliefs. The actual coping strategies reflect both the strengths and the stresses of black women. These include the actual or perceived strength of the family as recognized through a system of mutual support and aid; religion as a source of strength and the acceptance of Jesus as liberator; and an adherence to the American work ethic, which was espoused during their formative years as part of the American value system.

PERSONAL NETWORKS AS COPING STRATEGIES

An analysis of personal networks as coping strategies is incomplete without an understanding of the situational factors that lead to the formation of certain kinds of networks and the activation of particular links (for example, the choice of people). The kinship links are based upon role relationships and behavioral expectations that are predetermined by cultural norms, traditional values, individual personalities, and the kind of need that exists (for example, food, money, companionship, or advice). Extended family networks operate as an adaptive strategy within a system of mutual aid and support. With the exception of seven women who reported no living kin, aid in the form of goods, services, or money occurred in most families. The most frequent exchanges occurred between the older women and their adult children or their siblings. Women who resided with other family members often shared the chores and pooled their resources (financial or otherwise) to increase the total assets of the household. ·

The network was not limited to kin relationships. It included friends, neighbors, and service providers. In a new housing complex for senior citizens, the women formed peer friendships and networks to cope with specific problems. Sharing food, leisure time, and shopping errands served two main functions. First, these new friendships made life less lonely for individuals living alone. Second, the relationships and the communal sharing helped the women find a new sense of independence.

Networks are not new. Indeed, exchange networks and communal sharing have always existed as a means of "manipulating the system" in order to provide the basic necessities. These patterns of exchange are part of an ongoing process that has occurred repeatedly within black families and among friends for years. Stack (1974) describes the same patterns in her study of domestic networks as an adaptive strategy of urban blacks. Reciprocal relationships provide a strong support system that functioned in the past and continue to be operative in offsetting external pressure. More recently, McAdoo's (1978) empirically based analysis suggests that the primary criterion of black family strength, whether caring for the elderly or raising children, is the kinship network.

VALUE ORIENTATIONS AS A
SUCCESSFUL COPING STRATEGY

The most commonly found values and beliefs of individuals that are brought into play as problem-solving devices include religious beliefs, the virtues of hard work, self-help, and membership in the family (see Hill, 1972). Such strong value orientations lead to psychological and pragmatic ways of dealing with problems. Yet the values may be in conflict with what is actually happening. This is particularly true when the values of the elderly are no longer the primary values of society or when the values cannot be actualized (for example, consider the value of independence versus the reality of dependency in old age). Each of these values can be described in terms of their adaptive qualities.

First, the perception of the family as a major coping resource is based upon a value system that places a great deal of importance on the extended family and the continuity of life. Most of the women (94 percent) described the family as the most dependable source of aid. Among the eighteen women who were interviewed in depth, however, three cases were identified in which the family had been exploitative and/or negligent of the older woman. Conflicts were common in intergenerational households, and, in fact, the family was identified as a source of stress in three cases. It is precisely because of the value placed upon the family and the commitments that are made between members that some of the tensions exist. Further, the positive beliefs about the family may be the cause of women ignoring situations in which they have been abused.

Second, religion for most of the women has provided the solace they needed in times of distress and the impetus to go on when things were difficult. It was not a matter of becoming more religious in later life. Rather, religion as a coping strategy was always a source of aid for these women. Yet, women who had not been religious earlier were less likely to select this kind of coping mechanism. For others the power of prayer and the psychological release this might bring should not be overlooked. When solutions to problems are found, they have been attributed to God or Jesus as liberator or savior. Religious belief systems have a built-in explanation that allows individuals to accept situations when their desires are not achieved: It is simply God's will. Thus, their values and beliefs remain intact.

Third, the belief in the American work ethic, along with the basic values of self-help and independence, played an important role in the choices the women made during their lifetimes and in the kind of responses that they make during old age. There was a pride in "making do" in rough times (for example, during the Depression). This same ideal remains an important mechanism for dealing with current problems.

SUMMARY

For the women in this study the valuation of family, religion, and self-help is based on past experiences and cultural traditions that are firmly embedded in the mind of the individual. These cognitive perceptions are transferred to immediate situations, and they influence the behavioral responses.

The interdependence of all these factors contributes to the perceptions people hold about aging, the way problems are identified, and the choices made in order to cope. The value orientations, as well as the functioning of a viable support network, are part of an interacting system of coping.

Networks are extremely effective in situations where individuals or subgroups of people are denied equal access to the services and material resources that are needed to function efficiently and satisfactorily. Network manipulation is a tool for achieving basic goals and is learned as part of the biculturation process among black Americans. The network is the vital element in a cultural buffer system that operates to maximize individual or group alternatives in situations of limited choice.

Value orientations that emphasize faith, family, and a strong adherence to the American work ethic shape adaptive mechanisms and enable individuals to use kinship connections as problem-solving devices. The belief in the strength and support of the family, regardless of whether the family is supportive or negligent, is the primary strategy that allows older women to define aging as "no big thing."

Coping strategies may be real and observable mechanisms for dealing with day-to-day transactions; or they may represent an ideal that in effect exists within the mind of the individual. These kinds of strategies are by no means unique. It may be expected that all people draw upon a repository of past experiences and beliefs as cultural buffers. These experiences and beliefs have personal meaning and have proved to be successful in other situations.

THE QUESTION OF FAMILIAL AND SOCIAL SUPPORT

10

RELIGION AND THE BLACK ELDERLY: THE HISTORICAL BASIS OF SOCIAL AND PSYCHOLOGICAL CONCERNS

ALLEN C. CARTER

It is commonly accepted that religion has been a cornerstone of the black community. The history of the black church is almost a history of black people in America. The impressive victories of the civil rights movement and the political, economic, and educational progress of black people were all sustained by the black church. Furthermore, as shall become evident, the backbone of black religious expression has been the black elderly.

Despite the black elderly's impact on the black church, however, a review of the literature reveals that little has been written to document the role of religion in the lives of elderly black people. To be sure, some controversy abounds concerning religious activity and black people, but little good empirical evidence exists to document the importance of religion to older blacks. For example, Jackson's and Wood's (1976) conclusion of significantly greater religious identification among the black (relative to white) elderly is suspect inasmuch as the investigators failed to base their conclusions on credible statistical methodology; on the other hand, Jackson and Walls's (1978) conclusion of no statistically significant differences in religious identification by race is equally suspect, given the extremely small sample size. In addition, the importance of religion as psychological and sociological phenomena in the lives of elderly blacks has been almost ignored by scholars. The purpose of this chapter, therefore, is to trace the historical development of the psychosocial needs that religion has served and continues to serve for the black elderly. The central questions are (1) What functions have been, and are, served by religion in the lives of the black elderly? and (2) What evidence is there on the integration or participation of elderly blacks in religion and religious institutions? The discussion in this chapter constructs the foundation for arguments in subsequent chapters on the strengths and resources of the church for the formal delivery of social services to the elderly. That is, patterns of religious and church obligations to the aged, traditionally characteristic in the black community, shall be examined in subsequent chapters for their significance for the delivery of services to all elderly persons.

EARLY ROOTS OF BLACK RELIGIOSITY

It is the contention of several leading black psychologists that modern-day American blacks can be understood only in the context of their African origins. According to Nobles (1980), black psychology derives not from the negative aspect of being black in white America, but rather from the positive features of basic African philosophy that dictates the values, customs, attitudes, and behavior of Africans in Africa and the New World. His belief is based on the contention that there is an African (black) ethos that had its origin in West Africa and was consciously and unconsciously transported across the ocean in the minds and souls of the black men and women brought to America as slaves. This African ethos revolved around the concepts of "oneness with nature" and a collective, communal philosophy based on a belief in the "survival of the tribe."

Crucial to understanding this point is awareness that religion was not restricted to a ceremonial, ritualistic practice, but was in fact the total existence of tribal Africans. In fact, many African languages did not have a word for religion as such. The religion was the people—the community. Survival of the tribe, as a community, was directly dependent upon a deep sense of kinship that had sacred and reverent bonds. Linked to this concept of communal relationship were the belief in ancestral worship and a reverence for the elderly.

Here it is argued that in order to understand elderly black Americans, one must see their spirituality as an integral part of their everyday lives; and furthermore, to appreciate this spirituality, attention cannot be restricted to the institutionalized church. It is impossible, therefore, to analyze the sociology and psychology of blacks, particularly the elderly, without an understanding of the pervasive nature of this spirituality.

RELIGION AND PSYCHOSOCIAL NEEDS IN THE NEW LAND

Thrust into a new world, not of their choosing, and faced with a doctrine that emphasized individualism and materialism at the expense of the blood and sweat of the black individual, Africans had to fashion a philosophy that would sustain them through the horrors of slavery. The mold for philosophy was cast in Africa, but was shaped now by the religion of the European master.

As slaves, Afro-Americans were totally dependent upon the white slave master for their physical existence. At any moment a total arbitrary decision could be made about their existence. Death was thus an ever present and foreboding companion, for in the eyes of the white master the slave was mere property. For the black slave, then, death was often viewed as a positive refuge that had to be earned through suffering; and once earned, it offered a place where the arbitrariness and injustices of life were eliminated. Frazier (1964:24) alludes to this phenomenon when noting that the "best source of information on the manner in which the Negro adapted Christianity to his peculiar psychological and social needs is . . . found in . . . the Negro Spirituals." Consider, he notes, lyrics that plead for the divine to remove the individual from his or her present exasperating, real-life circumstances. Death could therefore be transformed through spiritual beliefs. Grier and Cobbs (1971) note that death, as such, was not just a reward for right living, but it was also a reward for suffering.

This flexible and often positive attitude toward death may be seen as another example of African remnants in the world view of the Afro-American. In Africa personal immortality was linked to the system of kinship and ancestral worship (Nobles, 1980). Individuals joined their ancestors after physical death, but remained linked to the living as long as they were remembered in name and spirit by them. This African concept of reverence for the elderly resulted in a positive attitude toward death that was also reflected in the New World religion. The Christian concept of heaven, for the Afro-American, often included the elements of joining with kin and older relatives.

Thus, in earthly matters the social organization of black life, which derived from the basic needs of survival, was served by religion. It was the primary avenue by which the black slave could give expression to his deepest feelings and at the same time achieve status and find a meaningful existence. C. Eric Lincoln (1974) states that the black man identified with his pastor, his church, or his denomination to the extent that it defined who he was. That is, the black church came to fulfill in many instances the needs and functions that were once met by the religion-based tribal and community organization of the African in his native land. The community, religion, psychology, and sociology of the black man were, in many instances, one and the same.

BLACK RELIGION AND THE BLACK ELDERLY

In the community life of the slaves it appears that the African tradition of showing respect and deference to elders remained as a cornerstone of that society. Frederick Douglass noted in 1885 that the young had to "approach the company of an older slave with hat in hand" (Gutman, 1976:218). In 1861, Lucy Chase, a white schoolteacher, supported Douglass's position: "They show great respect for age; they always call an older person Aunt or Uncle" (Gutman, 1976:24). This practice of addressing elders by kinship name served a psychosocial function by insuring a person of a secure place within a community. The title of Uncle or Aunt signalled respect and honor to those most esteemed in the community. This was another remnant of a spiritual bond that had its roots in the African sense of kinship and spirituality. This practice also served as a survival technique, because it promoted the psychological continuity of the slave to his ever changing environment.

Continuity of life was also shown in the naming ceremony. Recent scholarship indicates that elders of the community often named newborn children (Gutman, 1976). Usually names of older or deceased family members were chosen. Meyer Fortes argued: "The grandparents are felt to be living links with the past. Elderly slaves—fictive aunts and uncles among them—played that role among Afro-American slaves, a role given status within the slave community" (Gutman, 1976:185). Grandparents, therefore, served as role models, the carriers of tradition and morality, and were perceived as the living embodiment of spirituality. Not only were moral codes and judgments within their prerogative, but they also were the most direct linkages to ancestors and to the world of the spirits. Religion and spirituality thus were closely linked and identified with the elders.

The question that arises now is the present status of the relationship between the black elder and his religion. What is the nature of it, and is it still a sustaining influence in his life? Both Carter and Managroo (1979) and Watson (1980a), although finding that there was a significant expression of religious belief, also found that the eldest among the elderly attended church less than the younger among the elderly. Carter and Managroo (1979) found in their sample more than 92 percent of the elderly blacks holding membership in a church. Of course, this relationship is more often than not related to the degree of physical incapacitation associated with advanced old age.

Carter's and Managroo's (1979) study of rural elderly blacks also found that men did not value church organizations as highly as did women. Although their findings supported Watson's conclusions that no significant difference exists between elderly black men and women in regard to church attendance, their data reveal that the men felt that—other than the deacon board—little is left that is meaningful for a "man to do in the church." Dissatisfaction was expressed concerning the changing nature of the church, which did not allow for masculine influence. This finding was interpreted in light of the black church's serving as a psychological support for the black man, an institution that would reinforce his feelings of competence and meaningfulness whenever he needed to remove himself from the inhumanity and indignation of the white world. For most white men, feelings of control and dominance have been and are a constant part of their lives. However, for black men, racism and their minority status prohibit any form of power or dominance. One of the institutions that the black man felt was in his domain and power was the church. In this institution he was permitted to express himself freely and exercise power and influence. Dougherty (1978) notes, however, that when the opportunity is not present for males to occupy positions of leadership within the church, they do not attend in great numbers.

This trend, however, does not keep males from expressing strong religious beliefs. Unquestionably, the significance of and the satisfaction received from a religious life are by far one of the more important benefits of living for both the elderly black male and female. For black people, young and old, the ability to put trust in something other than oneself has been the important ingredient in the survival of the race.

The essence of any psychology of oppression is this mysterious ability to ransform conditions for survival's sake. In summary, because the oppressed person—whether oppression is due to race, class, sex or age—is forced into a condition of viewing life differently; because he is forced to know the life of the oppressor as well as the oppressed; because he must deal with the ever present threat of death; and because he conditions himself or is conditioned to be able psychologically to release and separate himself at a moment's notice from objects and other people, the only source of strength left for the oppressed is his trust in an unseen, just higher power. In this respect, therefore, it is important for the survival of an oppressed people that religious traditions remain vibrant. It is also important that the lessons of these traditions are shared and passed from one generation to the next. Typically this role has been played by those having the greatest experience with the surviving functions of religion: the black elderly.

11

THE BLACK "GRANNY" AND THE SOVIET "BABUSHKA": COMMONALITIES AND CONTRASTS

GARI LESNOFF–CARAVAGLIA

The biological or nurturant role imposed upon the female both by nature and by society has lasting reverberations that continue through advanced old age and are terminated only by death. Such role obligations vary, but in old age they assume a particular character that rests in part upon the role assumptions experienced by women over the life span and, in part, upon the fact of age.

The assumption of particular roles in societies occurs not by happenstance, but in response to a need that society directs toward those members most likely to be responsive. This is particularly evident in the role of "granny" in black American culture and in the role of "babushka" in Soviet culture, both of which have evolved as pivotal roles for women in old age to provide balance for the survival cycle of generations. In both instances these roles developed primarily from an economic basis with activity centered about grandchild rearing (Scanzoni, 1971; Lesnoff-Caravaglia, 1978; n.d.).

The black older woman in America has held a central role, one that predates the Civil War, in the survival of the family over generations (Billingsley, 1968; Myers, 1980). The role of older Soviet women had its initiation during a war that changed the face of the Soviet nation, the Great Patriotic War, or World War II.

The Soviet Union, in the eyes of the Soviets, is a developing or emerging nation. Past history is largely discounted, and the Soviets look upon their current state as having been born out of the 1917 revolution and as being only

Soviet research sponsored by the Fogarty International Center under the U.S./USSR Agreement for Technical and Scientific Cooperation.

some sixty years of age. As citizens of a newly emerging nation, the Soviets feel that many of the problems that beset their country are due primarily to its youth. Soviets make constant reference to the fact that things are better than they were and that they will unquestionably improve even more in the future. The babushka role, as will be shown, is one of the primary agents for dealing with such change and, at the same time, for providing a sense of continuity.

There is also a historical similarity between conditions in Soviet society and in the black experience with respect to the recent increased participation by blacks in American society, as well as their earlier relatively more disadvantaged position (Stanford and Alexander, 1981). The newness of this experience makes of history a personal study often foreign to increasing numbers of today's black youth. The black granny provides linkages to the past within black families.

The energy, courage, and devotion that black and Soviet women exhibited during times of national and group stress have earned them a reverence and esteem that has persisted over generations. Part of the respect paid to the Soviet babushka relates to the fact that women (along with men) were responsible for the rebuilding of the nation following the war, as well as the fact that babushkas had lived under the tyranny of the czars, had endured inequities of every description, and had been deprived of medical care and educational opportunities.

In both American and Soviet instances, the mothering expected by society is never absent from the description of what it means to be female. Although in both cases women have worked outside the home and often in professional capacities, particularly in the Soviet Union, the societal expectation still clings (Staples, 1978). Reassuming the care of children, albeit in the grandparenting role, is socially acceptable as an option for women as they grow older, even though they may have spent years of their working lives in totally different settings (Laslett, 1972).

The significance of the granny and babushka roles is probably felt most in the area of childrearing. Their concern for the young often takes the form of instruction in proper behavior and moral attitudes. In both cultures the young are regarded as being different from the older generation and difficult to manage. Further, the tradition in old Russian society—and this holds true in the Soviet Union today—focuses on the role of the old in the instruction of the young. The same expectation of the black granny is common (Frazier, 1966). Hill (1978) reports that two-thirds of all black families headed by women 65 years of age and over—relative to one-tenth among their white counterparts—had children under 18 years living with them. Hill and Shackleford (1975) note that two-thirds of black children under age 18 and living with relatives are grandchildren of the head of the household.

Because of extreme economic pressures, the black granny often was regarded as the economic mainstay, with family members treating her as the focal point in the family assistance scheme. Money and goods were often given her as she was regarded as the just distributor to those family members in greatest need. As implied by Jones (1973), since employment opportunities have often been greater for the black female than for the black male, the role of breadwinner has fallen to women out of necessity. Thus women often had to assume the financial burden of the children. The older woman, as the most experienced in dispensing meager resources, was looked upon as the head of the extended family. She continued to play this role until death, with no thought of retirement from either this capacity or as an active contributor to the family economy. The all-encompassing nature of her role leads family members, regardless of blood relationship, to address her simply as "Momma."

For Soviet women, professional roles have been possible for some time. As one example, 76 percent of the Soviet physicians are women. This ability to enter the professions on a par with men is the result of the decimation of the male population during World War II, when women were called upon to rebuild the nation. Women have continued in such professional capacities and have enlarged the spheres in which they can perform. There is virtually no occupation closed to women in the Soviet Union.

Although Soviet women officially may retire at the age of 55, few retire from their familial responsibilities or their work roles. Many women continue in the same capacity as they did before reaching retirement age. Some may take on a new position, but the opportunity to continue working is not only present, but encouraged because of the severe labor shortage. To take on the role of babushka is also an option that is much encouraged, for it frequently frees a younger woman to initiate or continue a career. Babushkas pride themselves on their daughter's achievements and the achievements of their grandchildren.

In the Soviet Union the older woman, upon her retirement, receives a pension that is usually more than adequate for her needs. Her assistance to the family economy is in more of an auxiliary role. Her greatest contribution to the family is in fully establishing the grandparent role by moving in, usually with her daughter's family, and taking complete charge of the grandchildren.

Since the retirement age for women in the Soviet Union is 55, this young grandmother is generally free of any disabilities and can take over the position as housekeeper, as well as babysitter, with no difficulty. The babushka, in effect, takes full responsibility for her daughter's home, freeing up both daughter and husband to participate unhampered in the work force. Her own pension allows her considerable independence, and it is not unusual for the grandmother to assist her children and grandchildren financially. With free health care supplied through the national health care system, the grandmother is thus financially independent. Women freely choose the babushka role as a form of work, rather than continuing to work outside the home. This voluntary assumption of the babushka role is, in part, a reflection of the love that frequently transcends the generations.

There are a number of reasons that women give up outside employment at retirement age. Some Soviet women feel that they have fulfilled their obligation to the state as citizens; some may retire because of poor health; and others see this as an opportunity to play an active role in rearing their grandchildren. Those women who choose to continue working do so because of challenging career opportunities; their salary is better than the reduced benefits that they would receive as retirement income; or their living quarters were assigned to them as part of their salary.

The system of student stipends permits Soviet students the opportunity to live independently of family; and with both parents employed and the babushka receiving a pension, the Soviet family members, unlike many blacks, can really exist independently of one another. The reality, however, is that they, like large numbers of black families, live in close family units and pool their resources to the material advantage of all family members. Thus the Soviet family is drawn together more by affectional ties than economic need. Manuel (1980d) similarly found the family to remain a strong affectional and care-giving resource for the black aged even under conditions of improved economic circumstances among the aged's offspring.

The expectation in Soviet society is that everyone will work, and this includes older persons as well. The notion of amusement or, simply, recreation as part of the older person's work is a foreign concept. Older persons themselves wish to continue to work and to be useful. This attitude is shared by the black granny.

Generations of black people have grown up in situations where it has been normal or typical for women to work and to take on the role of provider. To a certain extent, female employment has become established or institutionalized within black society and, as such, forms part of the granny role.

Black society regards the granny in a very positive fashion, while the Soviets actually give national recognition to the significance of this role. A holiday, Women's Day, is celebrated annually on March 8 to commemorate the contributions of all women to the nation.

Although the babushka is a positive representation of the growth and development of the Soviet Union, she is still regarded somewhat critically, as she also represents the past regime. It is commonly acknowledged that it is the babushka who introduces the religious emphasis into the home and serves as a bridge between old values and traditions and the new society. As mothers and grandmothers, women acknowledge the changes that have come about; and although they sew the uniforms for the children and grandchildren as they join the Young Pioneer groups of Soviet society, they also baptize them in the Orthodox church.

The option chosen by increasing numbers of Soviet women to remain in the work force has gradually diminished the numbers of babushkas available to care for grandchildren. In recognition of this gradual role change, the Soviet government has instituted a new law by which mothers can stay at home with newborn children for as long as one year on full salary. This change is a response to the fact that babushkas are somewhat less available and that there are too few nurseries to handle all of the children. In black society the increase in employment opportunities for black males has led to greater mobility among families and, correspondingly, some reduction in the importance of the granny.

In both the black American and Soviet families, however, families face housing shortages, and because of the fact that both parents usually work, or increasingly work, there are increases in the need for a caretaker of young children. For the black family, maintaining the granny in the home does not provide any advantages in terms of housing amelioration. In fact, including the granny may cause some rearrangement of the family composition. Many black grannies, however, have homes of their own into which they gradually accept grandchildren and returning children. The Soviet babushka, on the other hand, brings an added plus to the critical housing situation in that she has the right to a room of her own. The family that adds a babushka to their number has the privilege of applying for a larger apartment.

The housing shortage also makes for difficulties in relocation in both communities. The retention of the black family unit is often the result of external circumstances. Because of economic restrictions and lack of opportunity, blacks cannot locate at will. Many are forced to remain within the family support network in order to survive. In the Soviet Union everyone works for the state, and changes of job setting are dictated according to national need.

The material ambitions of black families, much like the Soviets', are high, but there is greater frustration in the blacks' inability to achieve some of their goals. The constant and frequent sharing with other family members limits the ability of a particular family segment to maintain material advantages. Once they have been recipients of aid, the understanding is that their own prosperity must also be shared with the extended family. The sharing of items large and small is the general rule, and such cooperation is often described by the expression "what goes round comes round" (Stack, 1974). The black grandmother plays a central position within this kinship system of mutual aid (Jackson, 1971a).

The role of providing for the family by the grandmother still has much to do with the provision of food for the table. For the black granny, food shortages are the result of a lack of money. For the Soviet babushka, the shortages of food are due more to poor distribution methods and the emphasis upon particular areas of production according to governmental decrees. One of the major tasks of the babushka is to stand in the long shopping lines, which can extend for blocks, for the purchase of a single food item (Lesnoff-Caravaglia, 1980).

Furthermore, both the granny and the babushka live in societies that operate according to the dictates of an ubiquitous authority—the white-dominated society or the Soviet government—that owns all and regulates all. Both participate in often drab, routine existences that have one goal: getting enough food or clothing and working hard for what little life provides.

The advantages of both the granny and the babushka roles lie in the fact that these roles are carried out within the bosom of the family (Martin and Martin, 1978). These women play meaningful roles within a social setting. Thus boredom and loneliness are often foreign to their experience, and their lives are not regarded as empty or futile. They are respected and cherished by family members until the moment of death. It is not surprising, then, that institutionalization is rarely regarded as an option when the elderly grand-mother has severe health problems or is at the point of death. The grand-mother has every expectation that she will be cared for by family members and thus has none of the anxieties of being removed from her home in old age and dying in the midst of strangers in a strange bed. This great sense of need has positive connotations, as the individual always has a role to play and figures prominently in the lives of many persons. Such expectations enrich the life of the older woman, but, as Bertram Cohler argues in the next chapter, the expectations also can be taxing and can limit freedom and personal develop-ment. Moreover, as Jackson and Walls (1978) show, although evidence points to the greater extensiveness of relations between black females and their grandchildren, it is also true that a greater percentage of the black aged (relative to the white aged) do not have grandchildren. Thus the preceding analysis should not be interpreted to mean that the black aged female is overwhelmed with extensive relations with grandchildren; rather, it appears that among those with grandchildren there is more extensiveness.

In the final analysis, however, one perspective suggests that the nurturant role of the grandmother may well provide satisfactory avenues that many groups of older women, including those in the nonminority American popula-tion, do not experience due to lack of family or lack of societal expectations for such role assumption. Not only the loneliness of old age and sense of an unfulfilled life, but the lack of esteem qualities associated with old age could possibly be mitigated by the introduction of positive participation of older women within the family life of their wider kin network.

12

STRESS OR SUPPORT: RELATIONS BETWEEN OLDER WOMEN FROM THREE EUROPEAN ETHNIC GROUPS AND THEIR RELATIVES

BERTRAM J. COHLER

Discussions of family life in contemporary urban society have sometimes suggested that maintenance of extended family ties may no longer be possible. Such conclusions contradict findings from more than two decades of research showing that the modified extended family is well suited to industrialization and that continuing contact and communication among relatives are characteristic of urban families.

Closeness across generations is particularly characteristic within families from traditional peasant societies such as those of eastern and southern Europe where existing patterns of intergenerational collaboration have been strengthened by migration and subsequent problems in adjusting to life in a new land. While such close ties among family members are generally viewed as important in mitigating the effects of stress and strain associated with urban life and in promoting more positive morale, the reciprocal obligations and responsibilities imposed by such continuing ties have their own cost: Ironically, the very family ties that are believed to mitigate strain may also be a source of strain. While the present chapter explores this paradoxical perspective among samples from three European ethnic groups, the conclusions are relevant for qualifying the current preoccupation with conceptions

Research reported in this paper was carried out with the assistance of a grant from the Administration on Aging (93-P-57425) and a grant from the Social Science Division Research Committee, the University of Chicago.

of the family as an automatic and positive source for coping among the minority aged.

ETHNICITY AND EXTENDED FAMILY TIES

Findings from studies of families across social strata and within diverse subcultures suggest that the model family arrangement in American society is not the nuclear, one-generation unit so often portrayed in critical sociological formulations. While not sharing a common household, as is often the case in traditional peasant societies, family members continue to live close to each other and exchange both tangible resources and assistance (Sussman, 1959; Uzoka, 1979). Litwak (1965:291) has described this kind of family unit as a "modified" extended family, which "consists of a coalition of nuclear families in a state of partial dependence." Within American society, while high levels of visiting and exchange of resources may be found across social strata, reliance upon family members for assistance is particularly striking among working-class families (Fried, 1973). Working-class subculture tends to emphasize informal rather than formal social ties and personal rather than impersonal definitions of status and social identity (Paterson, 1964). Reliance upon family rather than outside sources of assistance is preferred and expected.

Family ties emphasizing interdependence and mutual assistance and support are of particular significance among working-class families who have recently emigrated from abroad. Both the desire to maintain older traditions in the new land and the problems involved in successfully adapting to a culture whose traditions are often perceived as alien lead to isolation of first- and second-generation families within ethnic neighborhoods in which informal family ties replace formal assistance from extrafamilial institutions in providing assistance and support in time of need.[1] Reports from a number of field and interview studies of central and southern European groups have shown the importance of such family ties, often extending into the third generation (Cohler and Grunebaum, 1981).

Current patterns of family life among members of immigrant families and their descendants must be understood in terms of both the culture of the native land and the patterns of immigration to the United States. Ethnicity, in the present discussion, refers not just to intergroup relations, but also to enduring differences in the manner in which persons resolve conflicting alternatives to universal human dilemmas, such as the relationship between man and his fellows (Spiegel, 1971). Such variation in value orientations are transmitted across generations in ways that differ between the country of origin and that of immigration.

Not only the fit between the traditions of the country of origin and those of the new land, but also the pattern and timing of immigration have an important impact upon how these competing alternatives are ordered within particular ethnic groups. Irish immigration to the United States was concentrated heavily in the first half of the nineteenth century, while that of eastern and southern European groups, such as the Polish and the Italian, was heavily concentrated during the first years of the twentieth century. Irish immigrants were most likely to immigrate alone, usually as a result of complex family decisions regarding inheritance of the family farm (Arensberg and Kimball, 1968). Since there was little work available in Dublin, the only alternatives were either joining the church or immigrating to England or America. English labor surplus, particularly acute during the years 1840–1860, contributed to the decision to immigrate to America.

A closer fit was possible between the world view of Irish immigrants and American society than was true among eastern and southern European immigrants, as problems of language also contributed to problems in adapting to American society. Particularly among Italian immigrants, who were accustomed to living in dense villages established to maximize the amount of land that could be cultivated, immigration to the United States was a result of a chain process in which one or more within a village emigrated and then returned or wrote back, urging fellow villagers to emigrate (McDonald and McDonald, 1964). In traditional Italian peasant society, relations between members of the extended family had been a source of tension; as a result of scarce resources, it was assumed that relatives sought only their own economic gain (Bianca, 1974).

The result of chain migration was that villagers settled close to each other, often in the same apartment building. The advantages of continuing contact with others sharing a common world view, together with the necessity of depending upon others for help with such problems as finding work, led to increased reliance upon members of the extended family for advice and assistance. The result was a more effective intergenerational family unit than in the old country. While significant differences can be found between patterns of immigration between eastern and southern European groups—including the relatively greater importance of formal institutions such as the Catholic church in the settlement pattern and subsequent use of community resources of European groups (Fandetti and Gelfand, 1976)—similar positive impact of immigration upon the development of an extended family system may be observed.

ETHNICITY, AGING, AND THE SOCIAL WORLD
OF MIDDLE-AGED AND OLDER WOMEN

Within working-class families such as those of the Italian and Polish ethnic groups, much of the day-to-day contact and exchange of resources is enacted by women who generally serve as the family "kin-keepers" (Firth, Forge, and Forge, 1970). The daughter's kin-keeping activity, within both her own parental family and that of her in-laws, is an extension of her lifelong socialization into interdependence (Chodorow, 1978). Just as the young adult daughter is experiencing an increase in the number and variety of reciprocal obligations within the family, her own middle-aged mother is also experiencing dramatically increased expectations regarding her role as kin-keeper within the larger family unit. As the generation "in the middle," women at midlife are expected by their adult offspring to provide assistance and support during transition into such adult roles as marriage partner and parent. At the same time, there are increasing demands from older parents, parents-in-law, and other relatives for assistance and care. The high degree of interdependence that is characteristic of working-class families, particularly those from eastern and southern European ethnic groups, intensifies the role strain and overload so often reported by women at midlife.

Maintenance of close ties with relatives and friends is believed to foster personal adjustment, reducing the impact of otherwise stressful life events through provision of increased support and care at times of personal crisis (Mueller, 1980). However, this assumption must be qualified for middle-aged and older persons. Findings concerning the impact of aging on personality (Neugarten, 1979) have shown that, accompanying the transition to late middle age, both men and women experience greater "interiority," reflected in measurable increases in an inward orientation and measurable decreases in the extent of interest in outer-world events. Cohler and Lieberman (1979) have reviewed the empirical literature supporting such increased interiority with age and note that this interiority is expressed by men primarily as increased passivity and interest in satisfaction of basic needs, while among women it is expressed primarily as increased egocentrism and aggression. Cohler and Lieberman report increased introversion among both men and women beginning with the middle years, together with increased preoccupation regarding satisfaction of personal needs. A similar formulation has been provided by Gutmann (1975) who notes that, with children grown and no longer at home, women seek increased time and energy in order to resolve issues associated with their own aging.

The results of studies of the significance of personality development on the perceptions of older women regarding family ties are consistent with conclusions from Cohler and Lieberman (1980). They report on findings concerning social relations, role strain, and morale among middle-aged and older first- and second-generation men and women from the Irish-, Italian-, and Polish-American ethnic groups. Among women in the Italian- and Polish-American ethnic groups, living in communities characterized by particularly dense social networks and complex patterns of reciprocity and obligations with adult offspring and other close relatives, there is a significant negative relationship between extent of social contact and both self-reported life satisfaction and psychological impairment.[2]

Cohler and Grunebaum (1981) have provided more detailed support for this finding on the basis of extensive interviews with older women and their relatives within modified extended Italian-American families. Feelings of resentment regarding burdensome obligations, including demands for assistance and support from close relatives, were particularly characteristic among these middle-aged and older grandmothers. Daughters, socialized since childhood into interdependence, which included the expectation of continued help from their own mothers as they struggled to manage their adult lives, reported being confused and offended by their mothers' reluctance to provide support and assistance. Close relatives reported similar feelings of disappointment at the reluctance of these middle-aged and older grandmothers to continue kin-keeping activities.

Other studies have reported similar findings regarding the views of women at midlife concerning family ties as a source of stress rather than support. Mostwin (1979) reports that older persons from eastern and central European ethnic groups prefer "intimacy at a distance," in the terms of Rosenmayr and Kockeis (1963). Jackson (1972a), in a study of older black women and their families, reported that those women living closer to their adult children were less likely to have contact with them than women living at a greater distance and that contact with friends rather than offspring was the most important source of increased life satisfaction. Consistent with these findings regarding aging, morale, and family ties in minority groups, Kerckhoff (1966) has reported morale to be highest among older persons having the least expectations of assistance from relatives, while Kutner and associates (1956) reported a negative relationship between positive morale among older parents and extent of contact with adult children.

CONCLUSION

Contrary to stereotyped portrayals of family life in contemporary urban society, relations among relatives both within and across generations involve complex, continuing patterns of contact and interdependent support, including both emotional support and that intangible financial assistance rendered by women through such tasks as baby-sitting and by men through such tasks as home repair. Interdependence is particularly characteristic of working-class families and may be further emphasized among those ethnic groups, such as Italian- and Polish-Americans, who come from societies relying upon extended family ties. As a result of chain migration, these immigrants and their descendants settle in close-knit urban neighborhoods in which the desire to maintain particular cultural traditions further supports separation from the larger society (Lieberson, 1963). Within such ethnic communities, women are particularly important in maintaining interdependence among relatives on a continuing basis. The traditional socialization of women from childhood for "expressive" roles within the family, notably that of kin-keeper for both the woman's own extended family and also that of her husband, increases feelings of responsibility and obligation that women experience within these ethnic communities.

As a result of intrinsic developmental personality changes at midlife associated with a sense of a foreshortened life span, resulting from the realization that there is less time left to be lived than has been lived already, the response of many middle-aged and older women to their role as kin-keeper is to feel such obligations and responsibilities as a source of increased strain. At just the time when these women are freed from day-to-day responsibilities for child care, their daughters seek increased support as they raise their own children. Strains are also experienced as a result of the demands of older parents for assistance, together with the strains of maintaining complex social ties with other close relatives.

Life in close-knit ethnic communities accentuates problems felt more generally by older persons in American society, as these older persons struggle to resolve conflicts regarding their own aging in the context of expectations for continuing interdependence. This perspective suggests a paradoxical response to life in ethnic communities. The richness and vitality of continuing ties between relatives may be important in mitigating strains among young adults. Among older adults, however, particularly women at midlife, continuing familial ties represent a source of decreased life satisfaction and are often experienced as the source rather than solution of strains associated with life in contemporary urban society.

NOTES

1. The increased reciprocal support from family members among these immigrant families may be due primarily to ethnicity rather than social status. Studies of black families living in urban communities do not show the same extent of mutual support and assistance as has been reported among immigrant and second-generation families (Jackson, 1972a).

2. It should be noted that there appears to be some correspondence between patterns of immigration and present understandings of the woman's role within the family. Among the Irish-American men and women, who early dispersed from original ethnic neighborhoods (Greeley, 1974), little association was found by Cohler and Lieberman (1980) between kin-keeping and personal adjustment. Significant negative relationships were found, however, between kin-keeping and adjustment among women within the Polish and, particularly, the Italian ethnic groups. In these two later ethnic groups, particular patterns of immigration led to the development of tightly knit communities characterized by a high degree of interdependence among relatives. Since women serve as the primary kin-keepers, they have assumed much of the responsibility for maintaining this interdependence. Increased expectations regarding interdependence further adversely affect the adjustment of women within the family (Cohler, 1981). Among men, and particularly within the Polish group, increased contact and communication with family members, including offspring, were positively related to morale. This sex difference may be due to the fact that many of the kin-keeping burdens are a part of the lives of women; men can enjoy contact with the same demands for assistance and support on a continuing basis.

SOCIAL DISENGAGEMENT: RETIREMENT, DEATH, AND DYING

13

RETIREMENT, ECONOMICS, AND THE MINORITY AGED

LODIS RHODES

Retirement is an economic concept that masquerades as a sociopsychological one; being old is a sociopsychological concept that, unfortunately, has come to define a person's capacity to cope with life's routines. Although chronological age is an important aspect of each concept, it is not the primary consideration in either one. This fact is obvious if one considers the case of professional athletes or military personnel who retire at a relatively young chronological age or cases wherein physiological and biological maladaptions make one old before his or her time. Neither the general public nor policy makers can continue to define the problems the elderly face during retirement as sociopsychological. The problems are primarily economic, and unless the problems are solved, the overall economy may be imperilled.

The purpose of this chapter is twofold: (1) to show that pension programs are used first and primarily as tools that are increasingly important in helping to shape the economy and (2) to dispel the popular notion that being old and retired is the same as being without dignity and lacking the ability to cope with the pressure of daily routines. Both points can be illustrated by examining the particular conditions of the minority aged.

Although retirement is an economic concept, that fact does not diminish the very real social and psychological problems confronting many retired people. Their problems arise largely from lack of companionship and failing health. Policy makers have tried to solve the problems by implementing an array of service programs for the elderly. The cost of programs such as Medicaid, Medicare, and meals programs, plus a changing demographic profile, have forced policy makers to seek more straightforward and cheaper economic solutions. These solutions are being sought by redesigning employment and retirement policies. The stated goal is to make the elderly less dependent on service programs. The less obvious one is to control better the impact that pension programs have on the economy. Thus, even brief consideration of a socio-psychological viewpoint, in defining retirement, returns the discussion to an economic perspective.

RETIREMENT: AN ECONOMIC CONCEPT

The number of old people in our society has become an important economic issue because of their dependence on retirement programs. Until recently, being old and poor was of little political or economic importance to elected officials. Few old people received pension benefits, and the total benefits paid to them were a small part of our economic output. A shifting age ratio and the levelling of overall economic productivity have forced these same officials to realize that an increasing proportion of the population is old and consuming goods and services rather than young and producing them. The change means that it costs more in both absolute and relative number of dollars to support the elderly population, given current retirement practices. The choice that policy makers face is twofold. The first is to decide whether to continue enforcing arbitrary standards about how long people can work—mandatory retirement. The second choice concerns who assumes primary responsibility for assuring that employees "save" for those periods in which they do not or cannot work. This is a choice over what balance should exist among public, private, and individual retirement programs and who pays their cost. The decisions are made more difficult by the relatively short time that public and private pension programs have provided most of the retirement income for older citizens. As a result, traditional pronouncements about the pension programs such as Social Security, rather than economic fact, provide the substance for debates on retirement policies.

There are two significant themes in debates about pension programs. One is that the working population is being required to pay more and more of its income to pay benefits to the retired population. The second is that most pension programs have incurred staggering cash commitments (debts) to cohorts of workers who have not reached retirement age. This means that what was a relatively minor concern of providing a cash income for a small number of retirees has grown into a major political and economic issue. Pension programs are at the heart of the issue because of the money flowing through them. It has been estimated that private pension programs paid out $101 billion during a twelve-month period spanning calendar years 1974 and 1975. During the same period those programs held assets of $270 billion (Federal Reserve Bank of Boston, 1976). These dollars, by any standard, are a significant part of our economy. The amount of money paid to retired workers has a profound influence on everyone through tax rates, the tendency to save, and the money that is available to businesses to borrow and respend. In addition, tax rates, the ability to save, and the way in which investment capital is generated affect subgroups of the elderly differently because of their different employment and income histories.

Even though pension programs already have the attention of elected officials and citizens because of their cost, the economic significance of the programs will continue to increase into the next century. This is so because of the bulge moving through the population as a result of the 1945–1955 baby boom. Those babies will not reach retirement age until after the year 2000, and it appears that an increasing share of the economic output will be needed to support them. The rise of pension programs to economic significance is even more surprising in view of their short history. They were launched by the relatively unobtrusive passage of the pension provisions of the Social Security Act of 1935. Provisions of that act set the stage for public programs to become the central fixture in the pension arena and to touch all citizens. Although a few public and private programs existed before that time, all were small and of little economic concern. Private programs, though older than public ones, have grown slowly since the turn of the century. Public programs now are larger than private ones in terms of dollars controlled and participants. They include Social Security (OASI), civil service, and military plans at the federal level as well as state and municipal plans. Private programs are growing at a faster rate now than public ones, largely because the Social Security program covers over 90 percent of the workers and because tax and investment incentives enacted in 1974 have made private plans more attractive investment options. The combined impact of public and private programs has changed how money flows through the economy. The specific changes involve how federal, state, and local governments manage their debts and how investment capital enters and leaves the money markets.

Since public programs are operated on a pay-as-you-go basis, the overriding concern of those managing the programs is to ensure that pay-in rates match pay-out rates. As long as the rates match, pension programs do not incur short-term fund deficits. Deficits are incurred, however, when the rate of paying benefits exceeds the rate of paying premiums, as is the case when the retired population receiving benefits grows faster than the working population paying premiums. Managing public debt now commands the attention of policy makers. It involves manipulating tax rates, revenue sources used to pay benefits, and retirement policies. Some public entities have resorted to buying issues of their own bonded indebtedness in one area with revenues from another area, though it seems that this technique is becoming less effective in controlling debt. On the other hand, vesting requirements and investment restrictions force private programs to balance their long-term financial obligations with current revenues, thereby avoiding these types of deficit problems. Ultimately, the pay-in and pay-out rates of pension programs are critical determinants of the overall productivity of the economy, because they affect the amount of money available to borrow and to be respent.

The point in discussing how the demographic profile of the population is changing and how money flows through pension programs is to underscore the fact that pension funds help sustain productivity in the economy. The funds provide a large share of the money that is borrowed and respent by the public and private sectors. Many argue that if the country is to produce more, then more capital is needed; capital is generated by individual savings and by the number of people who work and pay pension premiums. Controlling who works and for how long requires manipulating the labor force. The key devices for manipulating the size and profile of the labor force are education and retirement policies. The former controls access to the labor force; the latter controls exits from it. These stark economic facts seem quite removed from the emotional picture painted about the life circumstance of old people. They are, however, at the core of many of the policy issues regarding the elderly and the minority elderly. Two issues are particularly important for the current examination of retirement and the minority aged. These have to do with decisions about mandatory retirement and individual pension benefits.

MINORITY ELDERS: THE ECONOMICS OF RETIREMENT

Most wage earners are required to save through a retirement program, either public, private, or both. Compulsory savings, in turn, ensure that those same wage earners or their dependents are entitled to receive pension benefits. These benefits now go to the overwhelming majority of those 65 years of age and older. More importantly, 72 percent of that population receives at least 50 percent of its income from public or private pensions; one-third gets over 90 percent of its income from pensions (Grad and Foster, 1979). Although many aged Americans receive benefits, the percentages do not mean that the benefits paid to retirees are adequate or equitable. Individual benefits, in most cases, are neither. Many retirees live on incomes that are near or below the poverty line, and minority retirees have incomes that generally are below those of their white counterparts.

Although minority retirees have lower incomes than whites, it is not clear if or how the difference influences how minority elders adjust to retirement. On the other hand, it is clear that the pattern of preretirement employment and the wage history do determine source and amount of retirement income. The factors that make a difference are the sector—public or private—in which a person works, the occupational category of the job(s) held (professional, industrial, clerical, laborer), and the longest time worked at a particular job (job tenure). The first factor is important because it indicates the likelihood that a person has been covered by a pension program; public-sector employees are more often covered by a pension plan than those working in the private sector. If the type of job a person held is known, one has a fairly reliable measure of income. Finally, the longer a person holds the same job or works for the same employer, the more likely he is to receive pension benefits upon retirement.

These job-related characteristics differ for black and white retirees, and the difference results in different retirement incomes for the two groups. The differences in income hold across all types of family units (for example, married, male or female head of household, or unrelated individuals).

Another aspect of pension coverage that is important here is that both the rate and the amount of benefits increase as one moves from lower-paying laborer and service occupations to higher-paying professional, technical, and managerial occupations. Because of this, the percentage of higher-paid wage earners covered by a mix of plans (public and private pension plans) exceeds 70 percent, and relatively few blacks are in this group. Needless to say, retirees receiving pension benefits from two or more pension plans will have higher retirement incomes than those with benefits from one, usually Social Security.

A person's salary also makes a difference in the level of pension benefits he or she receives during retirement. Simply stated, if one has a relatively high salary during the working years, that advantage will carry over into retirement as higher pension benefits under most public and private programs. Pension programs, however, do specify maximum and minimum benefit levels in order to cap the amount of income going to any one person and to guarantee a minimum income for those who are entitled to receive benefits, but who had low incomes during their working years. Few blacks are penalized because of the ceiling on benefits; many black retirees have gained because of the minimum benefit provision in some pension plans. Blacks, however, are penalized by the wage provisions of most pension programs in two ways. First, blacks are and have been underrepresented in the higher-paying jobs that generate higher pensions: professional, technical, and managerial occupations. These same jobs require a lower contribution rate (a regressive tax) when measured against total salary than do lower-paying jobs—the jobs generally held by blacks and other minorities. The net effect of wage rates is that blacks pay proportionately more to participate in pension programs. The second penalty is that low-wage jobs constitute the least stable part of the labor market, and those who rely on them are more likely to become unemployed. Frequent and extended periods of unemployment disrupt pension coverage, and the breaks can disqualify a worker from receiving pension benefits. So not only do blacks pay relatively more to be covered by a pension program, they also receive less in benefits.

Finally, job tenure is the provision that has had the most severe impact on black retirees. Until the vesting restrictions governing private pension programs were eased in 1974 by ERISA (Employee Retirement Income Security Act), it was not uncommon to find that an employee had to work at the same job (with the same company) from ten to twenty years and had to reach a specified age before he earned a nonforfeitable right to benefits from a pension program in which he was required to participate. A similar vesting provision of Social Security stipulates that to be fully insured a worker must be covered for at least ten years (forty quarters). These time requirements are a distinct disadvantage for blacks for two reasons. Black retirees often had jobs that were not covered by Social Security or private pension programs, primarily low-paying service and day labor positions. Second, even when blacks held jobs that were covered by public or private plans, they were not likely to hold them for the extended periods of ten to twenty years required to qualify for a pension. Consequently, many blacks who contributed to a pension program during the years they worked never qualified for benefits because they switched jobs and were unemployed more often than whites. Ironically, many elderly blacks who have literally worked their entire lives in a series of low-paying service jobs now find that their Social Security pension, assuming they receive benefits, must be augmented by SSI (Supplemental Security Income) to *raise* their retirement income so that it is closer to the poverty level.

The current shape and operation of pension programs place black retirees in triple jeopardy. In other words, many black retirees are excluded from pension programs by reason of occupation; when covered, they pay relatively more of their income for that coverage; and stringent vesting requirements often prevent those who are covered from collecting pension benefits once they retire. The degree of jeopardy is illustrated by the following statistics. Eighty percent of blacks are private-sector wage earners; 11 percent are public employees; and 9 percent are self-employed. There are two points that must be made about these percentages. First, although they total 100 percent, that does not mean that they include all black workers. In fact, they reflect only those workers who have established a work record. Second, sector of employment indicates, in part, the extent that blacks are or have been covered by pension programs. Public pension coverage is more nearly universal than private coverage; private coverage has traditionally had more stringent vesting requirements; and self-employed workers are the least likely to be covered by a pension plan. The overwhelming majority of black retirees and soon-to-retire black workers (aged 58–63) have never met job tenure and pension vesting requirements. *They are or will not be eligible for private pension benefits.* Put differently, 43 percent of white as compared to 20 percent of black workers were covered at some point in their work career by a private pension. Of that cohort of workers that was covered, a little more than half (52 percent) of the black workers as compared to 77 percent of white workers actually collected private pension benefits. Equally impressive is the fact that 50 percent of black retirees have income from all sources that is less than $3,000, and only 2 percent have retirement income of $15,000 or more (Grad and Foster, 1979; Thompson, 1978, 1979). These figures illustrate that the job characteristics that increase pension incomes eluded black retirees during their working years. It is impossible to tell whether these job-related characteristics that drive pension benefit levels will disadvantage future cohorts of black retirees in the same way that they have affected current retirees. Ironically, these same job characteristics may provide the edge for blacks to adjust better to retirement than white workers.

BLACK RETIREES: DO THEY COPE?

There is little question that black retirees are less well-off economically than their white counterparts. Because of this, one could argue that retirement policies should be changed to account for these differences. For example, some have proposed that different age standards be used to determine when a person can receive pension benefits. This change has been proposed to compensate for the shorter life expectancy of blacks and, by extension, for other ethnic minority groups as well. Some have suggested that pension premium rates be made progressive rather than regressive so as to equalize the proportion of income a worker must pay to be covered by a pension program. This proposal is offered as a way to balance the disproportionate share of pension costs carried by low-paid workers. Not surprisingly, the actions taken by Congress to stabilize Social Security — namely, increasing the tax rates and the income base as well as the related action of increasing the mandatory retirement age from 65 to 70 years — indicate that such race-specific proposals are more symbolic than practical. Considering the earlier conclusions regarding the impact of changes in public and private pension programs on how investment capital flows through the economy and how federal and local governments manage their debts, it is understandable that such proposals are likely seen not only as flying in the face of the economic solvency of many of the programs to which they would apply, but even as imperilling the overall economy. Moreover, proponents of race-specific proposals such as those mentioned should realize that economic well-being seems to have little direct relationship to how well blacks adjust to retirement and that different health, income, and employment patterns are changing as rapidly within the black population as across ethnic groups. Since it is hard to predict the ultimate impact of these changes, it may be wise not to use race or sex as a basis for reformulating retirement policies. In fact, one can argue that many black retirees are more favorably situated now because they have been hardened for the unstable and uncertain economic plight of retirement through successful struggles with similar conditions during their working careers. Since few black retirees were able to climb much beyond a most basic and frugal standard of living before they retired, they have the advantage (relative to white retirees) at retirement of not needing to change abruptly the way they live. Many black retirees report that they can readily cope with their daily routines. They view their work and professional lives with a pride and satisfaction that belie the hardship that most faced at earlier points in their life. Most black retirees have, earlier in their lives, convinced themselves in some way that to think they can cope means they can and will cope with scarce resources (Reynolds and Kalish, 1974). Coping ability seems to be a critical factor in determining whether a black elder adjusts to retirement. The ability belies the apparent reality that black retirees have significantly less money than whites. Do we know, and should we convince black elders, that they are supposed to feel less successful in retirement because of our sense of their economic and social circumstance?

14

SOME SNAPSHOTS OF DEATH AND DYING AMONG ETHNIC MINORITIES

BERNICE CATHERINE HARPER

Dying is like life. It affects each individual and their families differently. And while the needs of dying persons and their families have universality, the dying and their families vary in their conception and attitudes toward death according to ethnic and class origin.

Although little evidence exists to substantiate the hypothesis for the ethnic minorities within the United States, it is clear from a cross-cultural perspective that death—because of its universality, as well as its uncertainty—often is perceived as threatening to the very existence of the society or group. Thus, it is not surprising that all groups incorporate cultural values and beliefs defining, formally or informally, appropriate adjustment patterns to the death event (Blauner, 1966). Because, as has been demonstrated in earlier chapters, death rates are high in minority groups (relative to the majority), the factors of universality and uncertainty take on added importance due to the group's perceived lack of control over the mysterious circumstances producing the frequent incidence of death. Blauner (1966) argues that adjustment among groups having a constant uncertainty about death has traditionally taken the form of the development of elaborate rituals or superstitions. These rituals, along with superstitions and other psychological and social coping strategies, not only serve for the adjustment of the group or family to the loss of the dying individual, but function also in the psychological adjustment of the dying individual. In the following snapshots of death and dying within selected ethnic minorities in the United States, this rationale is well illustrated; also illustrated are the conflicts that can result when these subcultures apply their definitions within the larger American society.

THE NATIVE AMERICAN

Tribal affiliation is the native American's most basic identification. The tribal teachings and experience determine to a great extent the personality, values, and life goals of the individual, including the meaning of death and customs surrounding the burial of the dead. According to Hanson (1978), health professionals working with native Americans must take account of the culturally related feelings of the patient and his or her family.

One dramatic report describes a young Hopi man experiencing auditory hallucinations after a family death. The local psychiatric emergency ward erroneously interpreted the hallucination as a psychotic symptom rather than part of the symptom complex associated with unresolved grief. Native American mental health personnel intervened, and the man was returned to the reservation to participate in a series of rituals and tribal ceremonies appropriate for the burial of the dead. Shortly after the ceremony, he was free from the hallucinations. The young man could have been hospitalized in a state mental hospital as a psychiatric patient! Obviously, the ritual functioned for the bereaved young man as a coping resource, facilitating his transition back to reality. The ritual brought home the reality of the death of the loved one.

Some tribal cultures have been also accustomed to having wakes for the family of the deceased; a few tribes have a specific number of days set aside for the mourners to grieve. During this time all work ceases among the mourners. Friends of the family take care of the cooking and other necessary housekeeping chores. Other tribal beliefs require the deceased to be buried within twenty-four hours. This, of course, creates problems for native American families in urban areas when funeral directors are not sensitive to these beliefs and fail to cooperate. The Indian desires to be seen as a human being, with feelings of pride in his heritage and a desire for others to respect his beliefs and cultural traditions.

THE BLACK AMERICAN

It is said that blacks and other minorities do not serve as volunteers in hospitals and other health care facilities. This may be the case in terms of belonging to formal volunteer groups (Olsen, 1970); but, typically, studies fail to consider that minorities frequently serve each other, informally, in their homes and neighborhoods and through their churches, lodges, fraternal and social organizations. Black men and women take communion to the sick and terminally ill, prepare specific ethnic foods, clean up the homes, wash dishes and clothes, keep the children and do babysitting, visit during the day, sit up with the sick at night, bathe and shave the dying patient. They put dollar bills in "wish you wells," and they send sympathy cards. When funds are not available, they contribute financially toward helping family members go to the funeral, or they help to open a grave site; and they prepare meals prior to and after the funeral. Different blocks of neighbors in the community may take responsibility for various aspects of the meal planning and follow through in all aspects, seeing that each person (mourner, preacher, guest, or helper) is fed. And when the meal is complete, they clean up afterwards.

Relatives also come from long distances and take turns in caring for the sick and terminally ill. For example, a distant relative might come from Texas one week and another from Kansas or Mississippi the next week. In contrast to the dominant pattern for increased institutional responsibility for the care of the dying (Saunders, 1967)—as evidenced by the hospice movement (Sage, 1978)—care providers for the dying black may not be able, or perhaps may prefer not, to utilize the dominant society's health care systems; they do, however, provide for the sick, the dying, and the bereaved of the dead. These activities do not qualify for the volunteer structure in the dominant society; no hours are kept, no awards are given, no documentation takes place, and no research is done. These volunteer activities are given on the basis of love, friendship, and caring. They are factors that do need to be recognized, studied, and evaluated in terms of meeting minority cultural needs for the terminally ill.

THE CHINESE AMERICAN

The Chinese family traditionally has been viewed as a close-knit social unit from which its members derived support, security, and a means of meeting their needs. The Chinese elderly were cared for by their families; moreover, respect for the aged was considered a virtue in the Chinese tradition. The aged represented life experiences, knowledge, authority, and status.

The general veneration of the aged in China carried over into America among immigrants from China. In recent years, however, as the number of elderly has increased and as the influence of cultural norms and traditional structures has diminished, the problems of older Asians have multiplied. Inadequate income, reduced physical capabilities, social isolation and discrimination, poor health, and poor housing often make old age and terminal illness a time of degeneration, misery, and extreme suffering. Cheung and associates (1980) have noted that contact barriers between the elderly and their children were frequent, given that children either were living far away or were too busy with their own families. Conflicts with daughters-in-law were also found important as a barrier. These obstacles tended to interfere with family support for the Chinese elderly. Thus responsibility for transportation and care for the bedridden fell on the elderly themselves or their spouses. To a lesser extent, relatives, friends, or neighbors could be depended on. Children of the elderly tended somewhat to assist with the purchase of drugs and with respect to contact and care assistance. Thus with Americanization, elderly association with the family gradually appears to be eroding.

THE PUERTO RICAN IN AMERICA

The family as a care giver for the elderly infirm, however, is not to be dismissed as a dying phenomenon among the minority aged. Marquez (1970) and Paz (1959) have noted that Puerto Rican familial norms serve the dying and elderly most adequately during crisis situations. Flexibility, greater capacity to sustain disruptive situations, and receptive tolerance for any emotional manifestation make these families better prepared and capable to confront and cope with the crisis situation. Their open, more expressive communication and less regulated and less differentiated systems of codes help the family deal with apparent disorganization without much fear of threat or disruption. For these family members any event will serve as a sufficient reason for getting together; the house becomes a very strong focus of solidarity. It is the place in which all the family members together will make the decisions, discuss any problems, without separating the moments of happiness from those of sadness and misery. In order to maintain their mutual family image, the period of crisis is restructured in terms of minimizing disruption and maximizing members' effectiveness in meeting the practical needs of the elderly member's pain or death.

SUMMARY

In conclusion, the terminally ill patient's and his or her family's reactions to the illness and death appear to be strongly influenced by ethnicity. While ethnic minorities have many patterns in common with the dominant society, they also have several varying features. The preceding snapshots are intended to suggest some of the variety of these patterns. It remains for scientific research to indicate the significance of several of these differences, however. What extent are there, for example, variations in Glaser's and Strauss's (1968) "trajectory of dying" in awareness of dying? Or are, say, black Americans, with the experience of higher death rates, more accepting of death and thus less characterized by Kubler-Ross's (1969) stage conceptualization of dying, whereby one accepts death in a gradual, emergent process, first by experiencing denial, then anger, bargaining, and finally depression, followed by acceptance?

In order to develop effective and equitable care-giving programs for minorities, both differences and similarities in subcultural patterns must be studied and taken into consideration. Dying, like aging, is without question not a homogeneous phenomenon.

Part 4

PUBLIC POLICIES AND
SOCIAL SERVICES:
PLANNING FOR
THE MINORITY AGED

INTRODUCTION TO PART 4

The physical and sociopsychological comfort of the elderly in the United States has become an integral dimension of public responsibility. Today, for instance, the provision of public care for the elderly constitutes approximately one-fourth of annual federal expenditures. While care giving for the elderly has, hitherto, been the domain of familial, charitable, and local sources, the increasing numbers of elderly have supposedly overwhelmed this traditional system. But to what extent can public responsibility for the aged be continued? Still increasing numbers of elderly—in conjunction with a reactionary turn in political leanings of public officials—threaten also to overwhelm public and governmental responses to the elderly.

When considered in the context of the circumstances surrounding the minority aged, as these were discussed in the preceding chapters, what do these developments portend for the care of the minority aged? A review of the history of minority aging advocacy and the social policy process suggests to the first contributor in this section, Fernando Torres-Gil, that value premises traditionally underlying minority aging advocacy may not be the most effective ideology for responding to current sociopolitical developments. To assume, for example, that minorities must concentrate on minority problems, to the exclusion of supposed nonminority concerns, may be antiproductive in coming years. Why? Because, according to Torres-Gil, the assumption, while necessary in order to focus attention on critical unmet needs, limits minority participation in efforts to effect improvements efficiently for all elderly, including minorities. For example, given the greater prevalence of health problems among the minority elderly, advocates for the minority aged must begin fighting, as diligently as the next person, to promote a national health insurance. The proposed national health insurance is a program that will benefit the general population and in the process is directly beneficial to the doubly jeopardized circumstances of the minority aged.

While Torres-Gil's commentary applies to general policy issues, Donald Snyder narrows the topic to income maintenance policy. His question is, What policies are likely to be most effective in reducing the excessive retirement income discrepancies between the minority and nonminority elderly? After a thorough examination of strategies to reduce income discrepancies (private pensions, personal investments and assets, Social Security, and income transfer programs), Snyder concludes that the greatest long-range social dividends, at the lowest cost, would result from policies that insure the availability of

educational and occupational opportunities throughout life. Policies to promote employment gains for minorities would significantly impact on elderly
minorities through higher personal savings, Social Security benefits, and pension coverage.

Snyder recognizes, however, that current elderly cohorts of the minority
elderly are critically dependent upon income transfer programs. For example,
he observes a decrease of 44 percentage units (from 60 percent to 16 percent)
in the proportion of elderly, nonwhite, female-headed households below poverty when both income and in-kind services are used to supplement Social
Security benefits.

The three concluding chapters in this part proceed from the question of
policy development to actual programmatic issues in social service delivery.
First, Solomon Jacobson addresses the concept of equity in the delivery of
public benefits. Equity is defined as the "impartial distribution of benefits
according to a formula of fairness." There are three equity formulas: numerical
(service use in relation to numbers in the population); need (service use in
relation to need); and merit (service use in relation to contribution). Depending upon the formula applied, one may or may not conclude that a service has
been delivered equitably. Jacobson avers that the need formula is most appropriate for elderly minorities inasmuch as they (relative to their nonminority
counterparts) are significantly more likely to be impoverished. When this
formula is applied to such programs as the Supplemental Security Income
(SSI) or low-income public housing, Jacobson demonstrates that the minority
elderly are not necessarily receiving an equitable share of benefits.

How can a more equitable distribution of services be arranged? Oliver
Slaughter and Mignon Batey suggest a variety of strategies in chapter 18.
Although based on their experience in delivering mental health services to the
minority aged, Slaughter's and Batey's suggestions for increasing service utilization are applicable to a large array of services. Special sensitivity to the
impact of years of racism, neglect, and cultural differences is necessary, the
authors observe, even when introducing a service to a community. Rather than
outreach efforts, which use formal media such as the newspaper or television, for
example, a more informal approach with the minority aged appears to be
warranted; church and community organizations offer such a medium.

Service delivery often begins in the home, a pattern that, according to
Slaughter and Batey, is consistent with the visiting neighbor tradition within
black and minority communities. Even after service delivery has begun, a
sensitive and flexible strategy is crucial to program success. Thus, the authors
find the traditional, insight-oriented model of psychotherapy less effective than
activity-oriented modes, such as recreational or movement therapy. In sum,
utilization of services can be expected to increase, given adequate sensitivity to
the special needs of the minority elderly.

John Colen extends this notion by championing a new model of service
delivery. Colen advocates the linkage of formal services to informal, naturally

existing care networks. The traditional reliance of minorities on their naturally existing institutions (the family, church, and community) was studied in earlier parts of this book. Colen asserts that these networks of care giving should be exploited in the delivery of services, say, health care or referral activities. Central to the concatenation of formal and informal service resources, Colen concludes, are individuals in the community who can effectively link the service agency to the community workers and, eventually, to the elderly in need.

Colen's instructive essay brings the discussion full circle. Thus, rather than overwhelming either informal, familial, and charitable structures or the formal, governmental system, the increasing numbers of elderly can serve as a motive force for proposals that combine the advantages represented by both systems. Again, it is evident that resources for adjustment, differentially observable in the elderly minority community (for example, the family and church), can be useful in formulating new models for the care of all elderly persons. Indeed, it may be reasoned that the informal coping patterns, proportionately more evident in the elderly minority community, offers the predominant American culture an alternative model via which to respond, creatively, to the personal and social needs of the elderly. Slater (1976) argues that mobility, technology, and individualism have alienated, if not destroyed, the relationship of the individual to his kinship and primary group network in American society. Consequently, the basic human needs for community (cooperative, trustful relations), engagement, and dependence are frustrated. Thus the drive for individualism limits the structure and functionality of the family or church in providing dependent, cooperative relationships. The nuclear family, unlike the extended, for example, is less able to respond to the needs of the elderly in the kinship network.

The strength of the extended family or the church is that it constitutes a structure whereby the human needs for engagement, dependence, and community are realizable. It is these functions that permit Stagner (1981), Staples and Mirandé (1980), and Myers (1978) to conceive the minority family and other informal, community-level groups as coping resources. What is needed, according to this rationale, is public policy for the aged, all of America's aged, that reinforces or builds on the strengths of these naturally existing, informal institutions.

PERSONAL NEEDS
AND SOCIAL POLICY

15

THE SPECIAL INTEREST CONCERNS OF THE MINORITY PROFESSIONAL: AN EVOLUTIONARY PROCESS IN AFFECTING SOCIAL POLICIES FOR THE MINORITY AGED

FERNANDO TORRES–GIL

In recent years the problems of older minority members have captured the attention of government, the public, and the media. This awareness has developed through the efforts of advocates who have pressured, lobbied, and otherwise attempted to influence government to provide greater resources to minority elderly persons. Increased funding for programs serving older minorities, legislative and regulatory preferences to low-income and minority elderly, and the increase in research in this area are all products of advocacy on behalf of the minority aged. Thus these advocates have been, to a large extent, successful. However, it is time to assess their efforts in light of contemporary changes in social policy regarding aging and in light of political events now affecting the federal government. The election of a Republican administration and so-called taxpayer revolts are indications that future policy directions will emphasize increased attention to cost efficiency, fewer government services, and greater use of block grants by local governments. These changes will force a critical examination of aging programs as they have developed over the years. The number of older blacks, Hispanics, Asians, and Indians will increase dramatically, and their ability to receive services and cope with aging in a dignified manner will be affected by the changes occurring in government policies toward the elderly. These developments require minority advocates to examine past activities in order to determine if new strategies are necessary for promoting the concerns of older minority persons during the upcoming decade.

By focusing on the interplay between minority aging advocates and the policy arena responsible for shaping the social policies that affect the delivery of services to elderly minority members, this chapter seeks to raise the level of analysis and debate concerning the mechanics and goals associated with social policy for elderly Americans. This will be done through a review of the history of minority advocacy and an assessment of its impact. An examination of the value premises inherent in these efforts and suggestions for new strategies in minority aging advocacy are also considered.

MINORITY AGING AND SOCIAL POLICY: A HISTORY

Alexis de Tocqueville once observed that "Americans of all ages, all conditions, and dispositions constantly form associations" (de Tocqueville, 1945). With increased attention to problems of the elderly, a plethora of organizations have developed to advance the interest of elderly Americans. From the development of the Townsend movement in 1933 and the McLain movement of 1948, which respectively fought for old age pensions and for the revision and liberalization of programs of public assistance to the aged, advocates for the elderly have attempted to impact social policy in order to benefit this special population. Currently, through the efforts of a variety of organizations, such as the National Council of Senior Citizens (NCSC), National Retired Teachers Association (NRTA) and American Association of Retired Persons (AARP), and the Gray Panthers, older persons have developed considerable political leverage to influence legislation, funding of programs, and public attitudes concerning older persons (Putnam, 1970; Cottrell, 1960; Holtzman, 1954; Pratt, 1974).

In the same manner that the plight of older persons has generated a plethora of organizations and individuals advocating, supporting, and otherwise representing the overall elderly population, organizations have developed to advance the needs of older blacks, Hispanics, Asians, and native Americans. With the rise of minority aging as a policy concern and the development of aging organizations, the perception of the elderly as a homogeneous population has given way to an awareness among government officials, academics, and service providers that differences in language, culture, and ethnicity have a significant effect upon the needs and resources available to the aging individual.

The history of minority advocacy involvement in minority aging policy issues is rather brief, spanning only the past ten years. In one of the few articles to examine policy and the minority aging, Bechill (1979) describes the responses made by the Administration on Aging (AoA) over the years to the needs of minority and ethnic aged. Although his analysis begins with the creation of AoA in 1965, he concedes that the most significant accomplishments benefiting older minorities occurred after 1971. Prior to this date only a few individuals, primarily academics, were concerned about this area. A brief review of the literature about older minorities shows that the preponderance of articles prior to 1971 were published by nonminorities. In terms of political advocacy as well, minority members remained unorganized on a national level and, hence, lacked visibility and influence in the formulation of national policies on aging until 1971.

The 1971 White House Conference on Aging represents a historical watershed in the development of minority aging advocacy, despite initial underrepresentation of ethnic minority groups at the conference. Owens, Torres-Gil, and Wolf (1973) and Bechill (1979) describe criticisms about the "over politicization" of the conference by the Nixon administration and the apparent exclusion of groups that did not meet a political "litmus" test. Black advocates for the elderly who felt they had been excluded staged a counterconference to protest the lack of attention by the conference to minority concerns. The result was the formal creation of the National Caucus on Black Aged, organized to advocate and represent the black elderly. Similarly a number of Hispanics, Asians, and native Americans pressured the conference to address the concerns of their respective groups; many of these individuals later played important roles in the development of national groups representing Hispanic, Asian, and native American elderly.

Since 1971, federal agencies have committed greater resources for research studies, demonstration programs, and model projects. AoA, for example, in addition to funding and assisting national minority organizations developed to advocate on behalf of older persons (for example, the National Center on Black Aged, the National Indian Council on Aging, the Asian Pacific American Coalition, the Associacion Nacional Pro Personas Mayores, and the National Hispanic Council on Aging), has conducted a national competition to permit several area agencies on aging to implement special affirmative action programs.

A fundamental limitation in promoting policies for minority elderly has been a lack of information about the needs, problems, and life styles of older minorities. In the last several years a proliferation of studies and publications has occurred, funded in large part by AoA. A bibliography developed at the University of Southern California lists over 270 articles and publications on black and Mexican American aging (Ragan and Simonin, 1977). In addition, a Minority Research Associate Program was initiated to strengthen the participation of minority scholars in the field of aging research (Administration on Aging, 1980). From the approximately nine hundred projects funded by AoA between 1968 and 1978, about thirty-three projects were directly related to issues affecting older minority persons.

In addition to these efforts, other events have indicated that minority concerns are gaining attention. The Older Americans Act (1978, as amended) has noted the special needs of older minorities and has given special preference

to low-income and minority elderly and to those with the greatest economic
and social needs. Title VI of the act authorized a new discretionary program of
direct grants to Indian tribes. The drafting of the regulations for these amendments serves as an example of the act's cognizance of minority aging and the
influence that minority aging organizations have been able to develop and
exert. The 1978 amendments gave preference under Title III to those with the
"greatest economic and social needs." Several definitions that would broaden
or limit the population of older persons meeting this preference were allowed
under a notice of proposed rulemaking. After intense lobbying by minority
groups, and in spite of overwhelming support by most aging organizations for
a broad definition, the Department of Health and Human Services decided to
define economic needs to cover a limited population, thus benefiting low-
income and minority elderly persons. In addition, a reference to those facing
"cultural and linguistic barriers" was included in the definition of older persons
with social needs. Politically, minorities have also increased their visibility. The
1981 White House Conference on Aging took special note of minority aging and,
in direct contrast to the 1971 White House Conference on Aging, ensured representation of minorities on the advisory and technical committees. Each group
was allowed to sponsor a mini–White House conference and was assured that
they would have proportional representation at the national conference.

The above-mentioned areas provide examples that on a national level the
federal government is taking heed of minority aging and that minority advocates have had an effect. Within the context of an almost total lack of attention
paid to minority aging ten years ago and the almost total lack of individuals,
minority and nonminority, advocating for minority older persons on a national
level, these efforts represent clear signs that given time, sophistication, and
resources, minority advocates can have significant input into policies affecting
older persons. However, current political developments presage marked changes
in government funding of social welfare programs. With inflation, funding
cutbacks, and efforts to have local communities determine the needs and
problems of the elderly, the executive branch and the Congress have argued
that government cannot afford the luxury of special preferences to specific
ethnic groups. Thus, it is doubtful if subsequent amendments to the Older
Americans Act will continue to give preference to low-income and minority
elderly populations. These circumstances, at this early stage in the brief
history of minority aging advocacy, provide an opportunity to examine the
impact that minority lobbyists have made on national aging policy, to raise
questions about the direction they have taken, and to discuss the intended and
unintended consequences of their efforts.

PREMISES AND STRATEGIES

According to Gil (1976:27–39), "the dominant beliefs, values, and ideolo-
gies of a society . . . exert a significant influence on all decisions concerning . . .

social policies." Furthermore, he notes: "Clarification of value premises underlying the objectives of given social policies ... is of crucial importance for social policy analysis and development." When one examines the strategies that minority aging advocates have used in pursuing their objectives, it is useful to examine the underlying value premises that minority professionals appear to have utilized. While each of these value premises is a generalization subject to debate and disagreement, each serves the heuristic purposes of this article.

The values inherent in the strategies used by minority advocates are based on the premises that:

1. Minorities best understand the actual needs of older minorities.

2. Due to the pressing needs of older minorities and the limited time and resources available to address these needs, minorities must concentrate on minority concerns to the almost total exclusion of nonminority concerns.

3. Differences in culture, language, and ethnicity among minority groups exist and, thus, justify treatment of minority groups as a distinct population from other ethnic groups (for example, Italians, Poles, Germans, Irish) who allegedly have assimilated into the general population.

4. The current cohort of older persons provides the experiences and information to plan for future cohorts of minorities.

These value premises help explain efforts by minority advocates and organizations to develop specific legislation and regulations that separate the minority populations from the nonminority population. They have led to demands that research and training programs give special attention to minorities, to pressures for separate and distinct services based on language, culture, and race, and to demands that minority practitioners be hired to work with minority older persons. Although these efforts can be considered part of the larger struggle for equality and civil· rights, they take on special significance because older persons in minority communities most strongly reflect subcultural life styles and the influences of tradition, history, culture, language, and race. This view of "integrated pluralism" recognizes the preexistence of ethnic and racial diversity and argues that America is not a melting pot, but a society made up of numerous ethnic and racial groups and, hence, a plurality of subcultures (Trela and Sokolovsky, 1979).

The accomplishments by minorities in influencing legislation, funding, and programs flow from this thesis. At present, it is safe to conclude that minority advocates, by and large, adhere to the above-mentioned value premises and will continue to advocate policies and services that promote integrated pluralism. However, doubts have been raised about the extent to which advocates should pursue policies that segregate minority older persons. When this question is addressed, several challenges must be brought forth about the premises and strategies used by minority advocates.

ISSUES

First, do minority professionals reflect the actual needs of older minority persons? It is an axiom among minorities who have successfully competed in the larger society while maintaining linkages with their own communities that they best understand the needs of their populations and will accurately reflect them. As an axiom it provides a justification and raison d'être for minority advocates' representing older minority members. It also reflects a backlash against Anglo researchers who were the first to do research in the area of minorities and aging (in fact, this provided the motivation for many minorities to enter this field). However, without having more than an opinion and observations on which to base deductions, it is this writer's belief that in the heady world of Washington politics, policy formulation, and professional organizing, minority advocates attempting to serve two worlds (minority and nonminority) face the risk that they may lose direct contact with their community and may develop a self-centered sense of the realities of those they purport to represent. Kasschau and Torres-Gil (1975) examined this issue and provided data that, although not conclusive, nevertheless raise some doubts about the representativeness of the new minority elites. Kasschau and Torres-Gil used a large survey of white, Mexican-American, and black elderly in Los Angeles County to examine whether ethnic decision makers were more aware of the problems of ethnic elderly persons than were majority, white decision makers. Findings from the study indicate that ethnic decision makers in some cases (most notably in regard to income, health, and housing problems) appeared more sensitive than white decision makers to the special problems confronting the minority aged. In other policy areas (most notably crime, access to transportation, and lack of education) ethnic decision makers displayed the same gaps in perception of the ethnic elderly's problems as did white decision makers, suggesting that they were not better informed about the problems of the ethnic elderly.

Second, is there too great an emphasis on minority issues? The emphasis of minorities in aging to date has been on promoting the concerns of minority groups, almost to the exclusion of all else. Due to the few individuals active in this area, and to the insensitivity by some service providers, practitioners, and academics, it has been necessary to concentrate scarce time, talents, and resources on minority issues. Yet this approach has its risks. Those involved in advocacy have become labelled as "minority experts," a convenient excuse to exclude minorities from participation in large public policy issues. In time, they become recognized as professionals with narrow interests and a narrow set of skills related only to minority aging issues. At a time when many critical concerns exist in areas other than aging, and when not enough minority professionals are involved, their talents and energies are not being fully utilized.

Third, are minority aging professionals ignoring larger policy issues not directly related to minority aging? The field of policy and aging is undergoing significant challenges. For example, Neugarten and Havighurst (1977) question the relevancy of chronological age in developing standards of eligibility for participation in programs targeted at elderly beneficiaries and call for a reassessment of criteria for determining the targeting of social services. Binstock (1978) suggests that the political system is perpetuating a disservice to the elderly by developing all-inclusive aging legislation and providing scant funds that suffice to serve only a few. Others are questioning the wisdom of age-segregated programs in favor of a new system of age-integrated services (Estes, 1979). Although these challenges are in the main discussed by an elite of intellectuals and advocates, they will have a profound effect on the political debates and policy changes in the years to come (Binstock, 1974).

In some respects, minorities interested in aging appear to be unduly affected by traditional advocacy stands that call for more money and more programs to meet the needs of older persons. Furthermore, the early development of a politics of minority aging indicates that the traditional evaluation of specific interest groups promoting specific policies, irrespective of the wider implications, prevails. That is, minorities are content to fight for more attention and preferences, more dollars, and more programs for older minorities irrespective of the consequences for national policies on aging.

It is important for the small cadre of minorities interested in this area to understand and engage in questioning and challenging the existing status quo. As they advocate and promote their policies, they must be fully aware of the long-range consequences, intended and unintended, that may surface.

Minority professionals should actively engage in contemporary political issues, which may on the surface appear irrelevant to older minorities. The reauthorization of the Older Americans Act, attempts to promote national health insurance, and the need to balance the federal budget are all concerns that require attention by minority professionals. Whether these professionals are engaged in gerontology, law, business, or social welfare, the fact is that in the aggregate they are few in number and must expand their horizons. Thus, until minorities become more numerous, they must integrate their policy needs with policies and debates that may not be focused directly on elderly minority interests.

CONCLUSIONS

In conclusion, it is important to state that minority advocates have had a beneficial impact on the reallocation of resources to older minorities. Their strategies for having done so were, in the main, necessary for that particular time and period. The value premises inherent in these efforts served to concentrate energies and talent on some critical unmet needs and to a large extent were successful in drawing attention to these issues. However, it is now time to reassess the efforts of the last ten years and to question these value premises. Do elderly minority representatives now need to develop new strategies by becoming involved in larger issues that affect all elderly, including the minorities? Will the benefits be greater than the risks of ignoring many needs that are still unresolved? Will the increasing numbers of minorities in this field have greater flexibility to deal with nonminority aging issues? If minority advocates continue to focus on minority issues, will they be guilty of promoting "reverse racism" and "ageism"? These questions cannot be fully answered in this short piece. But it is hoped that the discussion at least has raised the level of analysis and debate in this very important area.

Minorities are expected to grow in numbers in the coming years; and in some sections of the country, such as California and Florida, they are expected to dominate numerically. In addition, the continued influx of refugees and immigrants, legal and illegal, will further increase their numbers. The manner in which policies and political issues affecting older minorities are handled will have a major impact on the minorities who will reach old age in the coming years and the refugees and immigrants who will become elderly in this country.

16

SOCIAL POLICY AND ECONOMIC STATUS: REDUCING INCOME DIFFERENCES BETWEEN ELDERLY WHITES AND NONWHITES

DONALD C. SNYDER

Current disparities in the income of white and nonwhite elderly families are well documented (Abbott, 1977; Grad, 1977; Schiller, 1980). Several of the chapters preceding this one have documented the doubly jeopardized status of the black and minority elderly. Statistics show that minorities or nonwhites receive lower Social Security benefits, fewer (and lower) private pension benefits, and little income from assets. In addition, they more frequently rent, rather than own, their residences. What is uncertain is how the nonwhite elderly will fare relative to their white counterparts in the future. Will nonwhites achieve parity with whites? If not parity, then how close to parity with white income will elderly nonwhite income be? What parity goal should society pursue, and what types of government policies can be prescribed to achieve greater parity? Is 100 percent reasonable? Eighty percent? These questions are important because they bear upon how society treats its elder citizens and, in particular, how society can (help) achieve a more equitable distribution of income between white and nonwhite elderly households.

These questions must, in turn, be considered in view of the fact that the income of persons of retirement age (defined here as age 65 and over) depends upon their work history, whether they were covered by a pension plan before they turned 65, and how much they earned during their work life. The most critical factor determining a family's retirement income is preretirement earnings, because this value determines the accumulation of savings, the likelihood of home ownership, and the size of (available) Social Security and pension payments.

PRERETIREMENT EMPLOYMENT AND UNEMPLOYMENT TRENDS OF NONWHITES

At first blush, reaching parity appears highly idealistic, even farfetched, because nonwhites do not earn as much as whites. Consider, as shown in table 16.1, that nonwhite unemployment rates are nearly twice as high as white rates. High unemployment rates among nonwhite youth are particularly discouraging, because early job experience is a critical determinant of lifetime earnings. The fact that current Social Security formula and pension benefits are based on prior work history and work attachment patterns during early years of work means low achievement throughout the work experience and low retirement income. Time out of the labor force reduces Social Security and retirement benefit payments at retirement. Moreover, frequent spells of unemployment during the ages 18 to 24 increase the probability that a worker will experience high unemployment during his or her later work life. The more frequent and more prolonged are the periods of unemployment experienced by workers, the lower will be their retirement benefits. Consequently, nonwhites will continue to receive lower Social Security and private pension income when they reach retirement age.

One can find evidence, however, that nonwhites have made significant progress in improving their economic status during the last two decades. A study by Vroman (1977) revealed significant employment growth among black workers in high-wage industries during 1960–1970. Snyder (1979) found that nonwhite workers made substantial gains in pension-covered employment during the 1960s. Both studies show that the greatest employment and pension coverage advances are concentrated among younger workers, however, leading to the conclusion that resultant income gains of elderly nonwhites will not surface until after the turn of the century.[1]

This conclusion is important because it indicates three things: (1) Future white/nonwhite elderly income differences will narrow, but the distribution of income among nonwhites will widen; more nonwhites will attain higher retirement incomes, but too many will still be buried at the bottom of the income ladder. (2) Public initiatives to create greater job opportunities for nonwhites have had some success. (3) However, other measures must be pursued to improve the future income status of older nonwhites who do not share the improved job prospects for younger workers.

PRIVATE PENSIONS

In 1974 the U.S. Congress passed legislation, the Employee Retirement Income Security Act (ERISA), containing a number of private pension system reforms. The intention was to improve the probability that workers would

TABLE 16.1
Nonwhite Male Unemployment Rates by Age and Race for Selected Years:
1960–1979

Race and Age	Year					
	1960	1965	1968	1970	1975	1978
White						
18–19	13.5	11.4	8.2	12.0	17.2	10.8
20–24	8.3	5.9	4.6	7.8	13.2	7.6
25–34	4.1	2.6	1.7	3.1	6.3	3.7
35–44	3.3	2.3	1.4	2.3	4.5	2.5
Total Aged 16 and Over	4.8	3.6	2.6	4.0	7.2	4.5
Nonwhite						
18–19	25.1	20.2	19.0	23.1	32.9	30.8
20–24	13.1	9.3	8.3	12.6	22.9	20.0
25–34	10.7	6.2	3.8	6.1	11.9	8.8
35–44	8.2	5.1	2.9	3.9	8.3	4.9
Total Aged 16 and Over	10.7	7.4	5.6	7.3	13.7	10.9

SOURCE: United States Department of Labor, 1979.

receive pension benefits accrued during their work life when they reach age 65. One requirement is that all private pension plans offer vesting (basically ten-year vesting) that increases the likelihood that an employee will receive a pension. The legislation also created a tax-sheltered savings plan known as an Independent Retirement Account (IRA). An IRA allows workers in firms that do not provide a pension plan to establish their own pension plans. The combination of increasing nonwhite employment in pension-covered estab-lishments and the increased ability to form one's own retirement account should improve the relative pension benefits available to the nonwhite elderly.

Additional pension reforms have been suggested. These include five-year vesting, break-in-service provisions, and automatic survivor's benefits. The first two proposals would improve the pension status of nonwhites, because their job tenure is shorter than whites and layoffs are more frequent. The latter reform aids all females whose husbands are covered by pensions, but particu-larly helps nonwhite women because nonwhite males have a shorter life expectancy than white males.

HOME OWNERSHIP

Home ownership is an important asset of older persons since it can be converted into income flow, through instruments like Reverse Annuity Mortgages, called RAMs (Carlson, 1979). When counted as imputed income, home ownership also reduces the relative incomes of nonwhites because of their relatively lower frequency of home ownership. For example, in 1974, 70 percent of all elderly nonwhite families owned their homes, compared to 84 percent among the elderly whites (Hill, 1978). Moreover, homes owned by older nonwhites are generally lower in value and in more dilapidated condition than homes owned by older whites (Koba Associates, Inc., 1980).

One way to reduce future income disparities, then, is to increase home ownership rates and the value of homes among middle-aged and younger nonwhite families. As income prospects of younger nonwhites improve, so will their home ownership rates. However, greater emphasis on government policies specifically designed to bring low-income home ownership rates and value in line with those experienced by whites will be necessary. It is important that such programs be initiated now, since their likely impact will not be felt for two to three decades.

SOCIAL SECURITY

As in the case of home ownership, Social Security benefit payments to nonwhites will rise as any employment gains are reflected in higher lifetime earnings at retirement age. The cumulative effect of employment gains that younger nonwhites are currently experiencing, however, will not yield higher Social Security payments to older nonwhites until after the turn of the century.

Another important dimension of the well-being of older nonwhites is how women are treated by the Social Security system. The treatment of women is important because the majority of elderly women live alone, and in many cases their Social Security benefits depend entirely on their husbands' work history. While nonwhite women compose a greater than proportionate share of elderly women living alone, their Social Security benefits are lower than white women because the benefits are based on the lower coverage and earnings of their spouses. Since over 60 percent of older persons are women, programs to narrow income disparities between elderly men and women are a potentially important vehicle to narrow the gap in income between older white and nonwhite families.

INCOME TRANSFER PROGRAMS

The U.S. government provides a minimum income guarantee for older citizens through the Supplemental Security Income (SSI) program. Those who are not eligible for Social Security benefits, or those whose benefits are below the official poverty line, are eligible for this program. A higher proportion of older nonwhites (than whites) rely on this program; hence, an increase in the minimum income guarantee of SSI would improve their relative income.

Other transfer programs also benefit a higher proportion of older nonwhites than whites. Housing subsidies, food stamps, and medical assistance programs aid low-income households and, consequently, nonwhites more than whites. The anomaly in the way income transfer programs work is that as nonwhite incomes grow prior to retirement, the income transfers they are eligible for at retirement age decrease.

Government programs providing assistance to the elderly, including in-kind transfers, are the vehicle by which a high proportion of elderly nonwhites avoid poverty. The impact of various government programs on poverty among older families in 1976 can be seen in table 16.2, which compares poverty rates before any transfers (column 1), after Social Security transfers (column 2), after other transfers (column 3), and after nonmedical transfers (column 4A) and medical payments (column 4B). The impact of different programs does not affect whites and nonwhites equally, as table 16.2 shows. Nearly 60 percent of families headed by an older nonwhite female were poor after Social Security payments. After all transfers are counted, however, their poverty rate falls to 16 percent. Thus, the structure and level of funding of the government's welfare programs are seen to be a critical element in the well-being of nonwhite elderly.

As the welfare program is currently formulated, states establish eligibility requirements and contribute optional payments to supplement those advanced by the federal government. That is, states may add to the federal floor of base payments at their own discretion. Some states add large amounts to federal payments, while other states add very small sums. Typically, states in the South add fewer dollars to benefits paid by the federal government than do states in the West, North, and East. Since nearly three-fourths of elderly blacks reside in the South, lower payments by these states further skew the income distribution downward for the elderly black population. A greater decentralization of welfare programs, as proposed by some conservative politicians, for example, would cause a greater disparity in those payments across the country (even after adjustments for cost-of-living differences). As a result, income from in-kind sources of transfers paid to nonwhites would likely fall relative to such transfers received by whites.

POLICY OPTIONS

The ownership of both real and human capital, as economic assets, is concentrated in the white population and will be transferred to their own future generations. The creation of human capital (labor market skills) occurs through schooling (general) and job experience (general and/or specific). Thus, one approach that society can pursue to reduce retirement income disparities between older whites and nonwhites in the future is to alter the determinants of lifetime earnings and asset accumulation. An idea of the impact of changes in the determinants of retirement income on the income gap

TABLE 16.2

Percentage of Elderly Families Below the Poverty Level Under Alternative Income Definitions by Race and Sex of Household Heads: 1976

Type of Household Head	*Alternative Income Definitions*				
	Pre Tax/ Pre-Transfer Income (1)	Pre-Tax/ Post-Social Insurance Income (2)	Pre-Tax/ Post-Money Transfer Income (3)	Pre-Tax/ Post-in-kind Transfer Income (4A)	(4B)
White Male	50.1	12.3	9.1	8.1	3.7
	(−75)[a]	(−26)	(−11)	(−48)	
White Female	67.4	27.8	22.4	19.9	8.2
	(−59)	(−19)	(−11)	(−52)	
Nonwhite Male	74.0	29.9	22.1	19.5	10.6
	(−60)	(−26)	(−12)	(−40)	
Nonwhite Female	88.1	59.6	45.5	39.3	16.0
	(−32)	(−24)	(−14)	(−51)	
All	59.9	21.5	16.7	14.0	6.1
	(−64)	(−22)	(−16)	(−47)	

SOURCES: Numerous tables in the Congressional Budget Office Report, *Poverty Status of Families, 1976*, and unpublished data tabulated by the Congressional Budget Office, 1977.

[a]The percentage reduction in poverty rates is included between columns for the reader's convenience.

between white and nonwhite elderly is provided by the results of a recent simulation study (Koba Associates, Inc., 1980). The simulation model operates on a data base of individual work histories generated by the Dynamic Simulation Model, or DYNASIM (Orcutt and associates, 1976). DYNASIM creates a simulated earnings history based on the characteristics of a sample of individuals who were aged 35 to 37 in 1970. These earnings records are then analyzed for the year 2000 (when the sample is aged 65 to 67) to determine the Social Security benefits, private pension eligibility and benefits, home ownership and value, and other asset holdings imputed to each individual based on his or her demographic characteristics and economic position in 1970.

The initial simulation results constitute a base run that represents how nonwhites would fare in the United States in the year 2000 if the current income and earnings patterns persist. The current institutional arrangements that determine how retirement income is determined can be changed and relative incomes recomputed. Institutional arrangements can be altered through public policy initiatives, for example, to prepare nonwhites better for more rewarding jobs or to increase their rates of home ownership and their Social

Security and pension coverage. The preliminary results of the analysis are very interesting. The effects of changing the current determinants of income result in the following (preliminary)[2] estimates for the nonwhite/white income gap in the year 2000: no change = 50 percent; home ownership = 35 percent; lifetime earnings = 40 percent; Social Security coverage = 45 percent; pension coverage = 46 percent; welfare programs = 46 percent; and all changes = 20 percent. A surprising result of the analysis is that improved home ownership represents the greatest potential source of income gain for older nonwhites. As expected, improved lifetime earnings are a powerful force in reducing the retirement income gap. But even when all income flows are improved, equal lifetime earnings will not foster equal retirement income, because whites will still hold the bulk of economic assets.

SUMMARY AND CONCLUSION

The income of the future elderly is determined by the employment and earnings of today's young and middle-aged workers. At the same time, however, persistent high unemployment among nonwhites indicates that major gaps in earnings, Social Security and pension coverage, and retirement income will persist among many nonwhites.

Simulations of alternative policies that could be pursued to ameliorate this predicted outcome show that government programs to improve ownership among low-income households would remove 15 percent of the current income gap. Policies to promote further employment gains among nonwhites would also have a significant effect on the future relative well-being of older nonwhites through the impact of higher wages on savings, Social Security payments at retirement, and pension coverage.

It seems idealistic to suppose that the income gap between older white and nonwhite families can be eliminated through government policies alone. To do so, younger nonwhites will have to achieve equal schooling and better jobs. They must also begin to prepare for retirement by establishing IRAs (if their employers do not have pension plans) or searching for pension-covered jobs. The sure way to a more equitable distribution of retirement income is to improve the quality of the jobs held by nonwhites during their work life.

NOTES

1. Neither study controlled for turnover, however; turnover among nonwhite workers would negate some retirement credits they would receive by maintaining continuous attachment to one employer or pension plan, though earnings would not necessarily be lower. A second dimension of employment, wage growth over an individual's career, was also not factored into either study.

2. Inasmuch as these are preliminary estimates, they should not be cited.

SERVICE DELIVERY
AND UTILIZATION

17

EQUITY IN THE USE
OF PUBLIC BENEFITS
BY MINORITY ELDERLY

SOLOMON G. JACOBSON

The concept of equity has particular relevance for minority elderly. As persons who developed into adults facing and overcoming discrimination, minority elderly persons were systematically denied benefits available to the general population. This discrimination has been recognized in legislation that requires that minority elderly persons must receive benefits that are, at least, proportional to their numbers in the population eligible to receive the benefit. It has also been argued, as it will be in this chapter, that minority elderly persons are entitled to a share of benefits that are beyond their proportion in the eligible population.

After defining several concepts related to equity, the chapter will examine the components that must exist in order to provide an equitable distribution of public benefits to the minority elderly population. The concepts will be applied to four federal programs to determine if they meet equity criteria and standards at the national level. As shall be shown, however, programs must also be examined and monitored at the state and local levels to assure that minority elderly persons have access to and full use of their equitable share of public benefits.

This chapter is based in part on research supported by grant number AoA 90-A-1662 from the Administration on Aging, U.S. Department of Health and Human Services.

DEFINITIONS

A primary concept in a discussion of equity is justice. "Justice" is a biblical concept; it means that the members of a society will deal with others in a fair and impartial manner. "Social justice" means dealing in a fair and impartial manner with groups within society. "Distributive justice" has a more specific meaning; it refers to the act of setting a fair and impartial formula for the distribution of social benefits among groups within a society. A different concept, "equality of opportunity," means that all groups will have the same chance to receive social benefits without partiality. "Equity" means that both the opportunity to receive benefits and the distribution of these benefits will be undertaken according to a fair and impartial formula. Finally, "barriers to equity" are those conditions that prevent the fair use of benefits by those eligible.[1]

As the chapter develops, the differences between these concepts will become more evident. The discussion will demonstrate that equity, the central concept, is a variable concept that must be carefully defined. There are certain equity formulas that provide a greater equality of opportunity and a more just distribution of benefits for minority elderly than other formulas.

Equity, as noted, is the impartial distribution of a benefit according to a formula of fairness. The distribution must be based upon relevant criteria in which persons are similar, including age, residency, income, or functional capacity. There are at least three formulas of equity. While it is possible that these formulas may be combined, they are presented here in uncombined form. These same formulas may be applied to the distribution of social benefits under a distributive justice scheme. But to be equitable, many distributive systems must concern themselves with the reduction of barriers that prevent equal opportunity to the benefit.

The first formula allows for equal shares of a benefit for all persons with a similar condition. For example, the formula may call for all persons living within a certain area to receive an exactly equal share of the benefit. This is a "numerical" equity formula. A second approach is to allow for an equal share of a benefit for all persons who have made a similar contribution. Here the formula would provide a benefit that is exactly equal for all persons whose incomes were under, say, $10,000 and who paid $500 in income taxes that year. This is a "merit" equity formula in that a person must have made some sort of contribution to become eligible for the benefit. The third formula, "need" equity, is based on the relative need of the recipient. Unlike the application of the numerical formula, it is not sufficient only to be a member of society in order to receive the benefit; one must also be in need. The formula would distribute exactly the same benefits to any person with an income, say, under $10,000 who must support five dependents on that income. All persons with equal needs would receive the same benefits.

Before applying an equity formula to public benefit programs, it is necessary to discuss in detail two related concepts. The first is "social justice." The second is the removal of barriers to the "just distribution" of the public benefits to minority group members. These two types of justice are a precondition for any equity formula.

THE CONCEPT OF SOCIAL JUSTICE

In order to be fair and impartial among groups in society, it is necessary that all groups be essentially equal along some critical dimensions. A most important dimension is equality of opportunity. There should be no group whose members face disadvantages simply because they are members of that group. Until very recently, a minority group member was denied opportunity based on race or ethnicity. Indemnity for past discrimination is basic to obtaining social justice. Affirmative action thus involves providing a different approach or treatment to group members who are disadvantaged because they are members of a minority group. This attitude implies, for example, that poor persons who have been disadvantaged by membership in a minority group will receive more access to opportunities or benefits than other poor people who do not belong to a disadvantaged group. A society can recognize that prejudice has deprived some groups of opportunities and that only preferential treatment will redress the disadvantages they now face.

In setting equity formulas, it is possible that the prescribed method may discriminate against a group of potential eligibles. An example of such potential discrimination is the use of chronological age as an eligibility criteria. An equity formula may be set that distributes exactly equal shares of a benefit to all persons over 75 years of age. While this may appear to be an application of the numerical equity formula, it is actually merit based, since the recipient must have reached age 75. The higher mortality rates of minority groups are, in part, a result of their generally lower income and less adequate health care. So, even if the shares of the benefit were distributed evenly and fairly to all persons aged 75, the scheme itself is inequitable since the formula means that fewer members of minority groups will survive to receive the benefit. Until each individual member of every group has an equal chance of surviving to obtain the benefit, any age-based eligibility is likely to be inherently inequitable.

Three solutions can redress the inherent inequity in using advanced age as an eligibility criteria. The first is the use of a death benefit. This solution, used by Social Security, provides payment to the survivors of a participant upon his or her premature death. A second solution is to use a needs equity formula. This formula provides benefits to those most in need. It insures that the surviving minority group members receive benefits based on their relative positions to majority group members (this solution will be discussed in more detail when the needs formula is applied to a public benefit program). A third solution has never been used, as far as can be determined, yet provides a possible remedy. In this approach the benefit is awarded on the basis of group characteristics. Although actuarial tables indicate that there are more or less equal chances of survival to age 45 among all groups in society, some groups have low survival rates beyond that age. Therefore, benefits can be calculated on the basis of the number of 45-year-olds in the group. The amount that would normally have been distributed to 75-year-olds, had they survived, is reserved for use by younger members of the more disadvantaged group. If survival to age 75 occurs at the rate of 500 out of 1,000 for the majority group, but only 200 out of 1,000 for a minority group, then the minority group is entitled to 300 units of benefits. The funds should logically be spent on measures to equalize the survival rate of the recipient groups.

REMOVAL OF BARRIERS TO JUST DISTRIBUTION

If an equitable formula is set, it may still fail to be delivered equitably. There are barriers to equity that may prevent eligibles from receiving their benefits. There are questions of access that must be addressed to determine if those delivering the benefit are administering the program in a manner that assures equality of opportunity to all eligibles, regardless of group membership. The questions include concerns about the quantity and quality of the benefit, as well as access to the benefit. Some of the questions, for example, might include, Do all minority groups within a service area have knowledge of the services for which they are eligible? Are services delivered at a time and in a manner that is acceptable to members of minority groups needing the service? Or do staff members have affinity for the minority group members served?

If there are barriers to equal access, then there can be no equity — even if there is an equity formula that is just and fair for minority group members. It is necessary to have both equality of opportunity and a just system of distribution to be equitable.[2]

SETTING EQUITABLE POLICY

In order for a government to set a policy that is equitable in terms of service delivery to minority group members, it must first set the basic equity formula and then determine if the eligibility standards set under the formula exclude any groups of potential participants. Next, the administrative structure of the program must be examined to determine if it contains requirements that would prevent program operators from applying the equity formula fairly. For example, if a program objective is to move poor persons into jobs, the program's operators may concentrate only on those poor individuals who may most quickly find jobs. This procedure would discriminate against the hard-to-employ, who most need the benefits of the program. After the administrative requirements have been established, possible barriers that may prevent eligibles from claiming their fair share of the benefit should be identified. A barrier would be created if, for example, a central office that could be reached only by automobile were used by a local agency.

The next step in setting up an equitable policy and program would be to develop a monitoring process that permits the testing of the fairness of the distribution. The exemplary questions on accessibility, introduced in the preceding section, would be among those asked in a monitoring approach. Finally, a method for analyzing the reasons that a program fails to meet its goals of equitable distribution should be established, so that ways can be found to improve a program's performance in meeting its commitment to equity.

There are at least four levels of government at which it is necessary to review both policy and program structure in order to determine if the benefit meets standards of fairness and accessibility: the congressional level, at which intent is set; the regulatory level, at which guidelines are set; the administrative level, at which operating procedures are set; and the contact level, at which the benefit or service is actually delivered to the recipient. These are the steps required and the levels at which the steps must be taken in order to test a program against criteria and standards for equity. It is not a simple matter.

The complexity and necessity of determining if the demands of equity are met may best be demonstrated by examining a single aspect—equity in terms of use of a service. What standard may be used to determine if the use of the service is equitable? Within a needs formula approach, there are two standards: comparison against need and comparison against relative disadvantage. In comparison against need the proportion of minorities within the eligible population is the appropriate rate for comparison. Thus, the users of the service are compared against those needing the service.

There is a variation of this basic needs equity formula that may be used if an affirmative approach is the basic intent of the program under consideration. The affirmative approach attempts to mitigate the relative disadvantage that accompanies membership in a minority group. In this approach, comparison against relative disadvantage, the proportion of the minority group eligible population, is compared with the proportion of majority group members who fit into the eligible category. In a socially just society, any advantage or disadvantage would be distributed evenly among all groups. The majority population may be set as the norm. There should be no group with a higher percentage of eligibles than the majority group. That is, the proportion of the minority group eligibles to the total minority population should be exactly equal to the proportion of the majority group eligibles to the total majority population. Any difference would be treated as a ratio that shows the extent to which the minority group is disadvantaged in relation to the majority group; hence, the terminology for this standard, "comparison against relative disadvantage."

When one utilizes this standard in applying the need equity formula, the minority group eligibles could use the benefit to a greater extent than the majority group eligibles in order to equalize the difference. This principle assumes that there should be equal odds, as has been previously argued in defining a socially just society, that any person in society could fall into a disadvantaged category and thus become eligible for a public benefit. If this were so, there would be fewer minority group members in a disadvantaged category than there are now. Instead of thirty minority persons disadvantaged out of one hundred, for example, there would be ten out of one hundred, as occurs among the majority population. The ratio, here, would be thirty to ten (30:10 or 3:1). To reduce this difference, the benefit could be extended to three minority group members for every benefit extended to a single majority group member. It could be argued that this is equitable, since minority group members have three times the risk of being disadvantaged, simply due to their minority status, than majority group members face. An equity needs formula that uses relative disadvantage as a standard attempts to equalize this basic inequity.

AN APPLICATION TO FEDERAL BENEFIT PROGRAMS

Formulas of equity can be applied to governmental programs. Since a needs equity formula is most appropriate for minorities, need-based programs will be selected for analysis. Three federal programs in which eligibility is determined by income level (means-tested) will be examined: Supplemental Security Income, Low Income Public Housing, and the Comprehensive Employment and Training Act (CETA) program. A fourth federal program, the nutrition program operated under Title III of the Older Americans Act, will be selected for contrast. The nutrition program is not means-tested, but consideration is to be given to minorities and those economically or socially disadvantaged. These four programs represent a range of income maintenance, housing, employment, and community service programs. The data used are based on 1977 figures, the earliest year for which comparable data are available. To simplify comparison, rates per thousand population are used. The beneficiaries of the programs are those persons aged 65 years or over who are at or below the poverty level. The exception is the nutrition program, which is available for any person over age 65.

Two standards are applied to test the equity of the programs: comparison against need and comparison against relative disadvantage. The first comparison is made by matching the rate of use against the rate of need within the eligible population. In the example given in table 17.1, for every 1,000 persons over 65 years who were at or below the poverty level in 1977, 764 were white and 236 were nonwhite. To be equitable, therefore, the use rates for every 1,000 elderly persons below poverty should be 764 for whites and 236 for nonwhites, or the ratio of whites to nonwhites: 3.2 to 1.0, or lower. It can be seen in table 17.1 that the needs-based programs meet this standard, but the nutrition program does not.

If relative disadvantage, however, is used as the standard for testing equity,

TABLE 17.1
White–Nonwhite Elderly Population "Poverty Rates" and "Benefit Use Ratios"
for Selected Federal Programs: 1977
(Rate per 1,000 of the population aged 65 and over at or below poverty)

| | Population Aged 65 or Over at or Below Poverty | | | | Selected Federal Benefit Programs | | | | | | | |
| | Rate per 1,000 below Poverty | | Adjusted Rate per 1,000 below Poverty | | Comprehensive Employment Training Act (CETA) | | Low-Income Public Housing | | Supplemental Security Income (SSI) | | Title III-C Nutrition Program | |
Race	Rate	Ratio	Rate	Ratio	Rate	Ratio	Rate	Ratio	Rate	Ratio	Rate	Ratio
White	764	3.2	525	1.1	609	1.6	622	1.6	698	2.3	772	3.4
Nonwhite	236	1.0	475	1.0	391	1.0	378	1.0	302	1.0	228	1.0

SOURCES: U.S. Department of Labor, 1979; U.S. Department of Housing and Urban Development, 1979; U.S. Department of Health, Education and Welfare, 1977, 1978.

there is a dramatic change in interpretation. This second comparison is made by equalizing the chances that nonwhite persons and white persons will be at a poverty level. This equalization is achieved by establishing a ratio of the rate of poverty for whites to the rate of poverty for nonwhites. Since there were 119 out of 1,000 whites in poverty in 1977 and 349 out of 1,000 nonwhites, the ratio is 349 to 119, or 2.93 to 1.00. This could be translated into the possibility that out of every 1,000 eligibles, nonwhites should be drawn at a higher rate than would happen by chance, since they are disadvantaged at a higher rate than whites and that is not a result of chance. An affirmative approach to overcome this disadvantage, then, would be to increase the chance that a nonwhite would be a beneficiary by the same ratio that they are disadvantaged.

In the example of table 17.1, the 236 nonwhites per 1,000 eligible would be multiplied by 2.93—this represents the fact that elderly nonwhites are 2.93 times as likely as whites to be in poverty—yielding a result of 692 (236 × 2.93 = 692). In order to get a new rate, the new number for nonwhites, 692, is added to the number for whites, 764, to get a total of 1,456 eligibles. Both figures, 764 and 692, are divided by 1,456 to get an equalized rate of 525 white users per 1,000 eligibles and 475 nonwhites per 1,000. This contrasts with the nonequalized rates of 764 whites and 236 nonwhites per 1,000 eligibles.

The equalized rates then become the rates expected if an affirmative approach is taken to distributing the public benefit. This new rate now serves as an index for determining relative disadvantage. If applied to actual use rates, it will show how far below or above the actual rate falls, when compared with the rate expected if the relative disadvantage of nonwhites were equalized to those of whites. These calculations are also displayed in table 17.1.

It can be seen that all programs now fail this proposed standard of equity. As anticipated, the greatest discrepancy between expected and actual delivery to minorities occurs in the nutrition program, which is not means-tested. The income maintenance program, the Supplemental Security Income program (SSI), has not reached enough persons to equalize their relative disadvantage. On the other hand, the housing program and the employment program (CETA) do relatively well in overcoming the disadvantages faced by minority elderly persons. The purpose of this exercise is to demonstrate that it is possible to serve minority elderly in exact proportion to their numbers in poverty and still not be equitable, if the standard selected to determine equity is the reduction of relative disadvantage among groups of users.

In the preceding discussion, the needs equity formula was compared against need and against relative disadvantage for users of four federal programs. There are several other criteria that must be examined to determine accurately if a federal program is equitable. The questions raised earlier in conjunction with equality of opportunity must be asked about the program under consideration. These questions relate to the dissemination of knowledge about the program, representation of minorities in program decision making, delivery of service in a manner acceptable to minorities, appropriateness of the amount and type of service in meeting minority needs, and staffing patterns that reflect an affinity for minority group users. It is unfortunate that these questions cannot be directly answered at the federal level. Data collected at the federal level are primarily concerned with the number of users of a service and the dollar amounts expended on the service. Any monitoring of equitable delivery would have to be made at the contact level or at the state level. It is possible, however, to review federal documents that establish the programs in order to determine if they require program operators at the contact level to meet standards of equity.

A content analysis of the laws and regulations that govern the preceding four programs reveals several interesting findings. The CETA program has the highest number of direct references to equitable performance in its basic laws and regulations. However, the Low Income Public Housing legislation, which also attempts to meet the needs of minority eligibles, does not provide strong support for equity considerations in its basic documents. Public housing units, however, are usually located in areas of greatest need, and the regulations specifically bar any form of racial or ethnic discrimination in renting the units.

The third program, SSI, hardly mentions race or ethnicity in its documents at the federal intent or regulatory levels. Aside from a statement that *every* eligible person is to receive benefits under the program, the Social Security Act provides little information responsive to the questions of equity raised in the content analysis. Finally, the basic documents of the nutrition program, Title III of the Older Americans Act and its regulations, are very complete in detailing how the program should be delivered equitably. For example, attention is given to ensuring that target groups are reached through information programs, given access through convenient location of sites, encouraged to participate in program planning, and provided meals that respect cultural, ethnic, or religious preferences.

SUMMARY

This analysis has demonstrated that determining equity is a complex process. It involves two parallel activities: setting a formula for equity that is fair for minority participants and removing barriers to equal access to program benefits. At the federal level a needs equity formula is fairest for minority elderly, since they tend to have a higher proportion of persons over 65 years in poverty than do nonminority elderly. Since the rate of poverty is nearly three times higher among nonwhites as compared to whites, this relative disadvantage should be accounted for in any equity formula. Based on this approach, four programs were examined and found to be lacking in their ability to make up for the relative disadvantage experienced by minority elderly.

There are limits to analyzing equity only at the federal level, however. The available data concentrate on utilization and amount of benefits. The data are most often incomplete, inaccurate, or misleading when it comes to measuring participation of minorities. Moreover, the elements of equitable delivery, such as dissemination of information and equality of access, cannot be measured at the federal level. Laws and regulations, however, may be examined to see if they direct program operators to deliver benefits in an equitable manner. Existing and proposed laws may be examined to determine if their eligibility requirements exclude minority participation through an emphasis on numerical or merit formulas. In the final analysis, equity must be attained at the state and local levels. The most equitable federal program will fail to reach eligible minorities if barriers to participation exist at the contact level. An examination or audit of federal programs could be instituted to monitor barriers to equal access and use. While there appears to be some progress toward dealing fairly and impartially in distributing public benefits to minority elderly persons, there remains the fact that the number of minority recipients must be increased before there is true equitable distribution.

Notes

1. For additional discussion on the meaning of these concepts see entries under "Justice" and "Equality: Moral and Social" in Edwards (1967). Both entries contain bibliographies that cover classic and recent discussion on the criteria that follow from the various definitions of these terms. It appears that the debate on equity remains to be resolved in each society according to its understanding of the concept.

2. Studies of barriers to service delivery, as the concept applies to elderly minority persons, constitute a small, but growing body of literature. In addition to the discussion in chapter 18 on barriers to utilization of services, the reader is referred to Anderson and associates (1975); Fuji (1976); Bell and Zellman (1976); U.S. Commission on Civil Rights (1978); and Manuel (1980c).

18

SERVICE DELIVERY AND THE BLACK AGED: IDENTIFYING BARRIERS TO UTILIZATION OF MENTAL HEALTH SERVICES

OLIVER W. SLAUGHTER AND MIGNON O. BATEY

In 1975 the Department of Health, Education and Welfare undertook one of the first and most comprehensive legislative actions to provide a program of specialized services for the aged throughout the nation's community mental health centers (CMHCs). The legislative aim was to strengthen and/or extend the range of mental health services provided to this underserved population. Thus, Title II of Public Law 94-63 was born with specific guidelines to curtail the growing numbers of aged unnecessarily uprooted from their communities to enter institutional care. With that thrust, community mental health centers began to receive funds to implement mental health programs for the elderly.

One of the most difficult tasks facing CMHCs then and now is how to increase the utilization of mental health services to the elderly. This situation was compounded when the catchment area was culturally diverse and outreach efforts for one group of people was not particularly effective for another. This chapter addresses some of the problems in extending services to culturally diverse populations. It specifically addresses the delivery and utilization of mental health services, within CMHCs, to the black elderly.

GENERAL FACTORS IN SERVICE DELIVERY
AND UTILIZATION

The study in this chapter is based upon the writers' experiences in two CMHCs, Central City Community Mental Health Center and Kedren Community Mental Health Center, both located in south central Los Angeles. Each has a catchment area comprised primarily of blacks and Chicanos. The latest population figures reveal that the catchment areas (regional geographic boundaries for service delivery) of Kedren and Central City each contain a senior population of over eight thousand, or 11.8 percent of the total community population. The typical profile of the elderly citizen in each of these communities reflects a black, widowed, female who is economically disadvantaged, has rural roots in the South, lives in a neighborhood plagued by high crime, and is poorly nurtured, resulting in a higher (than the general elderly population) incidence of deteriorating illnesses and death.

In 1975 the average number of elderly clients reported to have utilized Central City CMHC over the previous years was approximately 2 percent, and these were primarily admissions to the inpatient unit. Utilization of outpatient services was even less. This was not unique to the minority community, though; that is why the 1975 CMHC amendments were passed. There are, however, additional factors that uniquely affect blacks and minority utilization patterns. Why were utilization rates so low for the largely elderly minority community in the catchment areas? The National Institute of Mental Health (1976:21–22) lists many reasons:

Services for the elderly are not available in community mental health centers.

The elderly are unaware of services offered.

The center's staff may display negative attitudes toward the elderly.

The elderly have negative attitudes toward receiving mental health services.

The administrators of a center may be disinterested in providing special services to the elderly.

The services may not be easily accessible to the elderly.

Centers lack outreach programs.

The organizational structure of the center's programs may be a barrier to effective services.

The center's staff may lack the skills needed to work with the mentally ill elderly.

Policies that affect delivery or reimbursement for services may affect their utilization.

In a study of the utilization rates of the elderly in eight community mental health centers, Patterson (1976) found that the elderly within those catchment areas felt a strong sense of "self-reliance" and a great reluctance to think of themselves as having "psychological problems."

In the delivery of social services in general, Heisel and Moore (1973) studied 200 aged blacks in Newark, New Jersey, to explore levels of social interaction and isolates. They found that fear of young people and feelings of insecurity kept the black aged at home. There was little use of social services unless they were personalized. Sainer, Schwartz, and Jackson (1973) found that when the black elderly took an active role in establishing their own social services delivery system, utilization improved because the elderly were able to establish those programs they felt were needed most.

Solomon (1970) found that government agencies and institutions do not reflect the black experience and are not appealing to blacks. Billingsley (1969), Jackson (1972b), and Solomon (1970) all suggest that blacks may not utilize public services because of support received from the family. Sears and McConalay (1973) have pointed out that the designers of social service agencies have been middle-class Anglos whose values do not coincide with or reflect those of the black consumer. Consequently, blacks may be unable to get to the services, creating hostilities and a refusal to cooperate with these agencies. The situation is worsened when blacks are treated with disdain and contempt when they do attempt to utilize various social service facilities.

Stanford (1977:4–5) outlines ten suggestions for improving the delivery of social services to the black elderly:

1. Services must be delivered in a way that they preserve the personal dignity of the recipient. In order to do this, personnel must be involved on the basis of personal commitment as well as professional competence.

2. It is necessary to expand the scope of programs in order to accommodate some of the minority older persons.

3. Rules and regulations must be interpreted in a flexible manner because rules made for the average older person, by definition, do not fit the minority.

4. More attention must be given to looking at preventive as well as sustaining services.

5. Continuing efforts must be made to decentralize services to the degree possible. Service providers should not be afraid to establish services in areas where minority older persons live and work. It is important to have services nearby so that they seem less remote and the service provider can be more immediately responsive.

6. There must be stricter accountability for all service programs.

7.   Appropriate research personnel should be involved in the early stages of planning service delivery programs. It is appropriate to involve minority researchers who understand the life styles of the persons who are targeted to receive services.

8.   It cannot be denied that there is a need to develop an economic base for minority older people so that they can take advantage of private as well as public services.

9.   More attention must be given to the continued and further use of community persons who can serve as human service aides in a variety of paraprofessional roles. Community workers should be used in a wide spectrum of activities. The bureaucratic process has rendered the use of the indigenous community worker virtually useless.

10.   The involvement of minority elderly in continuing education programs can be a meaningful process. Such involvement enables the elderly to judge services and seek out services as they need them and become available.

Each one of these suggestions is imperative for the delivery and increased utilization of social services by the black elderly. Summarizing the preceding points, Levy's (1978) review of various surveys indicated that the minority elderly use the same service as other elderly groups. What is found to be needed by these various social service agencies is a special sensitivity to the minority elderly's different language, culture, and tradition.

ASSESSMENT AND TREATMENT FACTORS IN MENTAL HEALTH SERVICE DELIVERY

Ethnicity is a factor that cannot be ignored in the assessment of mental health. Dancy's (1977:6) interpretation parallels that of other researchers: "A clear framework of understanding may help the worker avoid the pitfall of generalizations and stereotypes which blind him or her to the variations that exist among the black aged." This is particularly found to be an accurate ingredient in work with the black aged at both Central City and Kedren Community Mental Health Centers. In the design of the program many unique factors that are specific to the needs of the black elderly were strongly emphasized in the implementation stages and continue as a major component of the overall program.

The preventive, as well as outreach, approach to the program was to identify the elderly with special mental health needs within community organizations, such as the church and other senior-serving agencies. Discussion groups were held on a twelve-week basis for seniors in congregate settings. Topics relative to aging, such as coping with loneliness, isolation, and so forth, were focal points of discussion. These groups provided the impetus for openly sharing common problems and needs in a familiar environment. From this setting individuals who appeared to need a therapeutic intervention, such as that offered by the geropsychiatry program, were thus able to enter the outpatient facility with greater ease and familiarity. The geropsychiatry program's operation began with several essential elements responsive to circumstances in the black community. First, the minimum age criterion for admission into the program was set at 55 years. This major factor is considered important within this predominantly black community and is based on the statistical data of life expectancy for nonwhite elderly: Black Americans can expect to live roughly five to six years less than white Americans.

Second, when referrals are received—be it by a family member, physician, community agency or other (the black elderly are rarely self-referred)—the first phase (three or four sessions) of treatment, prior to entry into the program, may begin in the home. This approach, first, provides staff opportunity to assess the home setting; second, it establishes rapport with the older person, thus alleviating many of their inherent fears toward discussing mental health issues; and, third, it identifies with the visiting-neighbor tradition within the black community.

At the point of formal entry into the geropsychiatry program, a diagnostic evaluation is made of each client and an appropriate treatment is designed. It is fairly well accepted that the symptoms manifested in many of the psychiatric disturbances are similar in their characteristics among both the black and white elderly. What is significantly different are the etiological factors, or causes. For example, many of the black elderly live in depressed areas of the city where crime runs rampant. Consequently, many are afraid to leave their homes to shop, let alone ride public transportation. This "healthy paranoia" may lead to a more pathological condition, where the elderly person is afraid to leave the home ever and becomes distrustful of most people. In this instance, as implied in chapter 8, treating the paranoid symptoms alone, without dealing with the cause, is "Band-Aid" treatment. The real treatment for this type of client may require the mental health practitioner not only to take note of the symptoms, but to also mobilize the necessary resources so that this fear will not again surface. Although there are many causes of depression, the environment—such as living in depressed areas of the city where crime runs rampant—is a major factor in the psychopathology of the elderly black. Thus the therapist is confronted with being not only a mental health practitioner, but a social worker as well. The therapist not only must provide assessment and treatment in the traditional sense, but must also coordinate other services that will improve the life situation of that client. Along with a therapeutic plan, it may be necessary, for example, to assist the client in receiving homemaker chores or a senior escort or in providing aid in obtaining Supplemental Security Income (SSI) or perhaps better housing.

In terms of other treatment factors impacting on the success of the service delivery, insight-oriented psychotherapies have generally been less successful than more activity-oriented therapies with blacks (for example, recreation, dance, music, and reality orientation therapies). McKay and Cross (1980) note that mental health services to seniors require not only sensitivity, but also flexibility so that the client is assured continuity of support. Emphasis, thus, is placed on group activities that are therapeutic, meaningful, stimulating, and appropriate to the individual's abilities and interests.

STAFF TRAINING AS A FACTOR IN SUCCESSFUL SERVICE DELIVERY

It is imperative that any treatment staff be representative of the community it serves in its ethnic composition. It is also important that both the professional and paraprofessional staff receive ongoing training in areas such as culture and personality, psychology of the aging process, psychopathology, and treatment modalities—all having a particular emphasis on the black elderly. Any such training program should without a doubt include a component that addresses that staff's sensitivity to and awareness of the population it serves. Staff must examine their own feelings about working with the black elderly—a client who is often likely to be nonverbal, hostile, and resistant to psychological interventions.

Some researchers have not yet realized that much of the behavior of the black elderly client is based on coping patterns that have evolved from inadequate and even nonexistent services from agencies and institutions. Dancy (1977) notes, as do several authors of chapters preceding this one, that inasmuch as blacks and other minorities have not traditionally depended upon public agencies for service, they have developed coping styles and resources that the practitioner will need to consider in order to serve them effectively. John Colen, in the next chapter, for example, demonstrates how naturally existing informal networks can be used to deliver services to the minority elderly.

SUMMARY

In order to provide services to the black elderly, special techniques must be employed, based on studies concerned with why blacks generally underutilize specific services. In the study of the effective delivery of mental health services, it has been observed in this chapter that to begin, special considerations are necessary in order to make community residents aware of the mental health center and the ways in which the center might service them. Among other things, this involves outreach, home intakes, and the creation of an atmosphere that is not contemptuous of the elderly black person. Years of racism must be taken into account, as well as culture and language differences.

Other considerations require the practitioner or therapist to be a coordinator of community resources and a social worker as well. And each therapist or practitioner working with the black elderly must examine his or her own attitudes to determine whether it is possible to function as more than just a therapist behind a desk in an office. With all these things kept in mind and put into practice—the proper attitude, outreach, ongoing training, and awareness of the impact of a unique culture, environment, and effects of racism— improved service delivery and increased utilization should be expected.

19

USING NATURAL HELPING NETWORKS IN SOCIAL SERVICE DELIVERY SYSTEMS

JOHN N. COLEN

Human service practitioners who work with the aged are increasingly aware of the potential role of informal, naturalistic helping networks in human service systems. This is true in terms of the impact of informal networks on help-seeking as well as care-giving behavior. Further, as Leutz (1976) notes, the influence of naturalistic systems comes not merely from the granting or receiving of aid, but also from the manner in which aid is given. The case in point is that of the minority elderly whose patterns of help-seeking and -giving, as shown by previous chapters in this volume, indicate a considerable reliance on natural helping networks. Thus the purpose of this chapter is to explore the use of these networks in social service delivery systems among and for elderly minorities.

THE CONCEPT OF SOCIAL NETWORKS

The introduction of family, indigenous workers, certain kinds of community organizers, and paraprofessional staff into the social service system has underpinnings in social network theory. Mitchell (1969) defines a social network as "a specific set of linkages among a defined set of persons, with the additional property that the characteristics of these linkages as a whole may be used to interpret social behavior of the persons involved."

Safier and Pfouts (1979) suggest that network components can be categorized according to structural and interactional characteristics.

According to this dichotomy, structural variables describe the basic morphological characteristics of the network. These variables include anchorage, range, density, and reachability. Anchorage refers to some specified individual whose behavior the observer wishes to interpret, while range refers to the number of persons included in the network. Density, on the other hand, refers to the degree to which individual members of a client network are in touch with other members. Reachability relates to the ease with which the central person is able to contact a network member.

By contrast, interactional characteristics include content, intensity, and frequency. Content refers to the significance that people in a network attribute to their relationships or the purposes for which links are established. Intensity or strength of a link in a personal network refers to the extent to which the individual experiences obligations or feels free to exercise rights implied by linkage with another person. Finally, frequency refers to the number of contacts among people within a network.

THE NATURAL HELPING NETWORK
AS A STRATEGY OF INTERVENTION

Social network analysis has been employed in a wide array of areas. In the past, usage of the concept was largely confined to research. More recently, various authors have reported on the practical application of social networks to service delivery. In terms of practice, Erickson (1975) suggests that the use of social networks falls into four general categories. Networks can be seen (1) as a curative grouping of individuals, thereby focusing on the therapeutic role; (2) as a location of resources in which patterns of mutual aid are emphasized; (3) as an interpreter of help-seeking behavior and utilization of services; and (4) as a mitigator of the effects of multiorganizational involvement with a family. He points out further, however, that these categories are not mutually exclusive, but vary in the degree of emphasis given.

Sarason and his associates (1977) and, more recently, Safier and Pfouts (1979) have delineated some of the more specific purposes to which networks have been put in practice. Several of those will be identified in the following section and will be discussed in terms of their applicability to the minority aged.

APPLICATIONS OF SOCIAL NETWORKS
FOR THE MINORITY AGED

While the application of informally based service delivery is in its early stages, various policy and programmatic recommendations relative to service delivery to the aged are grounded in the concept of social networks. Of particular interest is that natural networks have been recognized as an alternative means of service provision. From a macro, or programmatic, level Colen (1979) introduced the idea of "mechanism-specific" and "non-mechanism specific" services. A basic premise of this idea is that service providers often suffer from an orientation toward delivery mechanisms rather than concentrating on the services that are to be provided. For instance, many services such as counseling, information and referral, and the like are not mechanism-specific and can be provided in a variety of settings. Thus, these same services might just as easily be delivered through the black church, a naturally existing institution in the black community.

While the black church would be used as a service delivery alternative, it would not be subject to the same factors that have contributed to the underutilization and avoidance of the current social service system by elderly minority individuals. For example, in the black church elderly blacks would be more familiar with the institution; providers of services would be more sensitive to their cultural characteristics and communication patterns (Bell, Kasschau, and Zellman, 1976b); program procedures would more likely reflect their values and experiences; and it is unlikely that racial discrimination would be a barrier (Solomon, 1970).

In another realm, network structure has been cited as a key factor in identifying individuals and families at risk. Clearly, certain segments of the elderly represent high-risk groups. Thus, the Federal Council on the Aging (1976), in addressing the issue of the frail elderly, many of whom are minority, has promoted the use of "significant others" in service coordination, case management, and counseling for the frail elderly. A significant other, as utilized in the service delivery system, is a resource person who assists frail individuals with limited, but consistent aid. Such persons may be identified after studying the network system of these elderly, especially the interactional characteristics. Thus, individuals to serve in this role are not expected to be professionals; rather, they can be drawn from sources such as kin, friends, interested neighbors, or other members of an individual's informal network.

Similarly, social networks have been shown to impact positively on individual ability to handle stress. In this regard, Walker, McBride, and Vachon (1977) have offered evidence of the importance of natural systems in bereavement and other life crises. Speaking from the perspective of the extended kin network in the black community, Staples (1976) argues that this structure has historically managed to buttress psychological isolation and poverty of the black aged. Thus, he concludes that the elderly often rely on secondary kin and even "make-believe" kin. Illustrating the reciprocal care-giving and receiving quality of informal networks, he notes that in return for services needed, black grandmothers (real or make-believe) provide in-kind services, such as babysitting for their children.

Given the variety of ways in which social networks have been beneficial in service delivery within minority communities, it is important to discuss some of the efforts that have been made to integrate formal and informal service systems.

MECHANISMS OF INTEGRATION
BETWEEN FORMAL AND NATURAL HELPERS

A number of methods have been used in an attempt to integrate formal and naturalistic helping systems. Valle and Mendoza (1978) identified and operationalized the key actor in the naturalistic network system of elderly Latinos as the community service broker. These individuals were largely distinguishable from other helpers within service delivery systems by the extent of their activities and versatility. Not only did they demonstrate great capacity for information and referral activity and for crisis or emergency assistance, but they also frequently assisted agency staff to understand client needs better while serving as translator buffers between both. Overall, they operated as catalysts and links to the utilization of services and resources.

Two other levels of helpers were noted: the neighbor and the agency link person. The neighbor tended to be the individual who located the person in need or to whom the person in need would come for assistance at the neighborhood level. While the neighbor was not found to be much more knowledgeable about services than the ordinary population, they usually knew the community service brokers. The agency link person, on the other hand, generally had established key contacts in other agencies who were disposed to extending services to the community through culturally appropriate modes. Thus, the agency link person was critical in providing access to services in a style acceptable to the Latino consumer.

Using these components of the system, Valle and Mendoza were able to describe a critical path from person in need to either the neighbor or the community service broker. When the neighbor, or local link person, was the first contact, the community service broker was contacted next and subsequently linked the person in need with services. It is important to note that the authors point out that agency persons seeking to interface with the Latino elderly will find an extensive supportive network to assist them in making and maintaining contact. In addition, they note that providers will find that this system is generally supportive of, rather than competitive with, their program of services.

Several additional mechanisms have been identified by Collins and Pancoast (1976), as well as by Litwak and Meyer (1966), for integrating formal and informal service providers. Included among these are indigenous workers, natural opinion leaders, common messengers (individuals who are regularly members of both formal organizations and informal groups), and, in a more formal sense, detached experts (professional persons who act with relative autonomy and by direct participation in the primary group), such as a public health nurse who frequently is in touch with community members.

Colen and Soto (1979) report, drawing from their study of successful programs serving minority aged persons, that many of the factors that distinguished successful from unsuccessful programs were highly correlated with the integration of naturalistic helping systems. For example, one of the most striking findings of their study was the extent to which natural leaders (persons who act as brokers between community members and the larger social or service system, but who hold no such formal position) were used as mechanisms for consumer input into programmatic decision making. Additionally, natural leaders were used extensively in conducting personalized outreach activities.

CONCLUSIONS

The preceding discussion has illustrated some of the implications of minority cultures for service utilization and delivery. The ability to cope with crises, information dissemination, and, subsequently, help-seeking behavior are all affected by the existence of natural helping systems. Not only have these systems been shown to enhance service use, but they also have been found to affect the way in which services are used.

Persistently, policy makers, planners, and direct service providers have approached their tasks from the perspective of an individual-deficit model in which the "victim is blamed" (Ryan, 1971). More precisely, the tendency has been to focus on individual rather than organizational pathologies that often render services inaccessible to elderly minority clients. If barriers to services commonly experienced by elderly members of minority groups are to be eliminated, new and effective models of service delivery must be generated. One vehicle, it seems, is the development of complementary and reciprocal relationships between formal human service system and informal, naturalistic helping networks.

Part 5

THEORETICAL ORIENTATIONS AND THE STUDY OF THE MINORITY AGED

INTRODUCTION TO PART 5

The preceding chapters have emphasized the substantive and practical issues of minority aging. Proceeding from an introductory examination of the historical forces shaping minority aging in part 1, the discussion in parts 2 and 3 considered the demographic and sociopsychological circumstances resulting from these forces. Part 4 reviewed several of the issues in policy formulation and programmatic design portended by the conclusions of parts 2 and 3. In the concluding sections of this book the focus changes. The change is from a preoccupation with substantive and practical topics to a study of the tools by which the aforementioned conclusions are both derived (methodological issues) and generalized (theoretical issues).

The explicit note of a change of emphasis in the concluding sections is not meant to suggest any real division between theory (or research) and the preceding discussion. Rather, the strategy serves the purpose only of organizing the contents of this volume. Thus, while an immense gulf is often assumed to separate theoretical abstractions and practical, problem-oriented questions, this view indicates a misunderstanding of the nature of theory. Theory is an intimate aspect of practical, everyday problems. A good theory consists of a set of logically interrelated, empirically derived propositions that explain real, everyday phenomena.

Theory in social gerontology, therefore, should be concerned with systematically explaining the social phenomena underlying the aging process. Obviously, there are no social gerontological theories in the sense of logically interrelated sets of propositions. Rather, there exist a series of theoretical orientations, the latter representing a conglomerate of loosely fitting statements that are primarily useful as a framework for interpreting selected aspects of research conclusions.

The question confronting the gerontologist working with data on the minority elderly is that of determining the extent to which currently popular theoretical orientations—fashioned among middle-class, white samples—are relevant for understanding the aging behavior of minorities. Antonio Rey contends, in the first chapter of this section, that any theory that does not incorporate a historical perspective should be held suspect. Why? Because it clearly does not permit the examination of the impact of a lifetime of experience with prejudice and discrimination. Two alternatives are suggested by Rey's additional conclusion that neither of the traditional theoretical orientations in social gerontology (the disengagement and activity rationales) is relevant for describing the circumstances of the minority elderly.

First, there is a need for a general theory of aging that incorporates a historical perspective, reflecting the victimized experience of the minority aged. But, given the current paucity of data and empirical generalizations on the minority aged, this task must await further information gathering. In the meantime, a second alternative would emphasize the application of existing, predominantly extragerontological theoretical rationales to existing minority data. This approach is certainly not a new one for generating theory. As a matter of fact, this is the state of the art currently in theory constructionist efforts in social gerontology.

In the two remaining chapters in this section, Aaron Lipman and David Brodsky, respectively, apply this strategy for theory development to minority aging data. Lipman demonstrates the utility of the structural-functional and exchange theoretical models, as borrowed from sociology and social psychology, respectively. A functionalist explanation of the low socioeconomic position of elderly minorities, for example, emphasizes the functionality, for society, of a socially stratified population in which there is a pool of individuals to purchase used goods and inferior services.

On the other hand, the conflict perspective (borrowed from sociology) stresses the logical necessity of conflict between the economically differing minority and nonminority groups. Brodsky maintains that nonminorities who hold economic assets are in a position to exploit ethnic, age, and ethnic-by-age variations in order to promote their own interest.

In the aggregate, both Brodsky and Lipman provide stimulating directions for the development of theoretical rationales to account for the accumulating data on the minority elderly. One conclusion appears inescapable. Each rationale appears initially capable of assuming a historical perspective in order to explain the lifelong victimization experienced by the minority elderly. What is required in the application of each theory, however, is a more complete set of propositions in order to conceptualize a systematic array of the data on minority aging. Thus, while the rationale must be able to account for the disadvantaged position of the minority (relative to the nonminority) elderly, it must also be capable of explaining the circumstances of that segment of the elderly minority population whose position is not devastatingly characterized. Why, for example, are nearly 50 percent of the elderly minority population not living near or below poverty, according to functionalist terminology? Or, with reference to the conflict perspective, why are some elderly minorities who belong to the same social class as their nonminority counterparts characterized by a differential health status relative to the nonminority?

20

ACTIVITY AND DISENGAGEMENT: THEORETICAL ORIENTATIONS IN SOCIAL GERONTOLOGY AND MINORITY AGING

ANTONIO B. REY

Theories are tools for organizing information into sensible patterns of explanation and prediction. Central to all social scientific theory is the question, What is going on? All theories, moreover, rest on assumptions or beliefs. The merit of a scientific theory is its capacity for matching assumptions with observations in systematic, ordered ways that in fact seemingly explain what is observed.

The capacity of a gerontological theory to explain and predict what is going on among older people is a test of the theory's usefulness. Some theories, while inherently elegant and attractive, simply do not explain what is going on. Other theories may be conceptually less elegant, and perhaps emotionally unattractive, but provide better assessments of the dynamics shaping the actual circumstances of life of older persons.

Among minority older people, as among all other people in the United States, there is more going on than any or all known theories can explain. Yet, the critical question remains: Does a particular theory represent enough about what is going on to allow valid sense making to take place? The question is important for more than merely its scientific application. Public policy for the aged is and will continue to be made on the basis of social research; all social research ideally is based on implicitly or explicitly stated social science theory.

In this chapter an exploration is made of the two traditional, albeit increasingly less popular, orientations in gerontology: disengagement and activity theories. The discussion focuses on how useful the orientations are in explaining what is going on, and what is likely to occur in the future, among minority older people in the United States. In subsequent chapters in this section the utility of other theoretical frameworks will be considered.

It shall be shown that although North American social gerontology has been explicitly, and is implicitly, dominated by two antithetical ideas—disengagement and activity—the ideas have been controversial because of their inability consistently to demonstrate empirical support (Cumming, 1976; Lemon, Bengtson, and Peterson, 1976). While the controversy regarding activity and disengagement in the field of gerontology has concerned the consistency of empirical support for one or the other of the two theories, the central issue for minorities is the validity of both rationales. As a matter of fact, most theoretical orientations in gerontology—whether the central concept is "disengagement," "activity," "continuity," or "development"—ignore, or fail to treat sufficiently, the historically based differences between the majority culture and life in the minority communities.

DISENGAGEMENT THEORY

General theories are assumed to have universal application. Therefore, the theory of disengagement was initially assumed to apply across cultures. The theory also assumed the physical and economic well-being of all persons. That is, given the middle-class, white sample on whose data the theory was fashioned, it was implicitly assumed that variation by income and health was unrelated to the aging experience or adjustment to that experience. Finally, at the core of disengagement theory is the assumption that in the natural development of events, older people withdraw from work and other social activity and society "withdraws" from the older person. Moreover, disengagement theory assumes that society and the older person mutually acquiesce to this presumed natural development until the older person contently withdraws into death.

Disengagement theory suggests that society must go on. To do so, older people must abandon societal roles to prevent their death from disrupting the normal functioning of society. Therefore, the elderly withdraw, younger societal members assume the roles abandoned by the elders, and the society continues.

In U.S. society, to withdraw from social roles related to earning money is painful and therefore avoided by any number of people. On the other hand, however, some people are systematically, and have been historically, excluded from earning money. Critics of disengagement theory quickly point out that only recently have women and minorities been legally included in the money economy; their status in labor-market economic terms has been called "secondary" (Almquist, 1979). In contrast to the "primary" labor market, the secondary market has lower income, less security, lower status, and limited training. Therefore, the likelihood that many minority elderly or elderly women will have sufficient income resources from which to withdraw is small. One might ask, Disengagement from what? This circumstance, moreover, disallows the assumption of adequate income to be held in the application of disengagement theory. Without adequate income, the factors negatively influ-encing well-being obliterate the optimistic logic of the disengagement theorists.

Because disengagement theory, like activity theory, is a normative theory—focusing not so much on why people age, but rather on what must be done in order to age successfully—it is primarily studied in relation to measures of satisfaction with life. The theory suggests that the individual must withdraw from his or her productive roles before health fails so that personal reminiscing of one's previous role performance results in only favorable images of the self. This strategy, supposedly, will promote satisfaction. Thus, not only does failure to consider inadequate income impact negatively on the optimistic logic of the theory, but also the theory's usefulness is further eroded without a resourceful life history on which to reminisce—as is the case with minorities. Moreover, naively to seek out variations in life satisfaction among people struggling to survive stress and isolation is at best absurd and at worst inhumanely cruel. Disengagement theory provides a conceptual filter that can block out the day-to-day, as well as the historical, life experiences of older people; and as such, it alienates minority seniors from those who choose to pretend that all is rosy with the elderly to the very end.

ACTIVITY THEORY

Activity theory accounts for well-being in old age by the level of meaningful involvement sustained, rather than by successful disengagement. The more meaningfully involved the elderly are, the more "satisfied" they are. While an appealing idea, there is inconsistent empirical support, unfortunately. And, while meaningful involvement among the elderly can directly covary with happiness, it can also be frustrating and humiliating. Thus, there may be too many funerals to attend or too many grandchildren or grandnieces and nephews to nurture.

Meaningful involvement may also make people strong, determined survivors, but ones who are far from satisfied. Many minority persons live in spite of seemingly overwhelming obstacles. Why? Because to survive is their major drive in life. Is the will to survive necessarily synonymous with meaningful involvement or satisfaction? In the middle-class positivist view of the world, definitive emotional characterizations are permitted. Unfortunately, gerontologists have used these fictions to research older people. There is, however, no discrete state of personality development or human condition known as "satisfaction." There are no necessary golden years for elders, and this is particularly true for the minority elderly. There is, however, a theoretical construct called satisfac-tion that has too frequently been measured in relation to activity and has, therefore, been implicitly assumed to be caused by it. The lack of consistent empirical support for activity theory attests, in part, to the absence of a consistent, meaningful referent for the word *satisfaction* for most people. For the minority elderly, it is likely that life satisfaction, as a measure of successful aging, bears little relation to quality of life, as an alternative measure of successful aging. And, if so, the appropriate question, beyond defining quality of life, would be, What is the relation between quality of life and meaningful activity? Does meaningful activity promote successful aging? But, as suggested above, it is not clear what is meant by meaningful activity for the minority aged.

In the final analysis, problems related to the use of disengagement and activity are twofold. First, neither disengagement nor activity is a theory in the formal sense. They are contradictory ideas that continue to be used in spite of the fact that there is little observational support for them. Second, both concepts are assumed to apply to all people. Both theories systematically preclude understanding the ethnic minority elderly because both perspectives were and remain middle-class, Anglo-American ideas, ideas that do not reflect the historical or day-to-day living experience of elderly minorities. The humanity of minority people is ignored by looking at them only in relation to ideas originally conceived of, by, and for the white, middle-class majority in the United States.

21

MINORITY AGING FROM THE EXCHANGE AND STRUCTURALIST-FUNCTIONALIST PERSPECTIVES

AARON LIPMAN

The social facts that govern the lives of the aged within groups can be viewed from a number of different sociological perspectives; this chapter will examine aging from the conceptual frameworks of exchange theory and structural-functional analysis. In an examination of the basic postulates underlying these perspectives, two distinct questions are addressed: How may the experiences of the aged within minority groups be regarded from the standpoint of the life chances available to everyone in these particular groups, and how do these experiences of the aged in minority groups relate to those which are character-istic of the lives of the nonminority elderly? While the paucity of research in the area of minority group aging limits the application of these theories, and will require largely inferential conclusions, the exercise is useful inasmuch as it can (1) begin the process of theoretically focusing future research on the minority aged and (2) extend the explanatory domain of the theories.

MINORITY AGING: EXCHANGE THEORY

The philosophical background of exchange theory is firmly rooted in rationalism; that is, human beings tend to choose courses of action on the basis of anticipated outcomes from among a known range of alternatives. Underly-ing this rational view of human behavior is the principle of hedonism, expressed in the contention that people will tend to choose those alternatives that will provide the most beneficial outcome. Thibaut and Kelley (1959) elaborate these ideas in the form of two concepts: first, the comparison level through which an individual evaluates the outcome resulting from choosing or avoiding a given option and, second, the comparison level of alternatives, through which a person measures and evaluates the beneficial quality of the outcomes resulting from two or more possible courses of action. Throughout, the dominant notion prevails that persons will be guided in their choices by what they regard to be the best possible outcome from a given mode of acting.

Another proposition essential to exchange theory is the principle of reciprocity. In its simplest form it can be stated that a person should help (and should not hurt) those who have helped him. The principle of reciprocity further assumes that an individual chooses alternative modes of behaving by comparing the anticipated rewards, the possible costs that may be incurred, and the magnitude of investment required of him to achieve those rewarding outcomes. Accordingly, rewards in human social interaction should be proportionate to investment, and costs should not exceed rewards, or else the individual will shun that given course of activity. Homans (1961) has extended the principle of reciprocity to include this concept, which he calls "distributive justice." When rewards are not proportional to investments over the long term, he asserts, individuals tend to feel angry with social relations, instability is created, and the propensities for conflict increase.

Rewards may assume a wide gamut of forms: social approval; reduction of ambiguity in social interaction and in anticipated outcomes, such as the achievement of equality; attainment of similarity of beliefs and values with others; self-reinforcement of values through conformity; and attainment of those items that are highly valued in their culture, particularly economic rewards (Simpson, 1972; Ekeh, 1974; Heath, 1976; and Nye, 1978).

For the purposes of this chapter, the focus primarily will be upon how these exchange-theoretical propositions account for some of the major facts of life for the minority aged, especially regarding the manner in which their life chances and life perceptions are influenced by the operation of the principle of reciprocity in social relations. When the factor of inequality is introduced into the context of social relations, for example, there is the possibility that the norm of reciprocity will not be realized for many of the persons involved in the set of social relations. Thus, the genesis for tension, stress, instability, conflict, and ultimate dissolution of the interrelations is thereby provided. Stratification—especially when it is complex, enduring, and highly evident through inequity in the allocation of rewards such as power, privilege, and prestige—is a social fact that can have a highly disruptive social, as well as personal, potential.

The social and biological facts that accompany aging have been viewed in the context of stratification. The works of Riley, Johnson, and Foner (1972) suggest that for the entire population, age-graded roles may be viewed as an aspect of stratification in much of the same way as sociologists have regarded the crucial variable of class. In order for such a system to have stability, as we have noted from the exchange-theoretical perspective, it must be based on a system of reward allocation such that the aged, who have already invested a great deal in their lifetime in a variety of social relationships—familial (parental and marital), economic, and socioemotional—are insured that they will receive the rewards commensurate with such a volume of lifetime commitment.

One of the basic ways of defining minority group status involves the determination of which groups in a society have more or less power, privilege, and prestige relative to one another, with the minorities having less of each of these social factors than do other groups. Furthermore, a failure of the principle of reciprocity to achieve realization is likely to be most acute among the minority aged, especially if one considers the existence of an age stratification system in the entire society that operates to the detriment of the elderly. Thus, while older people in general have less ability to exercise power, to possess and control resources, and to be granted high levels of prestige, the situation of the minority aged represents a compounding of the disadvantages of an ethnic stratification and an age stratification system. Their social situation has been described as one of multiple jeopardy, and the feeling of many of the minority aged that any sort of reciprocity is remote may well be warranted. There is plentiful evidence to support the presence of the idea of cumulative disadvantage as a consequence of powerlessness, subordination, prejudice, and discrimination (Lipman, 1965, 1969).

At this point, attention should be given to the mechanisms through which the cumulative disadvantage experienced by the minority aged is reflected in an imbalance between investment and reward outcomes and may be mitigated through patterns of reward that are not so readily observable and quantifiable. Some recent discussions have focused upon the role of deference patterns as being reinforcing to the aged in the form of a nontangible reward. This is seen as compensating in part for the imbalance between the inadequate, more observable reward outcomes allocated to the aged and the magnitude of their investment in long-term interpersonal relations. Among certain groups there is evidence that ritualistic deference patterns that lend status to the aged can compensate to some extent for the gap between the magnitude of investment and the volume of reward (Lipman, 1980). Under certain conditions intrafamilial patterns of interaction may supplant whatever feelings of loss of power that the elderly experience. Among some groups of minorities, for example, the key role played by members of the eldest generation in a family, particularly female members, can substitute for more tangible reward outcomes. While it is evident that investigations must be made of the kinds of tangible supporting mechanisms (for example, income supports) that can be provided for the minority poor elderly, it is equally clear that when these mechanisms are absent or insufficient, attention should be drawn to how surrogate rewarding experiences might be duplicated or paralleled outside the family setting.

Recent evidence, which was designed to test the viability of the exchange-theoretical propositions in accounting for the presence of feelings of distributive injustice and the lack of realization of the norm of reciprocity, suggests that subjects who have these perceptions report lower life satisfaction and a higher degree of age consciousness (Dowd, 1978). Among the minority aged, blacks tended to have a high degree of age consciousness overall, which may be interpreted as a degree of perceived isolation from involvement in the society as a whole. Those who scored highest in age consciousness, however, were whites who felt distributive injustice and a lack of realization of reciprocity. This suggests that, in fact, among minority aged, other internal group mechanisms, such as extended familial deference patterns and support norms, as well as their perception of relative deprivation and distributive justice, may soften the impact of aging (Liang, Kahana, and Doherty, 1980). Clearly the evidence suggests that the exchange relationship between the aged and society differs within the minority populations from that within the general population. For these reasons the minority aged, from an exchange-theoretical framework, should be regarded as a special population.

MINORITY AGING: THE FUNCTIONALIST PERSPECTIVE

A differing and complementary perspective from which the aging process may be viewed is found within the theoretical context of structural-functionalism. In this section the attempt will be to integrate structural-functionalism and exchange theory with an orientation toward finding what common ground exists between these alternative approaches and how this commonality might lead to a more comprehensive and holistic understanding of life among the minority aged.

The epistemological sources of structural-functionalism have direct roots and analogies in sciences other than sociology, such as psychology, biology, and anthropology. For example, the key concept of "functional integration," which is a state of affairs in which institutions function in a complementary manner and in which conflicts are reduced to a minimum, is directly comparable to (1) the idea of equilibrium in psychology, in which a sense of consistency and consonance prevails within the personality structure of the individual, and (2) the idea of homeostasis in biology, a situation in which the various parts of an organic system function harmoniously in order to maximize the adaptive potential of an organism to its environment.

The variables that are of concern in studying the processes of social systemic creation, regulation, maintenance, and continuity relate to factors that are functional (that is, maintaining the stability of the social system) or are dysfunctional (creating conditions that are destructive for its long-term stability). Under certain conditions the functions of a pattern of social interaction may be either manifest (those which are intended, anticipated, and recognized) or latent (unintended, unanticipated, and unrecognized) or both. Under some conditions these manifest and latent functions will contradict and will often result in the emergence of a dysfunctional consequence that was clearly never desired (Merton, 1968).

As is the case with exchange theory, structural-functionalism is grounded in the rational tradition of philosophical thought. Within this tradition it is expected that manifest and latent functions will not contradict one another and also that the number of dysfunctions present in social action carried out within a social structure will be reduced to a minimum. As a result, the structural-functional perspective leads an investigator toward analyzing the sources of stability. Because of this orientation, investigators are often led to focus on stability-producing factors, ignoring that a course of social action may also have dysfunctional consequences. Certainly what may be functional for the adjustment of one group may be clearly dysfunctional for the adjustment of another.

STRUCTURAL-FUNCTIONALIST CONTRIBUTIONS

Historically, social gerontology has had a paucity of theories specific to aging. The only complete conceptual system related to aging, Cumming and Henry's (1961) disengagement theory, had its roots in the structural-functionalist perspective. Disengagement theory argues that since death is universal and inevitable, both society and the individual must adjust themselves to this fact in order to avoid conflict or disruption and to maintain homeostasis in the social system. Both society and the individual prepare for this ultimate fact of death through the mechanism of a gradual and mutual disengagement—a disengagement completed at death. Although not consistent, most research findings since Cumming and Henry, however, point to a positive relationship between social participation and morale among the elderly and fail to substantiate the major premises of disengagement theory on the level of its function for the individual (see, for example, Lipman and Smith, 1969).

To illustrate the duality of function that may emerge in applying disengagement theory, consider the consequences of retirement of the elderly on the young. Because of the scarcity of income-producing positions available to persons relative to the number of potential incumbents, it may be clearly functional for a society to have a long-range period of retirement for many elderly citizens, thereby reducing pressure on the job market and maximizing the chances for the employment of newcomers—especially youth. Since unemployed youth are often the source of many social problems for a society— among these being crime, delinquency, family instability, and social unrest in the form of civil disorder—the creation of a period of withdrawal from active work roles for elderly citizens can be seen as promoting social order by providing an avenue of economic mobility for youth. Among blacks, where there is great pressure on the occupational structure from large numbers of maturing youth, and in the absence of an expanding economy, the creation of a period of forced retirement for the aged may be even more critical for maintaining social stability within the group. However, while this retirement may be functional for the society and for the youth, it may have dysfunctional consequences for the elderly workers who were forced to retire.

In explaining behavior and attitudes, some social scientists, such as David Brodsky in chapter 22, argue that social stratification arising from achieved socioeconomic status is a more central and dominant variable than the ascribed status of race or ethnicity. In analyzing the existence of this social stratification, structural-functional theorists begin with the premise that different groups in society will get different allocations of the scarce resources of power, prestige, and services. They believe that social stratification comes about as a result of the distribution of differential rewards and is a functional necessity for individuals, the society, and organizations. For those roles that are functionally necessary for a society and that usually involve long periods of arduous training and dedication, society offers high privilege and prestige as a motivational inducement for differentially able individuals to train for and accept these demanding roles. Thus the structural-functional school, which considers itself to be value neutral, not only accepts inequality in the distribution of rewards and resources, but believes it to be both universal and adaptive for society.

To take a second illustration, consider the explanation of poverty as defined from a structuralist-functionalist perspective; this explanation is germane since many of the elderly poor were undoubtedly poor before they became elderly and since minorities constitute the largest percentage of both the poor and the elderly poor populations. Herbert Gans (1972) has described fifteen different ways in which the existence of poverty is functional for the larger society, subsumed under four general areas: economic, social, cultural, and political areas. Thus, poverty functions economically by providing a group of workers to perform the least desirable jobs, to buy used goods and inferior services, and to support occupations such as social workers and penologists. Socially and culturally, the poor serve as a benchmark for the better-off, giving the latter feelings of superiority and status. Politically, the poor absorb a large share of the economic and political costs of growth and change. Since they vote less and participate less politically than any other group, the political system can ignore their demands; in this manner the poor actually contribute to the stability of our political system. Here once again, structural-functional analysis has surveyed the role of poverty from the vantage point of societal adaptation, rather than its dysfunctional effects on the individual. However, to analyze functions in this manner does not necessarily mean to endorse them. There is no necessary contradiction between the statements that poverty is functional for the total social system and that attempts should continue to be made to eliminate or modify poverty on the basis that it is dysfunctional for the individual (Bromley and Longino, 1972).

The major problem attendant to the structural-functional perspective is the tendency to regard patterns of social action in a somewhat dispassionate, impersonalized, often conservative way, making it appear biased against radical social change. Structural-functionalists must begin, therefore, to identify the courses of action that will produce the most beneficial, manifest, functional consequences, will reduce the possibly harmful latent consequences, and, especially, will avoid deleterious dysfunctions. Since it is often the case that a course of action that has dysfunctions for some groups (in the present case, the minority aged) cannot be avoided, one typically enlists the most available alternative. Most critically, the need exists for the structural-functionalists to be more attentive to a wide range of alternatives in social action, especially as these relate to the adjustment and well-being of a population like the minority aged. Functionalists must also recognize that disequilibrium and, hence, social dysfunctions may be essential in achieving more equitable and humane institutions. Once again, the structural-functionalists will be in the position of evaluating the potentially rewarding or cost-producing outcomes of a wide range of policy and action program alternatives, in much of the same way as do theorists who are trained in the tradition of social exchange.

However, the traditions differ as to the degree of choice given to both society and to the minority aged individual in the evaluation of alternatives. Structural-functionalists tend to focus on the individual's need to adjust to already existing social structures and to patterns of social action. Since, as noted, society is likely to be the more powerful member in such a two-way relationship, structural-functionalists would be prone to emphasize the dominance of societal needs and requirements. However, exchange theorists tend to regard such a relationship between the aged and society as a reciprocal relationship based on the operation of the principles of reciprocity and distributive justice. While the structural-functionalists tend to regard the investment factor that the aged have provided to society during their lifetime as given, exchange theorists will regard this level of investment as an element in a bargaining relationship. Thus, exchange theory can be seen as being more dynamic an approach, emphasizing the role of mutual adjustment.

In the case of the minority aged, the question of which perspective dominates the approach of social gerontology becomes crucial. As has been shown, many of the minority aged have an acute perception of their differences in relation to the rest of society. This perceived uniqueness rests not only upon an existing pattern of age, but also upon the cumulative experience of minority group membership, which has determined the course and direction of much of their lives prior to late life. The minority aged have two important factors in their lives: lifelong discrimination and late-life age stratification influences. In order for either structural-functionalism or exchange theory to be an adequate explanatory tool, a dynamic model of aging, incorporating these realities, must be employed (Lipman, 1978).

22

THE CONFLICT PERSPECTIVE
AND UNDERSTANDING AGING
AMONG MINORITIES

DAVID M. BRODSKY

This chapter assesses the utility of a conflict perspective in understanding minority aging. First, the chapter briefly reviews problems with existing theories and research concerning aging among minority groups. Then it presents the essential elements of conflict theory and discusses research findings that suggest the applicability of this theory to the study of aging. Finally, the chapter offers an assessment of possible applications of conflict theory to the study of minority aging.

EXISTING DATA AND THEORIES

Since the mid-1960s, gerontologists have become increasingly interested in studying aged persons from minority groups. Despite this interest, a number of problems remain in assessing the status of the aging in various minority groups. These problems fall into two broad areas: those stemming from the lack of reliable *data* to describe accurately the minority aged and those relating to *theories* that seek to explain the aging experience of minority group members.

DATA PROBLEMS

Although students of minority aging have identified a number of data problems, several stand out. First, researchers to date have conducted relatively few cross-sectional studies and almost no longitudinal studies with sufficiently large samples of elderly minority group members. Second, even though the Bureau of the Census reports some separate data on blacks and Hispanics, most census reports prior to 1970 present data only for whites and nonwhites. Since 1970, census publications report data for whites, blacks, and other races. In some instances other races are absorbed in the white total. In either case these procedures obscure any differences among minority groups. And, finally, researchers have failed to report sufficient data about differences within minority group populations; this problem is compounded by the relatively small proportions of minority group members surviving to or beyond age 65.

THEORETICAL PROBLEMS

At a theoretical level critics have identified several inadequacies in current theories of aging. Contemporary gerontologists generally assume that such social problems as old age "have both their causes and solutions in the individual human conduct" (Dowd, 1980:9). As a result, they focus largely on the individual and his or her adjustment to old age and underemphasize the role of social institutions and structures in the development not only of the problems facing individuals, but also of their responses to these problems. Investigators have, until recently, treated the elderly as a relatively homogeneous group; this assumption leads them to highlight the similarities among older persons and to downplay differences that might exist across sex, ethnic, and class boundaries within age groups.

This lack of adequately developed theories of aging also causes researchers concerned with minority aging to compare groups primarily on the basis of race or cultural background. Consequently, if differences do appear, the analysis tends to attribute these variations to racial or cultural differences when, in fact, they may stem from the effects of such other factors as socioeconomic status. Students of minority aging frequently fail to test empirically the theoretical assumptions underlying their research or policy recommendations. For example, although the notion of "double jeopardy" informs much of the minority-oriented literature, only a few studies (one being Dowd and Bengtson, 1978) attempt to test this thesis empirically. These problems lead Jackson (1980) to the conclusion that "no body of theory about minority aging exists."

THE CONFLICT PERSPECTIVE: AN OVERVIEW

Although social scientists approach the study of conflict from a variety of perspectives, several shared assumptions form the basis of their work (see Turner, 1978). First, most students of social conflict characterize societies as collections of either individual or group actors with different and competing interests. Second, conflict theorists assume that because all societies have only limited resources and rewards at their disposal, conflicts inevitably arise as individuals or groups struggle over claims to status, power, and scarce resources. Third, groups who successfully assert claims to these scarce resources use their resulting advantage to dominate or constrain other groups in the society. Fourth, the conflict perspective assumes that social conflict represents goal-oriented behavior insofar as the competing parties seek to gain scarce values and to overcome resistance. And, finally, social structures and institutions provide frameworks that both limit and stimulate social conflicts. For example, federal and state laws structure and limit the conflicts that occur between labor and management. On the other hand, social structures may stimulate conflict by inequitably allocating the resources or the values that constitute the goals of social conflict. Moreover, a lack of flexibility within the institutional structure of a society may worsen the negative consequences of existing inequalities by preventing any meaningful change (Dahrendorf, 1959).

The applications of conflict theory to the study of aging that have been reported to date emphasize the importance of structural factors. Estes's (1979:2) analysis of the Older Americans Act stresses the importance of social structures in shaping public policies, and her research attempts to "make explicit how certain ways of thinking about the aged as a social problem (and the logical extensions of these views to social policies) are rooted in the structure of social and power relations." A number of authors focus on the relationships between the class structure of a society and the old age experienced by members of different social and economic classes. Rosenberg (1968) argues that class-related factors become increasingly important in old age and that a person's socioeconomic environment continues to influence his or her life circumstances beyond retirement. De Beauvoir (1972) views aging as a class struggle; this perspective is shared by Guillemard (1975:217), who writes that "each social class is destined for a specific kind of old age, reflecting the existing class relationships of a given moment in history." Henretta and Campbell (1976) also conclude that the social class inequalities present earlier in the life cycle continue into old age. Despite slight variations in emphasis, the conflict-oriented studies of aging reflect Dowd's (1980:ix) belief that "to understand the situation of aged people in any society, we must examine the relationship of society's stratification system to the aging process."

THE CONFLICT PERSPECTIVE AND MINORITY AGING

The conflict perspective is useful for understanding several of the conclusions from minority aging research. The concept of minority aging reflects conflict theory's concern with the unequal distribution of resources in a society and with the use of a stratification system by those in privileged positions to maintain their status. Crandall (1980:377) writes that "minority groups can be seen as groups with limited access to power and unequal access to certain opportunities in societies." Jackson (1980:2), on the other hand, emphasizes that minority groups are those "whose members have been singled out for differential and inferior treatment on the basis of such characteristics as their race, sex, nationality, or language."

From a conflict perspective Jackson's argument offers an incomplete understanding of the jeopardized conditions faced by the minority elderly. Jackson essentially ignores the broader social system in which racial and other cultural criteria exist and the impact of economic factors on the development of these criteria. In contrast, the conflict perspective sees these criteria as emerging

from prior economic struggles in which the propertied classes, those controlling the means of economic production, enjoy a power advantage relative to
the nonpropertied classes. The propertied classes use this power advantage to
shape public policies to serve their own interests, interests significantly different from those of the nonpropertied and the nonpowerful. Further, the
intensity of conflicts of interest among minorities within such population
groups as the old will vary with the minority's proximity to the control of
economic production.

The conflict perspective readily shows the importance of both racial and
economic factors in describing the conditions of the minority elderly; moreover, the conflict perspective offers a framework for interpreting obvious
differences in the conditions of the less powerful, including variations among
the minority aged. Thus, descriptions of the impact of minority status on the
minority elderly cannot depend upon racial or ethnic discrimination alone.
Rather, class distinctions must also be studied for appreciation of (1) the
substantial role that economic differences play in shaping social relations and
(2) the manner in which dominant economic groups exploit racial and ethnic
variations in order to promote their own interests, making race, in effect, an
intervening—rather than an antecedent—variable (Gomes, 1981).

How, then, can this broad perspective aid in the interpretation of data
reported for the minority aged? Consider, for example, that the proportions of
elderly blacks (35.5 percent) and Hispanics (26.7 percent) with incomes below
the poverty line far exceeds the proportion (13.2 percent) of aged whites in
poverty (see chapter 3). Abbott (1977) reports that although a relatively small
proportion of the elderly population receives public assistance payments, this
proportion includes a larger percentage of elderly blacks (30 percent) than
elderly whites (7 percent). He also finds that only 13 percent of elderly blacks,
in contrast to 53 percent of elderly whites, receive some form of asset income.
Golden (1980) notes that older minority group members, but especially
blacks, also have less education than whites and suffer more chronic illnesses
that prevent them from working. Findings of less income, more illnesses,
earlier death, poor housing, and, in general, direr socioenvironmental and
living circumstances have led several authors, in the preceding chapters, to
refer to the doubly jeopardized situation of elderly minorities, resulting from
the compound negative effects of being old *and* being a member of any racial
or ethnic minority.

Critics of the double jeopardy hypothesis, such as Bell, Kasschau, and
Zellman (1976b), charge that the literature either minimizes or ignores differences among the aged within minority groups. This oversight makes it difficult
to sort out the effects of discrimination due to race or ethnicity on the one
hand and such variables as class and socioeconomic status on the other hand.
These critics also suggest that influences that cut across racial lines may reduce
or level differences in patterns of aging. Thus, if the differences that existed
between middle-aged whites and their minority counterparts have narrowed

among the aged, the explanatory power of the double jeopardy thesis is lessened (Dowd and Bengtson, 1978).

Because class and race differences influence the type of old age a person will experience, the utility of the conflict model is suggested, combining the double jeopardy perspective and its emphasis on race with a class perspective and its emphasis on position in the economic structure of society. Such a model could first assess the effects of race and then control for such factors as "socioeconomic status," evaluated by such indicators as education, occupation, and income or "social class," assessed in turn in terms of relationships to the means of production and control over labor power (Wright and Perrone, 1977). The data generated would then enable one not only to distinguish between the experiences of the minority and the majority aged, but also to improve the ability to understand the heterogeneity of the minority elderly.

But understanding the current status of the minority elderly represents only a first step. Understanding, to have any value, must lead to real improvements in the living conditions of the minority elderly. However, improving their status will require a substantial redistribution of social and economic resources. How will these changes come about?

Unlike functionalism, which suggests that improved conditions for the minority elderly will gradually evolve through the increasing differentiation and subsequent integration of social and cultural structures, conflict theory argues that significant structural changes will fail to occur in the absence of intense conflict. For the minority aged this means that they, alone or in conjunction with other economically jeopardized groups, must first develop a sense of "consciousness," an awareness of their common economic (rather than racial) plight. This consciousness can then serve as a basis for the political mobilization of the minority elderly on behalf of policies focusing on shared economic interests rather than on narrow, racially or ethnically specific concerns. The extent to which the economically disadvantaged, including the minority elderly, develop a shared consciousness and mobilize on the basis of their common interests will influence the intensity of conflict and, hence, the potential for social and cultural change.

Part 6

RESEARCH METHODOLOGY AND THE STUDY OF THE MINORITY AGED

INTRODUCTION TO PART 6

Scientific research is a method for studying interrelationships among theoretically and practically relevant variables. The facts accumulating from this study must be explicitly demonstrated to have resulted from several meticulously planned steps.

But although the scientific enterprise depends on methodological rigor, the sociological imagination, of which sociologist C. Wright Mills spoke, demands flexibility, depending upon the research context. That is, the exact circumstances confronted in any one research context will vary to some extent from other contexts; the research strategy must be adaptable to the context. For example, awareness of the inverse relation between age and education, in the first instance, and the positive relationship between education and ability to conceptualize, in the second instance, could suggest that investigators should formulate interview measurement items in a manner consistent with this knowledge. Thus, contrary to typical Likert scaling procedures, it may be naive to expect the elderly to distinguish easily between "strong agreement" and mere "agreement" with an attitudinal indicator.

It is necessary to anticipate the research context for the study of even more specified categories of research respondents. There are several issues, for example, that make the context for scientific research with the minority aged unique to the context represented by the general aged population. While the chapters in the preceding section illustrated the need to incorporate varying theoretical propositions in order to account for the differential aging circumstances of the aged population in the United States, the chapters in this section document the need to recognize differential research strategies when studying the minority (relative to the nonminority) aged. Stated differently, the topics in this section illustrate some of the concerns that arise when interfacing rigorous research design, the sociological imagination, and minority aging research topics.

Linda Burton and Vern Bengtson capture the essence of this tripartite relation when noting, "research in elderly ethnic minority communities is not a simple undertaking. In keeping with the high standards of social inquiry . . . the [investigator] must acknowledge and be sensitive to the unique issues involved." The authors expand this theme as they discuss the problems and potentials of doing research in minority communities in chapter 23. There are four recurrent issues, they conclude, that permeate research on minorities and aging: the problem of context, the problem of comparability, the problem of investigative bias, and the problem of accountability to the community. Consider, for example, the problem of context; the authors ask, How do investigative perceptual and value contexts impact on research conclusions about the minority aged? Oftentimes, they note, the tendency to stereotype or over-romanticize the life experiences of the minority aged leads to faulty assessments. In the final analysis, they note, the solution to this and related problems rests in investigative self-criticism.

The problem of accountability to the community, to take another example, also illustrates the special research context constituted by the elderly minority population. This problem results from the perception, real or imagined, by the minority community of exploitation by research investigators. Thus, Burton and Bengtson assert that the investigator must not underestimate the power of community leaders to influence the acceptability of the research efforts in their community and, indeed, to influence the very continuation of the research. Community involvement, they observe, must be built into the research design.

Burton and Bengtson's analysis, in toto, illustrates well the type of sociological imagination that must be concatenated with good research design in producing valid conclusions regarding the nature, circumstances, and needs of the minority aged.

While Burton and Bengtson's chapter is concerned primarily with a representative number of the issues in collecting scientifically valid data, Schaie, Orchowsky, and Parham examine a problem that, although having implications for data collection, is primarily a problem of data analysis. The problem is one of measuring an aging effect. While cast in terms of a substantive research investigation, the authors effectively communicate the analytical decisions and processes that must be made in testing the *impact of aging* on criterion factors. In the case examined in chapter 24, the authors consider the relative effects of age, cohort, and race on the criterion of life satisfaction.

As Schaie, Orchowsky, and Parham illustrate, age—as an alternative explanation to race in accounting for variation in life satisfaction—cannot be studied alone in this analysis; provisions must also be made for the analysis of sociocultural changes, that is, changes due to cohort (or generational) and period (or time of measurement) effects. Moreover, each of these factors should be studied with controls for such other variables as may be deemed theoretically important. In their study these control factors include health and income. Using the sequential strategies developed by Schaie, the investigators illustrate the process for unconfounding age, cohort, and period effects so that the true impact of age can be observed. They conclude that, rather than age, differences between cohorts (regardless of race, health, and income status) explain most of the variation in life satisfaction.

Schaie, Orchowsky, and Parham's paper is an important study for all investigators of the age variable. It is especially important that those interested in the burgeoning study of minority aging not fall prey to the same mistakes that currently underlie much of the social science literature in studies of the age variable among nonminority samples.

Chapter 25 is an appropriate sequel to the discussion by Schaie, Orchowsky, and Parham. While the latter consider the precise measurement of "age" in the study of minority aging, Manuel expresses equal concern for the measurement of the "minority" component. Thus, Manuel asks the familiar question, examined in chapter 2: What does it mean to conclude that an individual is a member of a minority group? And extending the logic from chapter 2: Is it likely that one can tap the impact of the minority status by merely knowing the general label associated with an individual's supposed background? No, Manuel contends, it is unlikely that, say, all Mexican Americans have had similar experiences with the assumed minority background. That is, there are degrees in the extent of exposure of any individual to the minority experience. Proceeding from the definition of a minority outlined in chapter 2, Manuel introduces a set of empirically generated measurement scales that are in fact designed to reflect the extent of an individual's minority background experience. Utilizing these scales, it is maintained, will provide new evidence on how variation in ethnic-minority identification covaries with other important gerontological variables.

When conceived as a whole, the chapters in the two concluding sections—indeed, throughout the volume—provide a new perspective in gerontology generally and in minority aging particularly. The data, the conclusions, as well as the theoretical and methodological issues to which they give rise substantiate this basic conclusion. In sum, the minority aged, while victims of a lifelong and a continuing oppressed status, are beacons for charting new directions not only in policy formulations, but also in the theoretical and methodological study of the aged.

23

RESEARCH IN ELDERLY
MINORITY COMMUNITIES:
PROBLEMS AND POTENTIALS

LINDA BURTON AND VERN L. BENGTSON

Ethnic and subcultural variations within the population of the aged have been increasingly discussed within the past two decades. The yield of minority research in terms of quality and quantity, however, has been lower than many observers had hoped (see Jackson, 1980, for a recent bibliographic review). Why? Is the relative dearth of minority aging research an inevitable consequence of the complex issues involving the design or conduct of such research? Is the purportedly low scientific quality of minority aging research due to the researcher's naiveté or lack of adequate consideration of conceptual issues involved? Or is the lack of quality and quantity of minority aging research yet another reflection of social inequality (Solomon, 1977)?

The purpose of this chapter is to examine some recurrent issues and emerging potentials in the conduct of research on ethnicity and aging. In particular, the discussion focuses on four recurrent issues in minority aging research. The first concerns the context in which minority research is conducted. What is the unwitting and often unexamined role of stereotypes, of the "deviant perspective," of racism, and of elitism in minority research? A second issue is the crucial role of comparability. Why is comparability between groups so important and so elusive? How does one compare ethnic minorities with the white majority? The third issue concerns the plight of the researcher. What are some of the more general problems that recurrently face the white researcher, the minority researcher, and the indigenous researcher? What can be done to alleviate these dilemmas? A fourth issue revolves around community concerns about research. What are the frequent difficulties encountered?

CONTEXT IN MINORITY RESEARCH: STEREOTYPES, THE DEVIANT PERSPECTIVE, RACISM, AND ELITISM

Most observers would agree that in the past fifty years minority progress in America has benefited from the organization and application of research knowledge obtained from the well-intentioned researcher. But, despite the volume of data on the illness of racism (Kramer, 1970), there still are large numbers of Americans, including research investigators, who at varying levels of consciousness continue to incorporate racism, elitism, stereotypes, and the assignment of deviant perspective into their attitudes and orientations toward minorities. How do these perceptual and value contexts affect minority research?

STEREOTYPES

Sotomayer (1973) suggests that anthropologists, sociologists, and psychologists have written extensively about the Chicano as an underachiever, as a non-goal-oriented person, as an illiterate. Cuellar (1980) argues that most research on the older Hispanic has limited value because of researchers' tendency to stereotype and distort the former's life experiences. In Cuellar's assessment such research generally overromanticizes the importance of the extended family and the folk life, qualities of the urban barrio. Kitano (1969) notes that Asian Americans, on the other hand, have been stereotyped as having no pressing problems. Asians are also often described as individuals with a "reverence for hard work, achievement, self-control, dependability, manners, thrift, and diligence" (Kitano, 1969:76). These values are thought to be entirely congruent with American white middle-class perceptions.

The nature of human perceptual or cognitive limitations, simple naiveté, and the lack of genuine concern are precursors to research that create and perpetuate stereotypes. It might be assumed that research of this nature is contaminated from its onset because the researcher conducts his research selectively; no inquiry is value free. But, though agreed that values permeate choices and methodologies in social science research, it does not follow that stereotyping and its perpetuation are inevitable. Indeed, the methods of science, correctly followed, are in fact norms of validity and reliability in order to protect researchers from their own fallibility as recorders of social data.

THE DEVIANT PERSPECTIVE

Minority research has generally focused on the negative, or deviant, aspects of life circumstances, since it often operates from what has been called a "social problems" perspective. What Murray (1973) terms the "white norm, deviant minority" context is, unfortunately, particularly salient in minority aging research. For researchers one dismal implication of the preoccupation with deviance from the white norm is the potential for irrelevance—or, at best, inaccuracy. A deviance emphasis can create serious problems in developing relevant, reliable, and valid research. First, researchers may not identify the real issues in the community. When conditioned by the deviant perspective, investigators frequently gloss over important issues—say, unequal access to health care in the case of the elderly—while searching diligently for evidence to support the idea of behavioral variation from the majority norms.

A second concern in the deviant perspective involves respondent reactivity. When respondents become aware that the investigator is focusing on deviance, they often feel it is necessary to give socially acceptable responses; a variation of this form of respondent reactivity, "response acquiescence," is particularly noted among minority elderly respondents. The interview context may be such that unconscious pressure for conformity is put upon the respondent. The responses thus follow a modal pattern of yea-saying, a tendency toward agreement even when it involves a contradictory item (Ragan, 1975).

Individuals conducting research in the minority community need to exercise caution in evaluating the context in which they examine the community. The deviant perspective and related stereotypes are the result not of abnormality, but rather of minorities' experience in a system of inequality. The emphasis here is that research in minority communities is not a question of studying deviant groups, but rather a question of studying unique groups.

RACISM AND ELITISM

Why is minority research in modern society plagued with charges of elitism and racism? It is because the goals and abilities of many researchers are not always what they are stated to be (Moore, 1973), and minority advocates quickly perceive the inconsistencies.

Many researchers today see minority aging research primarily as an avenue for getting federal research grants, publications, and theses or dissertations. Quite often, many of these people who receive grants do not appear qualified to do minority research, especially in the eyes of minority advocates. Others lack the ability to perceive racist and elitist attitudes in themselves or in the society as a whole. Brazziel (1973:42) argues that "many of these researchers are not aware of their inadequacies; others take a cynical view of their responsibilities; for them it doesn't matter if instruments are inappropriate."

How can attitudes of racism and elitism be overcome in minority research? Such a feat may be rather difficult, as the field of social inquiry "reflects the biases and limitations of the 98 percent Anglo white composition of the profession" (Moore, 1973:66). However, careful scrutiny by government agencies funding minority research and the incorporation of minority research classes in the universities may help to alleviate some of the problem. At base, however, the solution lies in the awareness and self-criticism of the researcher.

THE CRUCIAL ROLE OF COMPARABILITY

Many researchers suggest, and advocates would agree, that ethnic minority elderly are, in fact, distinctive—in terms of problems as well as potentials—by virtue of their language, life style, socioeconomic status, and historical experiences in this country (Bengtson, 1979; Cuellar, 1980; Jackson, 1980). But how can one know this? Is this not also perhaps a stereotype in the service of personal values as advocates of minority elderly?

Although distinctiveness may be an assumption, it is also a proposition open to empirical test. The method of testing is in explicit comparative research between groups. Only by explicit and valid comparisons, using ethnically comparable methods, can adequate knowledge of minority aging be built. Comparability of methods is essential.

What are some of the requirements for comparative research? First, the researcher must not assume homogeneity among minority subcultures. The effects of cohort pools, regional distinctions, socioeconomic status, and cultural differences indicate the importance of this issue. For example, early Asian immigrants to the United States are quite different from recent ones in terms of historical experiences, affluence, and education. Mexican Americans in San Antonio, Texas, are quite different from those in San Diego (Cuellar, 1980). The Arizona Navahos have marked cultural differences as compared to the Oklahoma Cherokee tribe. Connelly (1980) notes that the "degree of Indianness" or level of white culture assimilation may also account for incongruencies in the Indian population. In short, it is naive to assume uniformity among minority populations.

A second issue involves the comparability of measures. Quite often measures are developed, refined, and validated within one group and then are applied to other groups under the assumption that their validity and reliability are stable across groups. This is, in fact, often an unwarranted assumption, as has been demonstrated by Morgan and Bengtson (1976) with respect to perceptions of aging.

Ragan (1973:9) suggests that "conceptualizations of social institutions may also be subject to ethnocentric errors." For example, definitions of the extended family structures among aged blacks vary from study to study. Bengtson and Burton (1980) define such a structure as "fictive kin," while Rubenstein (1971) calls the extended and augmented groups he observed "companionship households."

How can one surmount these problems in order to conduct reliable and valid, unique and explicitly comparative research? Most importantly, it is necessary to design explicit comparisons between groups (Bengtson, 1979). Research comparisons across race should be supplemented by comparisons across class, age, and sex strata. This strategy would help move the old value-laden "minority bad, majority good" type of research to a more refined, holistic view of each ethnic subgroup.

THE PLIGHT OF THE RESEARCHER

Today any group of researchers conducting a study of elderly minorities carries out the research in a climate of suspicion and resistance (Ragan, 1973). One of the reasons articulated for such resistance concerns the race of the researcher. Do problems encountered by the white researcher differ from those encountered by the minority researcher or the indigenous researcher? The general perception of white researchers by minority communities is that of inadequacy, insensitivity, or—to put it more bluntly—incompetence (Billingsley, 1970).

To be successful, research by the white investigator in minority communities involves four issues: first, obtaining community sanctions; second, dealing with the problem of reverse racism; third, having familiarity with the cultural milieu of the community (language barriers, slang); fourth, and most importantly, being able to eliminate suspicions that respondent confidentiality will be violated (particularly in the Mexican American community). These are significant challenges that must often be negotiated in the process of the research (Bengtson and associates, 1977).

Maykovich (1977) notes that a minority researcher is not any freer from problems than a white researcher attempting to carry on a project in a minority community. The minority researcher is, after all, expected to be an advocate of his or her community. One of the major problems encountered by the minority researcher involves the maintenance of social distance or objectivity. Faced with the prospects of ethnic loyalty and ethnic experiences similar to those of the respondent, the minority researcher runs the temptation of conducting research selectively. First, data may be excluded from the report for fear that it will have detrimental consequences for the group under study. Second, in identifying with the respondents, the researcher may feel he or she is exposing shared secrets, sentiments, and values to the white world. Third, the researcher may also view certain behavior as commonplace, while a more objective researcher would see it as problematic.

Weiss (1977) argues that the use of indigenous researchers, those who live in the community under study, can also be problematic in conducting minority research. First, it may be sometimes difficult to recruit indigenous researchers, for the perverse reason that they perceive they "know" so many "bad" things about the neighborhood that they are afraid to do the interviews. Second, indigenous researchers have been known to harbor resentment toward the researchers or the university conducting the study. If so, it would be understandable if they deliberately failed to collect accurate data in the field. (It should be noted that such falsifying of data is not documented in any publication to the writers' knowledge; nevertheless, instances have been suggested by at least one major survey research firm to the authors in defense of not employing indigenous interviewers.)

A third and final concern involving the indigenous researcher is that in many cases the respondent will identify negatively with the interviewer. Weiss (1977) reports that some of the respondents in her study looked at the indigenous researcher as an equal and were annoyed because they had not been selected to do the interviews instead.

CONCERNS OF THE COMMUNITY

Resistance to social research by minorities has been increasingly encountered in recent years (see, for example, Bengtson and associates, 1977; and Cromwell, Vaughan, and Mindel, 1975). Hostile sentiments that articulate this resistance involve community disenchantment and skepticism with the nature and conduct of minority research. Many feel that they have been exploited in the past by researchers, especially from elite institutions such as universities. Research has often resulted in the professional advancement and power gains for the researcher, while little, if any, demonstrable benefits have accrued to the community furnishing the data. The most adamant protest, however, that minority communities advance about social research concerns failure of investigators to consult with the community about research. It has been evidenced that community involvement in the entire research scenario is essential to developing an atmosphere that is conducive to research (Bengtson and associates, 1977). Yet many researchers either underestimate or deliberately ignore the concerns, as well as the power, of the communities and their advocates.

Experiences of the authors with a cross-ethnic research program at the University of Southern California illustrates the difficulties that can arise in research unless the community is actively involved. Because the history of this project illustrates direct confrontation between community advocates (sophisticated in community politics and highly motivated) and a university research staff (well-intentioned, but naive), it is useful to cite it as an example of what researchers should have considered, but did not.

Although the University of Southern California community survey did not follow the usual course of social science research, in which academics define the plan of study, gather data, analyze, and report findings, all within the confines of a scholarly community, its biography may be fairly typical of future cross-ethnic research. From the beginning the researchers became directly involved in the politics of community research with subsequent alterations in both the organization and the spirit of the program.

In fact, the program was suspended prior to its anticipated starting date because of community protest about the research. Representatives of the Los Angeles Mexican American and black communities formally protested to the funding foundation, requesting a role in setting policy for the studies so as to avoid the implicit racism and elitism that, they noted, had characterized other cross-ethnic research.

The major vehicle for gaining community involvement and trust was the establishment of the Community Research Planning Committee, comprising concerned members of the black and Mexican American constituencies. Over the five years of the project, the committee was the decision-making body at each stage of the program and at each level of project organization.

Regularly, quarterly meetings were held, reviewing each segment of the program and ratifying or modifying staff decisions concerning procedures. The major substantive goals of the program remained unchanged, while alterations were made in the means of data gathering and the targets of dissemination. The result was not only community support for the program, but also an unusual degree of confidence in its products: confidence that the inferences drawn from the data are valid and that the dissemination products are relevant beyond the usual academic audiences.

The costs of such unusual collaboration between academics and community representatives were high in terms of time and energy for each of the various interest groups involved (academic staff, community representatives, minority research firms, the funding agency, and the university). It is estimated that perhaps one year was added to the original time frame in order to build mutual understanding and trust, as well as to make necessary modifications in organization. But the rewards have also been high. The original concerns of the community advocates, greater minority involvement and greater effectiveness in dissemination of results, were achieved, at least to the satisfaction of the interest groups involved (Bengston and associates, 1977).

In sum, research in minority communities can be productive, and the process itself can be stimulating. But investigators must not be naive about the concerns and about the power of community advocates. Researchers must build community involvement into the process of the research and be prepared for both conflict and unanticipated benefits from the resultant collaboration. They must be aware of the new rules of accountability emerging in social research.

CONCLUSIONS AND SUMMARY

The conduct of social research in elderly ethnic minority communities is not a simple undertaking. In keeping with the high standards of social inquiry that call for valid, reliable, and relevant research, the individual conducting research in minority communities must acknowledge and be sensitive to the unique issues involved. First, the investigator must examine the context within which the research is conducted. Are the effects of stereotypes, racism, elitism, or the deviant perspective infiltrating the research? Second, it is essential that the researcher address the issue of comparability. In the comparison of minorities to each other and the white majority, are research instruments ethnically reliable and valid? Third, researchers must evaluate the effects of their race on the research. Finally, and most importantly, the researcher must not ignore or underestimate the power and concerns of the community involved. Community sanctions and involvement in the entire research scenario are essential to developing an atmosphere that is conducive to conducting research.

24

MEASURING AGE AND SOCIOCULTURAL CHANGE: THE CASE OF RACE AND LIFE SATISFACTION

K. WARNER SCHAIE, STAN ORCHOWSKY, AND IRIS A. PARHAM

The purpose of this chapter is to examine how some of the methodological concerns that have received much attention in the study of adult development and aging may affect analyses of data bases involving minority group concerns. More specifically, an example is presented on how cohort, age, and period effects might interact with racial identity. While the dependent variable, life satisfaction, encompasses a topical area that is a popular one in the gerontological literature, as can be determined from the preceding chapters, the concern in this chapter is not so much with this variable as with an illustration of an appropriate methodology for studying the impact of age, in relation to race, on life satisfaction. First, a brief exposition of the analytic model is given. Then the model is applied to a relevant case study in which survey data is examined on life satisfaction with respect to black/white differences, as well as their interaction with age, cohort, and period effects, respectively.

AGE, COHORT, AND PERIOD EFFECTS

Three major parameters are generally considered as index variables in studies of phenomena thought to be age-related. The first, chronological age, requires little explanation; the others are less well understood and require specification. For the purposes in this chapter cohort is defined simply as a group of persons who are born at the same point or within the same range of time; a period is the interval between two times of measurement or observation of the dependent variable of interest. These three concepts require consideration, because without strong additional assumptions it is impossible to estimate any one of them independently. That is, if one collects a cross-sectional data set in which two or more age groups are compared, these groups must belong to different cohorts in addition to being of different ages. Cross-sectional data consequently confound age and cohort effects. Likewise, when longitudinal panel data are considered in which the same individuals are followed over time, or when successive waves are sampled from the same cohort, it is clear that a period of time has elapsed between such data collections, and the resulting estimates of change will confound age and period effects (see Riley, 1973).

Why are these matters of concern when questions are asked with respect to race differences? Although there has been much discussion about the fact that there are racial differences in patterns of aging, much less attention has been paid to what should be even more obvious: namely, that social change has been differentially effective in its impact upon racial groups. The literature on age changes in intellectual competence, for example, shows a clear case where cross-sectional studies suggested the existence of an early decline; it was, in fact, no more than a substantial generational difference occasioned by dramatic changes in the educational system (see Schaie, 1979). But it can be suspected that generational differences among blacks have proceeded at a different pace and on a different time scale than for whites, and period effects are even more likely to be differentiable by race. What may be a period of dramatic change for one party of society may be stability or stagnation for another! As a consequence, it would seem important that studies of racial differences in attitudes, attributes, and behaviors pay close attention to the interactions between each of the terms defined here and the race difference variable.

SEQUENTIAL STRATEGIES

A number of strategies have been suggested to tease apart age, cohort, and period effects within univariate as well as multivariate contexts (for example, Fienberg and Mason, 1979; Schaie and Hertzog, 1982). All of these approaches require the assumption that one of the components, or at least several levels of one component, be set to zero or equality. An Analysis of Variance (ANOVA) approach has been suggested by Schaie (see for example, Schaie and Parham, 1974). In an approach that has become known as *sequential methods*, it is assumed that one of the confounds is of little interest to the researcher, respectively, for each of the sequential models. In that case three approaches are possible. The cohort-sequential strategy, preferred by developmental psychologists, assumes that period effects are trivial and is then able to separate age and cohort effects. The time-sequential strategy assumes cohort effects to be trivial and can then separate age and period effects. And, finally, the cross-sequential strategy, under the assumption of trivial aging effects, can separate period and cohort effects. A minimum of two measurement points and two ages or cohorts, respectively, are required for the cross- and time-sequential strategies. The cohort-sequential strategy requires a minimum of two cohorts carried over two ages, implying at least three measurement points.

It will now be argued that for studies of race differences, it is essential to give high priority to the study of race by period interactions, because it seems self-evident that sociocultural change proceeds at a different pace for different racial groups. In studies of ethnicity and aging, moreover, it would seem important to differentiate the age-by-ethnicity and period-by-ethnicity effects in variables known to be age-related and, similarly, to differentiate the cohort-by-ethnicity effect from the period-by-ethnicity effect, where generational differences are implicated. As a consequence, it would seem that the time-sequential and cross-sequential approaches are particularly useful for the study of ethnic differences in relation to the age variable (see Schaie and Hertzog, 1982). The following section will provide a case study applying these techniques.

LIFE SATISFACTION OF BLACKS AND WHITES

Research on life satisfaction in elderly individuals has frequently been concerned with the attempt to identify sociodemographic variables that are correlated with level of life satisfaction. Results of many of these studies, for example, have found a positive relationship between socioeconomic status and satisfaction (Bradburn, 1969; Edwards and Klemmack, 1973). Self-reported health has also been found to correlate positively with life satisfaction, especially in the elderly (Palmore and Kivett, 1977; Sauer, 1977).

Although results with regard to socioeconomic status and health have been quite consistent, this has not been the case with other variables. Studies that have examined sex differences in life satisfaction for men and women over 65, for example, have found that satisfaction is greater for women (Knapp, 1976; Spreitzer and Snyder, 1974). Other studies, however, failed to find this relationship (Bradburn, 1969; Palmore and Kivett, 1977). Specifying the direction of the relationship between life satisfaction and chronological age has also remained a difficult task. Some studies have found a positive relationship between life satisfaction and advancing age (for example, Czaja, 1975), but others showed a negative relationship (Bradburn, 1969; Edwards and Klemmack, 1973) or no relationship at all (Sauer, 1977). Larson (1978) in his recent review concludes that the majority of studies show slight decline in satisfaction in old age, which may be accounted for, however, by age differences in health and income. He also notes that "differences between birth cohorts may play a part in this association or lack of association between age and well-being."

There has been very little research on life satisfaction in elderly blacks (Jackson, Bacon, and Peterson, 1977). The few studies conducted on this topic report that while correlates of life satisfaction may differ for blacks and whites (Jackson, Bacon, and Peterson, 1977; Sauer, 1977), there are no differences in overall levels of satisfaction between blacks and whites when socioeconomic levels are controlled (Bradburn, 1969; Sauer, 1977).

The study presented here as an illustrative example was originally designed to explore the notion that cohort membership may account for more of the variability on life satisfaction ratings than does age and that this contribution will be differential across the two racial groups (Orchowsky and Parham, 1979).

METHODOLOGY

DATA SOURCE AND SUBJECTS

The illustrative study was a secondary analysis of data collected by the National Opinion Research Center (NORC) via interviews of a national probability sample of Americans aged 18 years and older living in noninstitutional settings throughout the country (National Opinion Research Center, 1977). The specific data to be reported on here were taken from the 1973 and 1977 NORC surveys. Only those subjects whose years of birth ranged between 1904 and 1943 (ages 30 to 73) were included. The resulting sample consisted of a total of 1,787 individuals, 922 of whom were interviewed in 1973 and 865 in 1977. There were 818 males and 969 females; 1,587 were white and 200 black.

DESIGN AND DATA ANALYSIS

Data from the two random samples were analyzed using both cross- and time-sequential strategies. For the former, respondents were grouped by birth year into ten consecutive cohorts, each covering a 4-year span. The youngest cohort, for example, consisted of individuals born between 1940 and 1943, and the oldest cohort's members were born between 1904 and 1907. For the time-sequential analysis, respondents were regrouped into ten 4-year age groups, with the youngest group aged 34 to 37 and the oldest group aged 70 to 73 years.

Since previous research consistently found life satisfaction to be related to income and self-reported health, an analysis of covariance (ANOVA) format included these variables as covariates in both types of analysis. The measure of self-reported health was the response to one of the NORC questions requiring perceived health to be rated as excellent, good, fair, or poor. Income was coded in twelve levels (from under $1,000 to $25,000 and over) based on respondents' self-reports of family income for the year prior to the survey.

Finally, race of respondent was included as an independent variable in both analyses. Thus the cross-sequential design had a 2 (races) × 2 (periods) × 10 (cohorts) ANOVA (N = 1,787) format, while the time-sequential design employed a 2 (races) × 2 (periods) × 10 (ages) ANOVA (N = 1,734) format.

LIFE SATISFACTION INDEX

The NORC surveys of 1973 and 1977 asked respondents to indicate satisfaction derived from seven different life domains: family, friends, health, place of residence, nonwork activities, work, and financial situation. The dependent variable used in the analyses was an overall index of life satisfaction created by summing across all components, dividing by the number of domains. The resulting scores could therefore range from 1 to 7, with higher scores indicating greater satisfaction.

RESULTS

AGE AND COHORT EFFECTS

Results of the cross-sequential ANOVA are given in table 24.1. The main effect for cohort was statistically significant, while the main effect for period and the cohort-by-period interaction failed to reach significance. Results of the time-sequential analysis are also shown in table 24.1. This analysis yielded significant main effects for age and period. How are these findings to be interpreted? Although attributions of sources of individual differences derived from sequential strategies generally require the a priori assumption that one of the effects is zero, there are a number of special cases when these assumptions can be empirically verified, as has recently been formally explicated by Adam (1978; also see Schaie and Hertzog, 1982). Violation of the assumption of the absence of age differences in the cross-sequential design will result in the observation of significant main effects for *both* period and cohort, provided there is no significant period-by-cohort interaction. Likewise, violation of the assumption of lack of cohort effect requires the finding of significant main effects for both age and period effects in the time-sequential design. In other words, given the absence of interaction effects, finding cohort but not time effects in the cross-sequential, but both age and period effects in the time-sequential analysis provides an empirical demonstration of the special case where cohort effects favoring the earlier-born cohorts are the only significant components of the presumed developmental difference (also see Schaie and Parham, 1974, 1976).

RACE DIFFERENCES

Both cross- and time-sequential analyses showed significant main effects for race of respondent and significant race-by-period interactions. The three-way interactions were pooled with the error terms because of the relatively small number of black respondents in this study. Mean life satisfaction scores for the effects involving race are shown in the table. In both years blacks reported significantly lower levels of satisfaction than did whites. Black respondents in 1977, however, reported significantly higher levels of satisfaction than did blacks in 1973. This period effect did not occur for the white respondents; and,

TABLE 24.1
Analysis of Variance Results of the Cross-Sequential and Time-Sequential Models of Life Satisfaction Scores

	Cross-Sequential Model				Time-Sequential Model		
Source of Variation	df	MS	F	Source of Variation	df	MS	F
Cohort (C)	9	6.77	10.23**	Age (A)	9	8.29	12.46**
Race (R)[a]	1	16.85	25.47**	Race (R)	1	15.82	23.79**
Period (P)	1	.55	.83	Period (P)	1	3.50	5.26*
C × R	9	.33	.49	A × R	9	.90	1.35
C × P	9	.32	.48	A × P	9	.29	.43
R × P	1	3.25	4.92*	R × P	1	2.67	4.02*
Error	1,754	.66		Error	1,733	.66	
Covariates				Covariates			
Income	1	60.11	90.85**	Income	1	53.93	81.10**
Health	1	153.10	231.40**	Health	1	153.47	230.80**

$*p < .05.$
$**p < .001.$

[a]The mean life satisfaction scores are blacks (N = 200) = 4.74 (1973) and 5.00 (1977); whites (N = 1,587) = 5.47 (1973) and 5.45 (1977).

in fact, whites in 1977 reported slightly lower satisfaction than they did in 1973. These differences remained significant even when controlling for effects of income and self-perceived health. In view of the absence of race-by-age or race-by-cohort effects in the two analyses, these differential findings can be clearly identified as true period effects.

DISCUSSION

The results of the above analyses lend strong support to the conclusion that generational (rather than age) differences account for a major share of individual differences in life satisfaction over the adult life span and that life satisfaction tends to be higher in cohorts born early in this century. More important for present purposes is the finding of the differential impact of sociocultural change depending upon the race of the respondents. The fact that only black respondents in 1977 reported significantly higher levels of satisfaction than was true in 1973, when controlled for age and cohort membership, might suggest that these respondents on the average were beginning to perceive positive societal changes, which affect their overall levels of life satisfaction. Perhaps 1973 was too early for black respondents to perceive positive changes that were to result from the turmoil of the late 1960s and early 1970s, changes that apparently were in evidence by 1977. Although economic gains made by blacks as a group during this period were largely limited to high-income recipients (Villemez and Wiswell, 1978), such gains may nevertheless have effects on modifying the perceptions of the broader black community. It is of interest to note in that context that a fine-grained analysis of the race-by-period interaction reported elsewhere (Orchowsky and Parham, 1979) found increased satisfaction from 1973 to 1977 for all seven domains contained in the life satisfaction index. However, these period effects were greatest for satisfaction with family, hobbies, and place of residence.

SUMMARY

The purpose of this chapter was to show that research on aging and social change affecting minority communities, or the study of differences between ethnic groups, needs to consider the interacting effect of race not only with age, but also with cohort and period effects. To illustrate this point, we presented life satisfaction data, collected for black and white respondents in 1973 and 1977, respectively. In this study it was determined that there were substantial cohort effects in life satisfaction favoring earlier-born cohorts regardless of race, even when state of health and income was controlled. However, there were significant race differences with respect to period effects, with life satisfaction remaining stable for whites, but increasing for blacks over the period studied. These results suggest that past experience may be an important determinant of current levels of life satisfaction and that cohort membership may determine to a great extent what the nature of that past experience may have been. The example studied provides a model for the application of sequential strategies to minority aging issues and provides references to the requisite technical literature.

25

THE DIMENSIONS OF ETHNIC MINORITY IDENTIFICATION: AN EXPLORATORY ANALYSIS AMONG ELDERLY BLACK AMERICANS

RON C. MANUEL

The impact of ethnic minority status upon behavioral, attitudinal, and need criteria is frequently examined in the contemporary gerontological literature. If it is assumed that comparative studies between specified groups of minorities and nonminorities are actually meant to reflect the minority experience, it is instructive to look briefly at the current literature. Paringer and associates (1979), for example, report significantly lower health status among the black (relative to white) elderly; Nowlin (1979), on the other hand, demonstrates little support for the conclusion that elderly blacks are less healthy than elderly whites. Cuellar (1980), summarizing literature on the Hispanic aged, identifies two distinct images of the impact of Hispanic culture on social and familial integration: One perspective views the elderly as respected and central figures in the family; and the second portrays them as abandoned and serving as the objects of intergenerational conflict in a youth-oriented culture. And in yet a third realm, conclusions on a variety of topical areas drawn from the National Council on Aging's nationally representative study of elderly Americans suggest that there are few elderly black and white differences in the United States (Jackson and Walls, 1978), despite a developing literature on the minority aged that generally implies the opposite conclusion (see Manuel, 1982b; Davis, 1980).

The research on which this chapter is based was supported, in part, by the Faculty Research Program in the Social Sciences, Humanities and Education at Howard University, Office of the Vice President for Academic Affairs.

These research findings are obviously inconsistent. The conclusions, in part, illustrate the meaninglessness inherent in current operationalizations of the "minority" concept.[1] Unfortunately, a reading of the literature on elderly minorities reveals a substantial number of ambiguous characterizations of the impact of ethnic minority status. The ambiguous conclusions regarding the explanatory utility of this concept undergirds the basis for this chapter. An underlying assumption, following from the discussion in chapter 2, is that minority-based ethnicity must be properly defined and its complexities explored before it can be applied in analyses that seek to unravel the ambiguous nature of its relation with other factors.

While the task of defining the criteria of an ethnic minority was sufficiently addressed in chapter 2, the relevance of the discussion for the current analysis justifies a brief restatement. Most importantly, the minority elderly, defined, are an ethnic group whose distinctive characteristics, within a sovereign state, have resulted in their (1) victimization by prejudice and discrimination by other, more powerful ethnic groups (the majority) within the sovereignty and (2) tendency toward intragroup interaction, thus strengthening the sense of peoplehood and resulting in a predominantly endogamous group with a common ancestral line. It was shown, when applying this definition to the United States, that four groups readily come to mind: African, Asian, Hispanic, and native Americans.

Although a relatively simple definition, it has not been simple to operationalize the concept. Traditionally, the methodology for measuring the impact of a minority status has rested on the assumption that an individual's mere application of a specified group label to himself could be used as an indication that he had experienced the sociocultural events generally known to be associated with the label. It has been assumed that the fact that an individual identifies himself—or is identified by the investigator—as, say, a native American is indicative that he has been a victim of various discriminatory practices that have been historically operative in American institutional processes. Studies were fashioned, therefore, such that one merely compared categories of ethnically distinct persons in order to identify variations between them on important criterion indicators. This methodology is represented in the studies that were cited in the introduction to this chapter; it is a methodology consistent with what Smith (1980) and Manuel (1982a) refer to, respectively, as the subjective and nominal approaches to measuring ethnic identification.

Ethnic minority identity must be seen as more than merely applying a label. Herman (1977) contends that questions must also be raised in regard to (1) what group attributes the individual sees in himself, (2) how he feels about these attributes, and (3) how he behaves in regard to the attributes associated with the group. Given the complexity of ethnic identification, which is suggested by the variety of answers to the above questions, it is obvious that some individuals' experiences will more closely resemble the experience of members of the majority, than will it resemble the experience of members of their nominally referenced group. That is, the visible heterogeneity of people composing a minority would suggest variation in the extent and manner in which members of this group have been victimized by the ethnic minority status. In the case of elderly black Americans, for example, can it be easily assumed that *all* members of this group have had significantly less of a chance than their white counterparts to participate fully in American institutions. To the contrary, it can be expected that there will be variation, thus resulting in differential circumstances of aging within and between various minority groups.

While measures of the strength of ethnic identification have been introduced in the literature, there have been, to this writer's knowledge, few measures of the extent of identification with an ethnic minority status.[2] But inasmuch as a minority status represents a special category of ethnicity, it is instructive to refer to the brief literature on the measurement of ethnic identification in preparation for constructing a measure of ethnic minority identification.

Although the works of Sandberg (1972), Driedger (1975), and Matsumoto, Meredith, and Masuda (1970) come immediately to mind, Smith (1980) provides the best summary of the current understanding on measuring ethnic identification. Smith observes natal and behavioral approaches, in addition to the subjective methodology, for measuring ethnic identification. The task using the natal approach is to study identification by studying the respondent's (or the respondent's parents') place of birth; ethnicity, following the behavioral approach, is defined according to specified practices, such as group memberships, friendship associations, or language usage. It is the behavioral indicators that most closely approximate measures of ethnic identification.

Unfortunately, as noted earlier, these measures have not been explicitly utilized for describing the minority impact that often characterizes the ethnic group. Moreover, the behavioral measures have not, in general, been standardized nor, as indicated, have they been systematically applicable for discriminating between ethnic populations.[3]

This chapter introduces a hitherto underdeveloped approach for the study of ethnic minority status among the elderly: the measurement of identification with specific minority-related experiences. In the final analysis this type of measurement rests upon insuring that each of the focal criteria, as outlined in the aforementioned definition of a minority, are in fact systematically observed.

There are three research objectives in this study that address this conclusion. The objectives are (1) to develop a measurement scale(s) that reflects individual variation in the extent of identification with a minority status among elderly black Americans, but is potentially applicable for summarizing the minority identification of any individual, (2) to describe the factorial dimensions, or conceptual subscales, of this measure and thereby derive an appropriate set of unidimensional measures of ethnic minority identification, and (3) to examine the validity, factorial stability, and internal consistency of the measure(s).

METHODOLOGY

DATA SOURCE

The responses from two different samples of elderly (50 years and older) black respondents served as data for responding to the research questions. The measurement scales were constructed, and for the most part standardized, on the basis of a nonrandom sample (N = 311) of black elderly residents in publicly subsidized housing in Washington, D.C. The cross-validity of the scales was studied among a nonrandom sample (N = 58) of black elderly participants in a church-based, senior citizens' center also in Washington, D.C. Both sets of sample respondents were identified by church and civic leaders in the community.

The age range was between 50 and 102 (N = 311), with a modal age of 74.5. Socioeconomic background varied little: 85 percent had less than a high school education, and over 80 percent had worked as service workers for most of their lives. The main sample for data generation (N = 311), like the cross-validity sample, was composed predominantly of individuals who were female, had been widowed, and perceived their health to be excellent to fair. A comprehensive sketch of the characteristics of both samples is presented in table 25.1.

DATA COLLECTION AND ANALYSIS

The initial problem consisted of the delineation of a series of empirical indicators. To begin, a large number of items was accumulated from prior studies of ethnic identity; measurement items were selectively borrowed from Sandberg (1972), Driedger (1975), Matsumoto, Meredith, and Masuda (1970), Zak (1973), and Hraba and Siegman (1974). In addition to modifications in these items, additional items were constructed on an a priori basis, designed to reflect the additional dimensionality of a minority status. All items reflected the criteria defining a minority status. These criteria are specified in detail in chapter 2.

An important criterion in the selection, revision, or construction of all items was to insure that the items were easily adaptable—with slight changes in a few key words—across ethnic groups. Consider, for example, the following item: "If I hear of a case of discrimination against blacks, I almost always feel that it concerns me"; with the substitution for the word "black" of another group label, the statement could be made applicable, theoretically at least, for Hispanic, Asian, native, and white American respondents. Due to limited resources, the analyses reported in this paper are based exclusively upon studies with elderly black Americans.

The items were pretested among a small group (N = 10) of elderly black women living within the Washington, D.C., metropolitan area. On the basis of interviews with this group some items were judged to be ambiguous or irrelevant; these were either revised or eliminated. A total of fifty-one forced-

TABLE 25.1

Percentage Distributions for Selected Demographic Characteristics, by Sample

Demographic Characteristics	Original Validation Sample (N)[a]	%	Cross-Validation Sample (N)[a]	%
Age				
50–59	49	16.4	8	18.2
60–69	79	26.5	11	25.0
70–79	114	38.3	20	45.5
80 and Over	56	18.8	5	11.4
Sex				
Male	63	20.3	6	10.3
Female	247	79.7	52	89.7
Level of Education				
Less than 6 Years	74	24.5	7	14.0
6–11 Years	184	60.9	24	48.0
12–16 Years	39	12.9	18	36.0
Over 16 Years	5	1.6	1	2.0
Occupation/Former Occupation				
Service, Laborer	206	81.7	42	82.4
Craftsmen, Operatives, Clerical	38	15.1	7	13.7
Professional, Managerial, Sales	8	3.2	2	3.9
Birthplace (Nationally)				
Northeast	7	2.3	3	5.2
Southeast	293	95.4	53	93.0
Midwest	6	2.0	0	0.0
Far West	1	0.3	1	1.8
Perceived Health				
Excellent to Fair	240	78.2	51	89.5
Poor or Very Poor	67	21.8	6	10.5
Marital Status				
Single	38	12.2	6	10.7
Married	47	15.1	10	17.9
Widowed	169	54.3	27	48.2
Divorced	57	18.4	13	23.2

[a]The numbers responding, per demographic indicator, do not necessarily sum to the total sample size because of missing data.

choice, Likert-scale (4 scale points) indicators, together with other measures designed to provide a broad demographic understanding of the sample, composed the final form of the interview schedule.

Ten trained interviewers, all elderly, black, and female—except one male—completed the interviews for the sample (N = 311, henceforth labelled the original validation sample) within a two-week period during the summer of 1977. The second sample (N = 58, henceforth referred to as the cross-validation sample) was studied during the summer of 1978. Each interview was completed, on the average, within twenty to thirty minutes.

An item analysis of data from the original sample left forty-five items for the scale construction task. In the rejection of each of the six deleted items, the measure failed to discriminate significantly (using the t ratio) between the 25 percent most identified among the sample (those having the lowest index score, when measurement items were summed across all items) and the 25 percent least identified.

The construction of the measurement scales consisted of identifying the dimensionality of the items and establishing the internal consistency and validity of each dimension. By means of the Statistical Package for Social Sciences (SPSS) software package, a principal-factor solution (commonalities in the principal diagonal of the correlation matrix), with varimax rotation, was used to identify the dimensional structure of the items in the original validation sample; factor comparisons between the original sample and the cross-validation sample were subsequently made in order to study the validity and stability of the measurement subscales.

RESULTS

RESEARCH QUESTION 1

The first task was to develop a measure that is potentially applicable for identifying extensiveness of minority identification for any group. Table 25.2 shows the first solution (unrotated). Rummel (1970) indicates that the first unrotated factor represents the most general pattern of relationships in the data. Accordingly, the fact that several of the measurement items correlate highly (.50 or greater) with the factor suggests, in fact, the presence of a general dimension underlying the battery of items. The factor accounted for 32.4 percent of the common variance and 16.3 percent of the total variance.

The raw score sample means and standard deviations for each item are shown in table 25.2.[4] The item means range between 1.4 and 3.1, with typical standard deviations being less than 1. Thus the sample basically straddles the attitudinal continuum (strongly agree, agree, disagree, strongly disagree).

The cross-ethnic applicability of the forty-five items, listed in abbreviated style in table 25.2, was described in the preceding section. The diversity of the content, tapped by these items, is obvious. There are items designed to reflect the extent of minority-related (1) endogamous intragroup relations (for example, items 19, 20, and 28; see table 25.2); (2) victimization by prejudice and

TABLE 25.2
Means, Standard Deviations, and Unrotated Factor Loadings on Factor 1 of Ethnic Minority Identification Items

Single-Item Measures of Ethnic Minority Identification[a]	Mean[b]	S	Factor 1
1. Schools should teach the black contribution	1.4	.59	.72
2. Need organizations to express black views	1.5	.15	.67
3. Blacks must retain culture	1.5	.69	.67
4. Proud of Negro spirituals	1.4	.59	.72
5. Always have had unequal chance to whites for jobs	2.2	.90	-.05
6. Always have had unequal chance to whites for education	2.2	.92	-.06
7. Always have had unequal chance to live as whites	2.2	.98	.06
8. Always have had unequal chance to do as whites	2.5	.80	-.29
9. Enjoy music by blacks more than that by whites	1.8	.93	.43
10. Feeling for blacks is in my blood	1.6	.80	.58
11. All blacks are my kin	1.9	.99	.50
12. Would vote for a black over a white	2.4	1.03	.38
13. For my own people first	1.9	.97	.41
14. Feel praised when other blacks are praised	1.7	.82	.61
15. Need to emphasize black pride	1.9	.94	.31
16. I have less chance to do as whites	2.5	.98	-.15
17. I have less chance than whites to buy things I need	2.5	1.03	-.26
18. I have less chance than whites to buy things I want	2.5	1.03	-.29
19. Relationships with blacks are warmer than with whites	2.1	.92	.38
20. Feel less at ease with whites	2.3	.93	.17
21. I search out crowds for blacks	2.1	.96	.34
22. Feel more at home with blacks than whites	2.0	.95	.30
23. Glad I am black	2.9	.86	.09
24. Would not like to be in a white nursing home	2.9	.89	-.04
25. Would not conceal my racial background	3.1	.79	-.26
26. All blacks experience discrimination	2.7	.96	.38

237

(TABLE 25.2 Continued)
Means, Standard Deviations, and Unrotated Factor Loadings on Factor 1 of Ethnic Minority Identification Items

Single-Item Measures of Ethnic Minority Identification[a]	Mean[b]	S	Factor 1
27. Like to learn about black history	1.7	.81	.51
28. It is better to marry within race	1.6	.89	.48
29. Discrimination is not black's own fault	2.4	1.06	.04
30. Washington needs more black newspapers	1.6	.80	.58
31. There should be all-black communities	2.4	.96	-.32
32. Blacks should be members of black groups	1.6	.72	.58
33. Blacks should assist other blacks in need	1.4	.70	.38
34. NAACP deserves support	1.5	.68	.58
35. I am especially interested in T.V. soap operas with black stars	1.7	.82	.58
36. There is antiblack feeling	2.8	.92	-.13
37. Discrimination is every black's problem	1.7	.84	.38
38. Race has blocked my opportunities	1.9	.88	.13
39. My food, clothing, shelter are not equal to whites	2.6	.80	.08
40. I must work with other blacks to get goals	1.1	.34	.32
41. Race has held me back	2.2	.83	.13
42. My friends are mostly my own race	1.9	.97	.12
43. I feel an attachment to all blacks	1.6	.79	.59
44. Blacks should not disagree among themselves when whites are around	2.1	1.06	.33
45. All discrimination against blacks concerns me	1.6	.80	.52

NOTE: Average N per item is 303.
[a]The item designations refer to key words from each questionnaire measurement indicator.
[b]Raw scores on each item varied from 1 (highest identification) to 4 (lowest identification).

238

discrimination (for example, items 5 and 6); and (3) power limitations (for example, items 17 and 18). There are also items that study general group identification (for example, item 34).

RESEARCH QUESTION 2

Although there were slight correlations between many of the items, there were a number of more substantial correlations ($r \geq .50$) distributed throughout the correlation matrix.[5] The problem was to determine if there were distinct clusters of highly interrelated items, indicating items sharing a common source of statistical variance. Factor analysis was used to determine these clusters or factorial dimensions.

Table 25.3 shows the varimax-rotated factor patterns. The factor solution initially indicated twelve uniquely defined clusters of intercorrelated variables, accounting for 50.5 percent of the total variation in the items. Several of these factors, however, were considered theoretically meaningless; on this basis, only those factors were accepted in which there were at least three items, each sharing, respectively, at least 25 percent (.50 factor loading) of its variance with the underlying source of variation. Six of the twelve factors were dropped from the analysis on this basis.

Generally, when orthogonal rotation is utilized, as in this study, it is intended to isolate clusters of intercorrelated variables that are distinct from each other, but are theoretically covariant within. As a theoretical criterion for considering the six remaining factors for further study, judges (Ph.D. candidates in an advanced statistics class) were asked to interpret each factor descriptively. A factor was included if at least two of the judges agreed independently on the name of the factor. Five factors, the first five produced by the rotated solution, were considered for further analysis. Only items associated with factor loadings of .50 or greater for these five factors (as shown in parenthesis in table 25.3) were used to compose the final factorial dimensions, henceforth called measurement subscales.

The items in each of the subscale sets of items do appear theoretically related. The first subscale, consisting of four items, measures "identity as a perceived need for subcultural continuity." In each case—teaching the black contributions; expressing black views; retaining black culture; or accepting, proudly, one's association with the "Negro spirituals"—the emphasis is upon retaining the culture of the group.

The second subscale, "identity as a perception of lifelong victimization by social injustices," and the fourth, "identity as a perception of existent current victimization by social injustices," were seen as mirror images of a broader concept: "identity as a perception of victimization." Items loading on the third subscale are similar inasmuch as they reflect a general measure of "identity as an awareness of self-group commonality;" that is, identity as an awareness of the unity of interest in self with interest in one's ethnic group. The last dimension or subscale is summarized as "identity as a tendency toward intragroup

TABLE 25.3
Varimax Rotated Factor Weights for Ethnic Minority Identification Measures

Single-Item Measures of Ethnic Minority Identification[a]	Conceptually Meaningful Factor-Based Subscales[b]				
	I	II	III	IV	V
1. Schools should teach the black contribution	(.85)	.04	.10	-.07	.01
2. Need organizations to express black views	(.80)	.03	.10	-.02	.07
3. Blacks must retain culture	(.55)	.07	.18	-.06	.27
4. Proud of Negro spirituals	(.63)	-.02	.27	-.13	.09
5. Always have had unequal chance to whites for jobs	.04	(.75)	-.02	.14	-.08
6. Always have had unequal chance to whites for education	.01	(.79)	.01	.16	.04
7. Always have had unequal chance to live as whites	.14	(.79)	.08	.28	-.02
8. Always have had unequal chance to do as whites	-.25	(.84)	.01	.19	.03
9. Enjoy music by blacks more than that by whites	.23	-.02	(.56)	.16	.02
10. Feeling for blacks is in my blood	.45	.02	(.51)	.10	-.01
11. All blacks are my kin	.16	-.02	(.56)	-.11	.11
12. Would vote for a black over a white	.17	-.01	(.50)	.03	.09
13. For my own people first	.07	.02	(.55)	-.20	.05
14. Feel praised when other blacks are praised	.39	.07	(.57)	-.05	.04
15. Need to emphasize black pride	.06	-.04	(.55)	-.00	-.06
16. I have less chance to do as whites	.01	.41	-.07	(.66)	-.04
17. I have less chance than whites to buy things I need	-.08	.26	-.03	(.84)	-.16
18. I have less chance than whites to buy things I want	-.08	.30	-.03	(.77)	-.18
19. Relationships with blacks are warmer than with whites	.21	-.02	.02	-.05	(.59)
20. Feel less at ease with whites	-.02	.00	.10	.00	(.50)
21. I search out crowds for blacks	.10	-.08	-.04	-.18	(.65)

(TABLE 25.3 Continued)
Varimax Rotated Factor Weights for Ethnic Minority Identification Measures

Single-Item Measures of Ethnic Minority Identification[a]	Conceptually Meaningful Factor-Based Subscales[b]				
	I	II	III	IV	V
22. Feel more at home with blacks than whites	.11	.08	.10	-.10	(.62)
23. Glad I am black	.03	.10	.01	-.03	.02
24. Would not like to be in a white nursing home	-.00	.07	.12	.20	-.05
25. Would not conceal my racial background	.26	.04	-.06	.10	.06
26. All blacks experience discrimination	.08	.23	.07	-.03	-.28
27. Like to learn about black history	.42	.03	.15	.11	.19
28. It is better to marry within race	.27	.05	.41	-.13	.20
29. Discrimination is not black's own fault	-.07	.11	.22	.11	-.19
30. Washington needs more black newspapers	.49	.05	.36	.01	.04
31. There should be all-black communities	-.21	.02	-.01	.05	-.18
32. Blacks should be members of black groups	.47	-.11	.11	-.05	.21
33. Blacks should assist other blacks in need	.31	-.03	-.05	-.08	.18
34. NAACP deserves support	.47	-.07	.09	-.12	.07
35. I am especially interested in T.V. soap operas with black stars	.41	-.02	.08	-.10	.26
36. There is antiblack feeling	-.11	.08	.03	.05	.02
37. Discrimination is every black's problem	.21	-.16	.09	-.09	.28
38. Race has blocked opportunities	.07	.22	-.13	.14	.25
39. My food, clothing, shelter are not equal to whites	.03	.15	.10	.24	-.08
40. I must work with other blacks to get goals	.25	-.01	.05	.00	.07
41. Race has held me back	.12	.10	.22	.16	-.10
42. My friends are mostly my own race	.01	.09	.19	.02	-.06

(TABLE 25.3 Continued)
Varimax Rotated Factor Weights for Ethnic Minority Identification Measures

Single-Item Measures of Ethnic Minority Identification[a]	Conceptually Meaningful Factor-Based Subscales[b]				
	I	II	III	IV	V
43. I feel an attachment to all blacks	.3 6	-.09	.18	-.00	.17
44. Blacks should not disagree among themselves when whites are around	.14	-.07	.27	-.02	.03
45. All discrimination against blacks concerns me	.49	-.03	.18	.09	.07

NOTE: Average N per item is 303.

[a]The item designations refer to key words from each questionnaire measurement indicator.

[b]Raw scores on each item varied from 1 (highest identification) to 4 (lowest identification). Weighted subscale scores varied respectively as follows: I, .70 (highest identification) to 2.83 (lowest identification); II, .54 to 2.17; III, .80 to 3.19; IV, .77 to 3.97; V, .59 to 2.36. Factor-based subscales I through V are named, respectively, "identity as a perceived need for subcultural continuity"; "identity as a perception of lifelong victimization by social injustices"; "identity as an awareness of self-group commonality"; "identity as a perception of existent current victimization by social injustices"; "identity as a tendency toward intragroup social interaction."

social interaction." Thus feeling warmer, more at ease, more at home, or more comfortable and secure in the company of other persons in the group suggests similar psychological benefits resulting from endogamous relations.

In summary, the analyses in this section suggest five distinctive conceptual dimensions of ethnic minority identification. The items, composing the respective subscales, when seen in toto clearly reflect the various features of a minority group: the endogamous nature of social relations, the victimized circumstances and power subordination, as well as the sense of group commonality.

RESEARCH QUESTION 3

In the final set of analyses, a study is made of the validity and internal consistency of the respective measurement scales. Actually, both of these criteria have been described to some extent by the definition of the factor procedure. That is, the construct validity of the subsets of items has been automatically established by the theoretical link characterizing each of the statistically produced set of items. But because replication of results is the basis for the development of scientific knowledge, it is advantageous to maximize the generality of the scaling endeavors. To begin the process of standardization for the preceding study, this section reviews the evidence from further analyses of the validity and internal consistency of the measurement subscales.

To examine the stability of the ethnic minority identification (EMI) measures, a study of the factorial invariance of the subscale patterns is completed with a cross-validation sample (N = 58).[6] The primary inquiry is whether the respective subscale factor loading patterns, as standardized on the original sample, are similar to patterns of loadings for the cross-validation sample. Pearson r was used to assess the extent of invariance between the two factor-produced weighting schemes for each subscale pattern. All analyses were calculated using the cross-validation sample data. Thus correlations were made between (1) the average subscale scores (N = 58) with each individual score weighted by the varimax factor loadings from the original validation study and (2) the same scores (N = 58), with each individual score weighted by the varimax factor loading derived from the cross-validation study. The coefficients appear in table 25.4; each indicates a high degree of invariance between the two weighting patterns for each of the measurement scales (the lowest: r = .93; and the highest: r = .99). Harman (1967) implies that coefficients equal to or above .93 should be accepted as indicative of factorial stability.[7]

Finally, table 25.4 presents the means, standard deviations, and measures of internal consistency for the original validation sample. The measures of internal consistency (Pearson r) describe the average degree of interrelatedness or correlation among the respective scale items. While it is evident that the items composing, respectively, subscales I, II, and IV are reasonably consistent, it is equally clear that items associated with subscales III and V are not highly intercorrelated. In general, these conclusions follow from the relative magni-

TABLE 25.4
Means, Standard Deviations, and Pearson r Measures for
Studies of Cross-Validation[a] and Internal Consistency (r_{ic})[b] of
Ethnic Minority Identification (EMI) Scales

EMI SCALES *Based on Varimax Factor* *Weights for Original* *Validation Sample,* *N = 311*		*EMI SCALES* *Based on Varimax Factor Weights* *for Cross-Validation Sample, N = 58*				
		I	II	III	IV	V
I		.98				
r_{ic}	.55					
$\overline{x}$	1.09					
s	.36					
II			.93			
r_{ic}	.67					
$\overline{x}$	1.08					
s	.21					
III				.99		
r_{ic}	.34					
$\overline{x}$	2.23					
s	.60					
IV					.99	
r_{ic}	.71					
$\overline{x}$	2.00					
s	.75					
V						.94
r_{ic}	.36					
$\overline{x}$	1.28					
s	.26					

[a]For each of the subscales Pearson r was used to assess the degree of invariance between the varimax factor weights derived from the original validation study and the weights derived from the cross-validation study. Correlations were made using only the cross-validation sample data (N = 58).

[b]Internal consistency (r_{ic}) refers to the average of the correlations between the items that compose the respective scales.

tude of the varimax rotated item loadings. Subscales I, II, and IV (relative to subscales III and V) are each more sharply delineated as distinctive clusters of interrelated variables. In future studies the development of additional indicators, reflective of the latter two dimensions, should contribute to clarifying or improving the internal consistency of subscales III and V.

SUMMARY AND CONCLUSIONS

The purpose of this analysis has been to introduce a variable, as contrasted to attribute, measure of ethnic minority identification. It was reasoned that a nominal or attribute approach to the measurement of a minority status—as is popular in today's gerontological and ethnic literature—leaves individual variation in identification with a minority experience unanalyzed and, as such, fails to weigh the considerable heterogeneity existing within the minority group. Consequently, a substantial part of the inconsistency in research conclusions regarding the explanatory significance of a minority status may be an artifact of the level of measurement sophistication. With this perspective three specific research objectives were outlined: (1) the development of a potentially versatile measure reflecting individual variation in the extent of ethnic minority identification among elderly black Americans, (2) the description of the conceptual dimensions of this measure, and (3) the examination of the measurement validity and stability of the measure, beyond the original validation sample.

Examining data from two separate samples of elderly black Americans, one may draw the following conclusions. First, from a clearly specified definition of a minority status, a forty-five-item Likert-scaled measure of ethnic minority identification was described. Although the current data did not permit statistical tests of the cross-subcultural validity of the items on an a priori basis, it would appear relatively easy to apply the items, with a few changes in wording, to other ethnic minorities as well as nonminorities. Most importantly, the Likert response categories permit the observation of variation in identification with ethnic minority criteria.

Next, based upon statistical as well as theoretical criteria, five distinctive statistical factors or conceptual subscale dimensions of ethnic minority identification were described. These include (1) "identity as a perceived need for subcultural continuity"; (2) "identity as a perception of lifelong victimization by social injustices"; (3) "identity as an awareness of self-group commonality"; (4) "identity as a perception of existent current victimization by social injustices; and (5) "identity as a tendency toward intragroup social interaction." Each subscale is based on those items with substantively significant varimax rotated factor loadings.

Finally, each subscale was studied in order to describe its validity and internal consistency. Excluding the internal consistency for subscales III and V, both the validity and internal consistency of the measures were generally impressive. Besides construct validity, as defined by the factor analytic procedure, evidence from the cross-validation studies indicates the stability of the factor-based dimensional structure of the items, across samples.

There are two interrelated, broadly defined sets of implications suggested by the conclusions of the research. The first is predominantly methodological and the second predominantly theoretical in orientation. Methodologically, while no claim is made to have perfected a scale for measuring ethnic minority identification among the elderly, it is assumed that the desirability has been kindled for a quantitative approach to a concept that figures prominently in the study of aging and the aged. It is imperative, however, in view of the nonrandom samples on which the subscales were standardized, that this study be followed by additional validational efforts. In addition to its application to random samples of black and other minorities, the individual items—or perhaps additional items that might extend the content reflective of the minority experience—should be studied among the nonminority population. Ideally, the measurement indicators should be worded generally so that they are easily applicable to varying groups.

Having standardized a measure of ethnic minority identification, investigators can begin to restudy the impact of a minority status on various criterion measures in social gerontology. Herein lies the major theoretical implication of the conclusions. In fact, a measure reflecting individual variation in minority background experiences may produce new evidence on both those factors studied as determinants, as well as consequences of a minority status.

This report thus proposes the replacement of the nominal approach to the measurement of minority status. Rather than dividing a sample into, say, elderly blacks and whites for comparative purposes, research investigators should consider incorporating variable measures, such as the subscales introduced in this paper, of the ethnic minority concept. In the final analysis, regardless of the relation between minority status and other relevant variables, a new level of confidence can be placed in the conclusions, given a more precise technology for observing the relations.

NOTES

1. The reader may wish to review chapter 2 inasmuch as the current discussion is a logical extension of the ideas introduced in that chapter.

2. In addition to ethnic identification, consideration of a related concept, ethnic consciousness— or, as more typically studied, race (or black) consciousness—is also important. Race or ethnic consciousness, or even conceivably "minority consciousness," when used in the sense of the latter concepts, is not synonymous with ethnic minority identification. While consciousness, like identification, refers to how a group of individuals define the situation they believe they face, it also, unlike identification, points to attitudinal commitments regarding how the group should react, collectively, to the perceived situation (see Pitts, 1974).

3. Manuel (1982a) has stipulated four criteria for measuring ethnic identification. In addition to describing extensiveness, the measure should reflect the multidimensionality of content inherent in the concept; third, the measure should be cross-ethnically applicable and, relatedly, must be statistically standardized. The reader is referred to Manuel (1982a) for a review and critique of current variation type measures of ethnic identification.

4. Scores on each item varied from 1 to 4; lower scores were consistent with higher ethnic minority identification. Although the abbreviated listing of the items in tables 25.2 and 25.3 are stated with consistent direction (agreement with the item is synonymous with identification), the direction of the items varied on the interview form.

5. Because of space limitations, the correlation matrix for the forty-five measurement indicators is not printed.

6. In addition to similar factor analytic procedures, the analyses with the cross-validation sample were based on the same measurement indicators as used with the original sample. See Mulaik (1972) for a discussion of the pitfalls in comparing factor studies; see Harman (1967) or Rummel (1970) for nontechnical reviews of methodological approaches to comparing factors; also see Meredith (1964) and Jöreskog (1971) for related theoretical considerations in the study of factorial invariance.

7. While Meredith (1964) and Jöreskog (1971) suggest additional criteria (for example, rotation to similarity) for increasing the association between patterns, it is reasoned that the factor comparison coefficients are of sufficient magnitude to eliminate the need for additional control procedures.

REFERENCES

Abbott, Julian
1977 "Socioeconomic characteristics of the elderly: some black-white differences." Social Security Bulletin 40 (7):16–42.

Achenbaum, W. Andrew
1978 Old Age in the New Land: The American Experience Since 1970. Baltimore: Johns Hopkins University Press.

Adam, June
1978 "Sequential strategies and the separation of age, cohort, and time-of-measurement contributions to developmental data." Psychological Bulletin 85 (November): 1309–1316.

Adams, David L.
1971 "Correlates of satisfaction among the elderly." Gerontologist 11 (Winter): 44–47.

Administration on Aging
1980 Use of Discretionary Resources Under the Older Americans Act, 1980. Administration on Aging, Washington, D.C. Office of Human Development Services, Department of Health and Human Services.

Allport, Gordon
1958 The Nature of Prejudice. Boston: Beacon Press.

Almquist, Elizabeth M.
1979 Minorities, Gender and Work. Lexington, Massachusetts: D. C. Heath and Company.

Althauser, R. P., and associates
1975 The Unequal Elites. New York: John Wiley and Sons.

American Psychiatric Association
1980 Diagnostic and Statistical Manual of Mental Disorders (DSM III). 3d. edition. Washington, D.C.: American Psychiatric Association, Division of Public Affairs.

Anderson, Ronald, and associates
1975 Equity in Health Services: Empirical Analyses in Social Policy. Cambridge, Massachusetts: Ballinger Publishing Company.

Arensberg, Conrad and Solon Kimball
1968 Family and Community in Ireland. 2d edition. Cambridge, Massachusetts: Harvard University Press.

Bahr, Howard M.; Bruce A. Chadwick; and Joseph H. Stauss
  1979   American Ethnicity. Lexington, Massachusetts: D. C. Heath and Company.

Barron, Robert A.
  1977   Human Aggression. New York: Plenum Press.

Beard, Virginia H.
  1977   "Health status of a successful black aged population related to life satisfaction and
         self-concept." In Wilbur H. Watson and Associates (eds.), Health and the Black Aged.
         Washington, D.C.: National Center on Black Aged.

Beatty, Walter M.
  1960   "The aging Negro: some implications for social welfare services." Phylon 21 (2):131–135.

Bechill, William
  1979   "Politics of aging and ethnicity." In Donald Gelfand and Alfred Kutzik (eds.), Ethnicity
         and Aging. New York: Springer Publishing Company.

Bell, Duran, and Gail Zellman
  1976   Issues in Service Delivery to Ethnic Elderly. Santa Monica, California: Rand Corpora-
         tion.

Bell, Duran; Patricia Kasschau; and Gail Zellman
  1976a Characteristics of the Black Elderly. Santa Monica, California: Rand Corporation.
  1976b Delivery Services to Elderly Members of Minority Groups: A Critical Review of the
         Literature. Santa Monica, California: Rand Corporation.

Bengtson, Vern L.
  1979   "Problems and issues in current social science inquiry." In Donald Gelfand and Alfred
         Kutzik (eds.), Ethnicity and Aging: Theory, Research, and Policy. Chicago: Springer
         Publishing Company.

Bengtson, Vern L., and associates
  1977   "Relating academic research to community concerns: a case study in collaborative
         effort." Journal of Social Issues 33 (4): 75–92.

Bengtson, Vern L., and Linda Burton
  1980   "Familism, ethnicity and support systems: patterns of contrast and congruence." Paper
         presented during the 33d Annual Meeting of the Gerontological Society, San Diego,
         California.

Bernard, Viola
  1972   "Interracial practice in the midst of change." American Journal of Psychiatry 128 (8):
         978.

Berreman, Gerald D.
  1972   "Race, caste and other invidious distinctions in social stratification." Race 13:385–414.

Bianco, Carla
  1974   The Two Rosettos. Bloomington, Indiana: Indiana University Press.

Bild, Bernice, and Robert Havighurst
  1976   "The life of elderly in large cities." Gerontologist 16 (1): part 2.

Billingsley, Andrew
  1968   Black Families in White America. Englewood Cliffs, New Jersey: Prentice-Hall.
  1969   "Family functioning in the low income black community." Social Casework 50 (Decem-
         ber): 287–337.
  1970   "Black families and white social science." Journal of Social Issues 26 (3):127–142.

Binstock, Robert H.
  1974   "Aging and the future of American politics." Annals of the American Academy of

Political and Social Science 415 (September):199–212.

1978   "Federal policy toward the aging: its inadequacies and its politics." In The Economics of Aging: A National Journal of Issues Book. Washington, D.C.: Government Research Corporation.

1981   "Summary Statement" (Proceedings of the Seventh National Institute on Minority Aging). In E. Percil Stanford (ed.), Minority Aging: Policy Issues for the '80s. San Diego, California: University Center on Aging, San Diego State University.

Blalock, Hubert
1967   Toward a Theory of Minority-Group Relations. New York: Capricorn Books.

Blauner, Robert
1966   "Death and social structure." Psychiatry 29: 378–394.

1970   "Black culture: myth or reality." In Norman E. Whitten and John F. Szwed (eds.), Afro-American Anthropology. New York: Free Press.

Bonavich, Edna
1972   "A theory of ethnic antagonism: the split labor market." American Sociological Review 37 (October):547–559.

Bozak, B. A., and E. Gjullin
1979   "Nursing homes and the black elderly." Paper presented during the 32d Annual Meeting of the Gerontological Society, Washington, D.C.

Bradburn, N. M.
1969   The Structure of Psychological Well-being. Chicago: Aldine Publishing Company.

Brazziel, William F.
1973   "White research in black communities: when solutions become a part of the problem." Journal of Social Sciences 29 (1):41–44.

Bromley, David G., and Charles F. Longino
1972   White Racism and Black Americans. Cambridge, Massachusetts: Schenkman Publishing Company.

Brown, Carol
1981   Personal conversation. Special Assistant for Minority Affairs to the Commissioner on Aging, Administration on Aging, U.S. Department of Health and Human Services.

Bullough, Bonnie
1972   Poverty, Ethnic Identity and Health. Englewood Cliffs, New Jersey: Appleton-Century, Crofts.

Butler, Robert N., and Myrna I. Lewis
1977   Aging and Mental Health: Positive Psychosocial Approaches. 2d edition. Saint Louis: C. V. Mosby Company.

Cahalan, Don; Ira Cisin; and Helen Crossley
1969   American Drinking Practices: A National Study of Drinking Behavior and Attitudes. New Haven: College and University Press.

Calhoun, Richard B.
1978   In Search of the New Old: Redefining Old Age in America, 1945–1970. New York: Elsevier North-Holland.

Carlson, Robert E.
1979   Retired Strategies: Income from Ownership. Washington, D.C.: Koba Associates, Inc.

Carp, Frances M.
1969   Factors in Utilization of Services by the Mexican American Elderly. Palo Alto, California: American Institute for Research.

Carter, Allen C., and J. Managaroo
  1979   "The psycho-social role of the church in a rural black elderly population." Unpublished paper. Psychology Department, Morehouse College, Atlanta, Georgia.

Carter, James H.
  1972   "Differential treatment of the elderly black, victims of stereotyping." Postgraduate Medicine 52 (5):211–213.
  1974   "Recognizing psychiatric symptoms in black Americans." Geriatrics 29 (November): 96–99.

Cheung, Lucia Yim-San, and associates
  1980   The Chinese Elderly and Family Structure. Public Health Reports 95 (number 5).

Chodorow, Nancy
  1978   The Reproduction of Mothering: Psychoanalysis and the Sociology of Gender. Berkeley and Los Angeles: University of California Press.

Clark, Margaret, and Monique Mendelson
  1969   "Mexican-American aged in San Francisco: a case description." Gerontologist 9 (2):90–95.

Clausen, John A.
  1956   Sociology and the Field of Mental Health. New York: Russell Sage Foundation.

Cohler, Bertram
  1981   "Personality, social context, and adaptation to motherhood." In Rebecca Cohen, Sidney Weissman, and Bertram Cohler (eds.), Parenthood as an Adult Experience. New York: Guilford Press.

Cohler, Bertram, and Henry Grunebaum
  1981   Mothers, Grandmothers and Daughters: Personality and Socialization Within Three Generation Families. New York: John Wiley and Sons.

Cohler, Bertram, and Morton Lieberman
  1979   "Personality change across the second half of life: findings from a study of Irish, Italian, and Polish-American men and women." In Donald Gelfand and Alfred J. Kutzik (eds.), Ethnicity and Aging: Theory, Research and Policy. New York: Springer Publishing Company.
  1980   "Social relations and mental health among middle-aged and older men and women from three European ethnic groups." Research on Aging 2 (December):445–469.

Cole, Johnetta B.
  1971   The Black Way of Life: An Anthropologist's Approach. University of Massachusetts Alumnus 2 (3):11–15.

Colen, John N.
  1979   "Critical issues in the development of environmental support systems for the aged." Allied Health and Behavioral Sciences 2 (1):77–90.

Colen, John N., and David Soto
  1979   Service Delivery to Aged Minorities: Techniques of Successful Programs. Sacramento, California: School of Social Work, California State University.

Collins, Alice, and Diane Pancoast
  1976   Natural Helping Networks: A Strategy for Prevention. Washington, D.C.: National Association of Social Workers.

Congressional Budget Office
  1976   Poverty Status of Families, 1976. Washington, D.C.: U.S. Government Printing Office.

Connelly, Richard J.
  1980   "An expanded outline and resource for teaching a course on the native American

elderly." In George Sherman (ed.), Curriculum Guidelines in Minority Aging. Washington, D.C.: National Center on Black Aged.

Cottrell, Fred
   1960 "Government functions and the politics of age." In Clark Tibbetts (ed.), Handbook of Social Gerontology. Chicago: University of Chicago Press.

Cox, Oliver C.
   1948 Caste, Class and Race. New York: Doubleday & Company.

Crandall, Richard C.
   1980 Gerontology: A Behavioral Science Approach. Reading, Massachusetts: Addison-Wesley.

Cromwell, Ronald E.; C. Edwin Vaughan; and Charles Mindel
   1975 "Ethnic minority family research in an urban setting: a process of exchange." American Sociologist 10 (3):141–150.

Cuellar, Jose B.
   1980 "An expanded outline and resource guide for teaching an introduction to Hispanic aging." In George Sherman (ed.), Curriculum Guidelines in Minority Aging. Washington, D.C.: National Center on the Black Aged.

Cuellar, Jose B., and John R. Weeks
   1980 Minority Elderly Americans: A Prototype for Area Agencies on Aging. Executive Summary, Administration on Aging, Grant No. 90-A-1667 (01). San Diego, California: Allied Home Health Association.

Cumming, Elaine
   1976 "Further thoughts on the theory of disengagement." In Cary S. Kart and Barbara B. Manard (eds.), Aging in America. New York: Alfred Publishing Company.

Cumming, Elaine, and William E. Henry
   1961 Growing Old: The Process of Disengagement. New York: Basic Books.

Czaja, Sara J.
   1975 "Age differences in life satisfaction as a function of discrepancy between real and ideal self concepts." Experimental Aging Research 1 (September):81–89.

Dahrendorf, Ralf
   1959 Class and Class Conflict in Industrial Society. Stanford, California: Stanford University Press.

Dancy, Joseph
   1977 The Black Elderly: A Guide for Practitioners. Ann Arbor, Michigan: Institute of Gerontology, University of Michigan–Wayne State University.

Davis, F. James
   1978 Minority-Dominant Relations: A Sociological Analysis. Arlington Heights, Illinois: AHM Publishing Corporation.

Davis, Lenwood G.
   1980 The Black Aged in the United States: An Annotated Bibliography. Westport, Connecticut: Greenwood Press.

de Beauvoir, Simone
   1972 The Coming of Age. New York: Putnam Books.

Demeny, P., and P. Gingrich
   1967 "A reconsideration of Negro-White mortality differentials in the United States." Demography 4 (2):820–837.

Dennis, Ruth
    1977   "Social stress and mortality among nonwhite males." Phylon 38 (3):315–327.

de Tocqueville, Alexis
    1945   Democracy in America. New York: Vintage Books.

Dougherty, Marilyn C.
    1978   Becoming a Woman in Rural Black Culture. New York: Holt, Rinehart and Winston.

Dowd, James J.
    1978   "Aging as exchange: a test of the distributive justice proposition." Pacific Sociological
            Review 21:351–375.
    1980   Stratification Among the Aged. Monterey, California: Brooks/Cole.

Dowd, James J., and Vern L. Bengtson
    1978   "Aging in minority populations: an examination of the double jeopardy hypothesis."
            Journal of Gerontology 33 (3):427–436.

Drakes, St. Clair, and Horace R. Cayton
    1945   Black Metropolis: A Study of Negro Life in a Northern City. New York: Harcourt,
            Brace and Company.

Driedger, Leo
    1975   "In search of cultural identity factors: a comparison of ethnic students." Canadian
            Review of Sociology and Anthropology 12 (2):150–162.

Du Bois, W.E.B.
    1909   Efforts for Social Betterment Among Negro Americans. Atlanta: Atlanta University
            Press.

Du Bois, W.E.B., and Augustus G. Dill
    1914   Morals and Manners Among Negro Americans. Atlanta: Atlanta University Press.

Dudley, Donald L., and Elton Welke
    1977   How to Survive Being Alive: Stress Points and Your Health. New York: Doubleday &
            Company.

Dunn, L. C., and Theodosius Dobzhansky
    1964   Heredity, Race and Society. New York: New American Library.

Edwards, John N., and David L. Klemmack
    1973   "Correlates of life satisfaction: a re-examination." Journal of Gerontology 28 (October):
            497–502.

Edwards, Paul
    1967   The Encyclopedia of Philosophy. New York: Macmillan and the Free Press.

Ekeh, Peter
    1974   Social Exchange Theory. Cambridge, Massachusetts: Harvard University Press.

Elling, Ray, and Russell Martin
    1974   Health Care for the Urban Poor: A Study of Hartford's North End. Connecticut
            Research Series, no. 5. Hartford, Connecticut: Connecticut Health Services.

Erickson, Gerald
    1975   "The concept of personal network in clinical practice." Family Process 14 (4):487–498.

Estes, Carroll L.
    1979   The Aging Enterprise. San Francisco: Jossey-Bass.

Fandetti, Donald, and Donald D. Gelfand
    1976   "Care of the aged: Attitudes of white ethnic families." Gerontologist 16 (6):544–549.

Faris, Robert E. L., and H. Warren Dunham
   1967   Mental Disorders in Urban Areas. Chicago: University of Chicago Press.

Feder, Judith, and John Holahan
   1979   Financing Health Care for the Elderly: Medicare, Medicaid and Private Health
           Insurance. Washington, D.C.: Urban Institute.

Federal Council on the Aging
   1976   Annual Report to the President, 1976. Washington, D.C.: U.S. Government Printing
           Office.

Federal Reserve Bank of Boston
   1976   Funding Pensions: Issues and Implications for Financial Markets. Boston: Federal
           Reserve Bank of Boston, Public Information Center.

Fienberg, Sam E., and William M. Mason
   1979   "Identification and estimation of age-period-cohort models in the analysis of discrete
           archival data." In Karl Schuessler (ed.), Sociological Methodology. San Francisco:
           Jossey-Bass.

Firth, Raymond; Jane Forge; and Anthony A. Forge
   1970   Families and Their Relatives: Kinship in a Middle Class Sector of London. New York:
           Humanities Press.

Fischer, David H.
   1978   Growing Old in America. New York: Oxford University Press.

Frazier, E. Franklin
   1964   The Negro Church in America. New York: Schocken Books.
   1966   The Negro in the United States. Chicago: University of Chicago Press.

Freeman, Joseph
   1979   Aging: Its History and Literature. New York: Human Sciences Press.

Fried, Marc
   1973   The World of Urban Working Class. Cambridge, Massachusetts: Harvard University
           Press.

Froland, Charles, and associates
   1981   Helping Networks and Human Services: Creating a Partnership. Beverly Hills,
           California: Sage Publications.

Fuji, Sharon
   1976   "Elderly Asian Americans and use of public services." Social Casework 57 (3):
           202–207.

Gans, Herbert J.
   1972   "The positive functions of poverty." American Journal of Sociology 78:275–289.

Garvin, Richard M., and Robert E. Burger
   1968   Where They Go to Die. New York: Delacorte Press.

Gelfand, Donald E., and Alfred J. Kutzik
   1979   Ethnicity and Aging: Theory, Research, and Policy. New York: Springer Publishing
           Company.

Gil, Davis
   1976   Unraveling Social Policy. Cambridge, Massachusetts: Schenkman Publishing Com-
           pany.

Glaser, Barney C., and Anselm L. Strauss
  1968   Time for Dying: Chicago: Aldine Publishing Company.

Golden, Herbert M.
  1980   "Black ageism: relative deprivation revisited." In Beth B. Hess (ed.), Growing Old in
          America. 2d edition. New Brunswick, New Jersey: Transaction Books.

Gomes, Ralph
  1981   "Changing perspectives on class and race." Black Sociologist Newsletter 10 (1):7.

Gordon, Milton M.
  1978   Human Nature, Class and Ethnicity. New York: Oxford University Press.

Grad, Susan
  1977   "Income of the population aged 60 and older, 1971." Staff Paper number 26. Washington,
          D.C.: Social Security Administration.

Grad, Susan, and Karen Foster
  1979   "Income of the population, 55 and over." Social Security Bulletin 42 (7):29.

Greeley, Andrew
  1974   Ethnicity in the United States. New York: John Wiley and Sons.
  1976   Ethnicity, Denomination and Inequality. Beverly Hills, California: Sage Publica-
          tions.

Grier, William H., and Price M. Cobbs
  1971   The Jesus Bag. New York: McGraw-Hill.

Gruman, Gerald J.
  1977   A History of Ideas About the Prolongation of Life. New York: Arno Press.

Guillemard, Anne-Marie
  1975   "Gerontology: a relatively new area of social science in France." Gerontologist 15
          (3):212–218.

Gutman, Herbert G.
  1976   The Black Family in Slavery and Freedom, 1750–1925. New York: Pantheon
          Books.

Gutmann, Davis
  1975   "Parenthood: a key to the comparative study of the life cycle." In Nancy Datan and
          Leeny Ginsberg (eds.), Life-Span Developmental Psychology: Normative Crises. New
          York: Academic Press.

Guttmann, David
  1980   Perspectives on Equitable Share in Public Benefits by Minority Elderly. Executive
          Summary, Administration on Aging, Grant No. 90-A-1617. Washington, D.C.: Catho-
          lic University of America.

Hanson, Wynne
  1978   "Grief counseling with Native Americans." White Cloud Journal 1 (2):9–21.

Harman, Harry
  1967   Modern Factor Analysis. 3d edition. Chicago: University of Chicago Press.

Harris, Louis, and associates
  1974   The Myth and Reality of Aging in America. Washington, D.C.: National Council on
          Aging.

Harris, Seymour E.
  1975   Economics of Health Care: Finance and Delivery. Berkeley, California: McCupchan
          Publishing Corporation.

Heath, Anthony
  1976   Rational Choice and Social Exchange. London: Cambridge University Press.

Heisel, Marsel A., and Margaret E. Moore
  1973   "Social interaction and isolation of elderly blacks." Gerontologist 13 (3):100.

Henderson, George
  1965   "The Negro recipient of old-age assistance: results of discrimination." Social Casework
          46 (4):208–215.

Hendricks, Jon, and C. Davis Hendricks
  1981   Aging in Mass Society: Myths and Realities. Cambridge, Massachusetts: Winthrop
          Publishers.

Henretta, John C., and Richard T. Campbell
  1976   "Status attainment and status maintenance: a study of stratification in old age."
          American Sociological Review 41 (6):981–982.

Henle, Peter
  1972   "Recent trends in retirement benefits related to earnings." Monthly Labor Review
          95:12–20.

Herman, Simon N.
  1977   Jewish Identity: A Social Psychological Perspective. Beverly Hills, California: Sage
          Publications.

Hill, Charles A.
  1970   "Measures of longevity of American Indians." Public Health Reports 85 (March):
          233–239.

Hill, Robert
  1972   The Strengths of Black Families. New York: Emerson Hall.
  1978   "A demographic profile of the black elderly." Aging (September/October):2–9.

Hill, Robert, and Lawrence Shackleford
  1975   "The black extended family revisited." Urban League Review 1:18–24.

Hollingshead, August B., and Frederick C. Redlich
  1958   Social Class and Mental Illness: A Community Study. New York: John Wiley and
          Sons.

Holzman, Abraham
  1954   "Analysis of old age politics in the United States." Journal of Gerontology 9
          (1):56–66.

Homans, George
  1961   Social Behavior: Its Elementary Forms. New York: Harcourt, Brace and World.

Hraba, Joseph, and Jack Siegman
  1974   "Black consciousness." Youth and Society 6 (1):63–89.

Iskrant, Albert, and Paul Joliet
  1968   Accidents and Homicide. Cambridge, Massachusetts: Harvard University Press.

Jackson, Jacquelyne J.
  1967   "Social gerontology and the Negro: a review." Gerontologist 7 (3):168–178.
  1970   "Aged Negroes: their cultural departures from statistical stereotypes and urban-rural
          differences." Gerontologist 10 (2):140–145.
  1971a   "Aged blacks: a potpourri in the direction of the reduction of inequities." Phylon 32
          (Fall):260–280.

1971b "Negro aged: toward needed research in social gerontology." Gerontologist 11 (Spring):52–57.

1972a "Comparative life-styles and family and friend relationships among older black women." Family Coordinator 21 (October):477–485.

1972b "Social impacts of housing relocation upon urban, low-income black aged." Gerontologist (1):32–37.

1974   "NCBA, black aged and politics." Annals of the American Academy of Political and Social Science 415 (September):138–159.

1980   Minorities and Aging. Belmont, California: Wadsworth Publishing Company.

Jackson, Jacquelyne J., and Bertram Walls
1978   "Myths and realities about aged blacks." In Mollie Brown (ed.), Readings in Gerontology. 2d edition. Saint Louis: C. V. Mosby Company.

Jackson, James S.; John Bacon; and John Peterson
1977   "Life satisfaction among black urban elderly." Aging and Human Development 8 (2):169–179.

Jackson, Maurice, and James L. Wood
1976   Aging in America: Implications for the Black Aged. Washington, D.C.: National Council on Aging.

Jaffe, A. J.; Ruth Cullen; and Thomas D. Boswell
1976   Spanish Americans in the United States. New York: Research Institute for the Study of Man.

Jahoda, Marie
1950   "Toward a social psychology of mental health." In Problems of Infancy and Childhood: Transactions of the Fourth Conference, Supplement II. New York: Josiah Macy Jr. Foundation.

James, Sherman, and Davis Kleinbaum
1976   "Socioeconomic stress and hypertension related mortality rates in North Carolina." American Journal of Public Health 66 (4):354–358.

Jericho, Donnie J.
1977   "Longitudinal changes in religious activity subscores of aged blacks." Black Aging 2 (4):17–24.

Jones, Faustine C.
1973   "The lofty role of the black grandmother." Crisis 80 (January):19–21.

Jöreskog, K. G.
1971   "Simultaneous factor analysis in several populations." Psychometrika 36:409–426.

Kasschau, Patricia, and Fernando Torres-Gil
1975   "Do ethnic decision-makers more accurately perceive the problems of the ethnic elderly than white decision-makers?" Unpublished paper. Andrus Gerontology Center, University of Southern California, Los Angeles, California.

Kerckhoff, Alan
1966   "Family patterns and morale in retirement." In Ida H. Simpson and John McKinney (eds.), Social Aspects of Aging. Durham, North Carolina: Duke University Press.

Kitano, Harry
1969   Japanese Americans: The Evolution of a Subculture. Englewood Cliffs, New Jersey: Prentice-Hall.

Klebba, Joan
1975   "Homicide trends in the United States, 1900–1974." Public Health Reports 90 (3):195–204.

Knapp, Martin R. J.
  1976   "Predicting the dimensions of life satisfaction." Journal of Gerontology 31 (September):595–604.

Koba Associates, Inc.
  1980   Condition Forecast: Economic Security and Productivity Among Black Aged in the Year 2000. Washington, D.C.: Koba Associates, Inc.

Kramer, Judith R.
  1970   The American Minority Community. New York: Thomas Y. Crowell.

Kubler-Ross, Elisabeth
  1969   On Death and Dying. New York: Macmillan.

Kutner, Bernard, and associates
  1956   Five-Hundred Over Sixty: A New Community Survey on Aging. New York: Russell Sage Foundation.

Kutzik, Alfred
  1979   "American social provision for the aged: an historical perspective." In Donald E. Gelfand and Alfred J. Kutzik (eds.), Ethnicity and Aging: Theory, Research, and Policy. New York: Springer Publishing Company.

Larson, Reed
  1978   "Thirty years of research on the subjective well-being of older Americans." Journal of Gerontology 33 (January):109–125.

Laslett, Peter
  1972   Household and Family in Past Time. New York: Cambridge University Press.

Lawton, M. Powell
  1972   "The dimensions of morale." In Donald Kent, Robert Kastenbaum, and Sylvia Sherwood (eds.), Research Planning and Action for the Elderly. New York: Behavioral Publications.

Leighton, Dorothea C.
  1972   "Cultural determinants of behavior: a neglected area." American Journal of Psychiatry 128 (8):1003–1004.

Lemon, Bruce W.; Vern L. Bengtson; and James A. Peterson
  1976   "An exploration of the activity theory of aging: activity types and life satisfaction among in-movers to a retirement community." In Cary S. Kart and Barbara B. Manard (eds.), Aging in America. New York: Alfred Publishing Company.

Leonard, Olen E.
  1967   "The older rural Spanish-speaking people of the southwest." In E. Grant Youmans (ed.), Older Rural Americans: A Sociological Analysis. Lexington: University of Kentucky Press.

Lesnoff-Caravaglia, Gari
  1978   "The 'babushka' or older woman in Soviet society." Paper presented during the 31st Annual Meeting of the Gerontological Society. Dallas, Texas.
  1980   "Attitudes and aging: US/USSR contrasted." In Gari Lesnoff-Caravaglia (ed.), Health Care of the Elderly. New York: Human Sciences Press.
  n.d.   "The babushka or older woman in Soviet society." In Gari Lesnoff-Caravaglia (ed.), The Older Woman. New York: Human Sciences Press.

Leutz, Walter N.
  1976   "The informal community caregiver: a link between the health care system and local

residents." American Journal of Orthopsychiatry 46 (4):678–688.

Levy, Jerrold E.
1967   "The older American Indian." In E. Grant Youmans (ed.), Older Rural Americans: A
        Sociological Analysis. Lexington: University of Kentucky Press.

Levy, Valerie
1978   "Self-reported needs of urban elderly black persons." Gerontologist 18 (5, part 2):94.

Liang, J.; Eva Kahana; and Edmund Doherty
1980   "Financial well-being among the aged: a further elaboration." Journal of Gerontology
        35 (3): 409–420.

Lieberson, Stanley
1963   Ethnic Patterns in American Cities. New York: Macmillan (Free Press).

Lincoln, C. Eric
1974   The Black Church Since Frazier. New York: Schocken Books.

Lindsay, Isabel Burns
1975   "Coping capacities of the black aged." In No Longer Young: The Older Woman in
        America. Institute of Gerontology, University of Michigan-Wayne State University,
        Ann Arbor, Michigan.

Lipman, Aaron
1965   "The Miami concerted services baseline study." Gerontologist 5: 256–259.
1969   "Latent function analysis in gerontological research." Gerontologist 9 (1): 33–36.
1978   "Ethnic and minority group content for courses in aging." In M. A. Seltzer and T.
        Hickey (eds.), Gerontology in Higher Education: Perspectives and Issues. Belmont,
        California: Wadsworth Publishing Company.
1980   "Prestige of the aged in Portugal: realistic appraisal and ritualistic deference." In Jon
        Hendricks (ed.), Being and Becoming Old, vol. 2. Farmingdale, New York: Baywood
        Publishing Company.

Lipman, Aaron, and K. J. Smith
1969   "Functionality of disengagement in old age." Journal of Gerontology 23: 517–521.

Litwak, Eugene
1965   "Extended kin relationships in an industrial democratic society." In Ethel Shanas and
        Gordon Strieb (eds.), Social Structure and the Family: Generational Relations. Englewood
        Cliffs, New Jersey: Prentice-Hall.

Litwak, Eugene, and Henry Meyer
1966   "A balance theory of coordination between bureaucratic organizations and community
        primary groups." Administrative Service Quarterly 11 (1): 31–58.

Lopata, Helena Z.
1971   "Widows as a minority group." Gerontologist 11 (1): 66–77.

Lowenthal, Marjorie F.
1964   Lives in Distress. New York: Basic Books.

Maddox, George L., and Elizabeth B. Douglass
1972   "Self assessment of health." In Erdman Palmore (ed.), Normal Aging, vol. 2. Durham,
        North Carolina: Duke University Press.

Manniello, Robert, and Phillip Farrell
1977   "Analysis of United States neonatal mortality statistics from 1968–1974 with specific
        reference to changing trends in major causalities." American Journal of Obstetric
        Gynecology 129 (6): 667–674.

Manton, Kenneth G.
  1980 "Sex and race specific mortality differentials in multiple cause of death data."
        Gerontologist 20 (4): 480–493.

Manton, Kenneth; Sharon S. Poss; and Steve Wing
  1979 "The black/white mortality crossover: investigation from the perspectives of the
        components of aging." Gerontologist 19 (3): 291–299.

Manuel, Ron C.
  1980a "An expanded outline and resource for teaching a course on the Sociology of the
        Black Aged." In George A. Sherman (ed.), Curriculum Guidelines in Minority
        Aging. Washington, D.C.: National Center on the Black Aged.
  1980b "Factors influencing the black elderly and their familial relationships." Paper
        presented at the 1980 Congressional Black Caucus during a workshop entitled
        "Black Families and the Black Elderly," Washington, D.C.
  1980c "Leadership factors in service delivery and minority elderly utilization." Journal
        of Minority Aging 5 (2): 218–232.
  1980d "Patterns of support for aged parents within black families: impact of intergenera-
        tional occupational mobility." Paper presented during the 33d Annual Meeting of the
        Gerontological Society of America, San Diego, California.
  1982a "Ethnic group identification." In David J. Mangen (ed.), Research Instruments in
        Social Gerontology. Minneapolis, Minnesota: University of Minnesota Press.
  1982b The Aged Black in America. Washington, D.C.: National Urban League.

Marquez, Garcia
  1970 Cien Anos de Soledad. Buenos Aires: Editorial Sud Americana.

Martin, Elmer P., and Joanne M. Martin
  1978 The Black Extended Family. Chicago: University of Chicago Press.

Martin, James G., and Clyde W. Franklin
  1973 Minority Group Relations. Columbus, Ohio: Charles E. Merrill Publishing Com-
        pany.

Matsumoto, Gary M.; Gerald M. Meredith; and Minoru Masuda
  1970 Ethnic Identification: Honolulu and Seattle Japanese-Americans 1 (1): 63–76.

Maykovich, Minako K.
  1977 "The differences of a minority researcher in minority communities." Journal of Social
        Issues 33 (4): 108–119.

McAdoo, Harriette
  1978 "Factors related to stability in upwardly mobile black families." Journal of Marriage
        and the Family 40 (November): 761–776.

McDonald, John, and Leatrice McDonald
  1964 "Chain migration, ethnic neighborhood formation and social networks." Milband
        Memorial Fund Quarterly 42 (January): 82–97.

McKay, J. B., and D. T. Cross
  1980 "Mental health services for older people living in the community." International
        Journal of Mental Health 8:117–131.

Meredith, William
  1964 "Notes on factorial invariance." Psychometrika 20 (2): 177–185.

Merton, Robert
  1949 "Discrimination and the American creed." In R. M. MacIver (ed.), Discrimination
        and National Welfare. New York: Harper & Row.

1968   Social Theory and Social Structure. New York: Free Press.

Metropolitan Life Insurance Company
1974   "Alcoholism in the United States." Statistical Bulletin (July).
1977   "Expectation of life among nonwhites." Statistical Bulletin (March).
1978   "Gains in longevity continue." Statistical Bulletin (July–September).

Millette, James
1971   The Black Revolution in the Caribbean. Curepe, Trinidad: Moko Enterprises Ltd.

Mitchell, J. Clyde
1969   "The concept and the use of social networks." In J. C. Mitchell (ed.), Social Networks in Urban Situations: Analyses of Personal Relationships in Central African Towns. Manchester, England: Manchester University Press.

Montagu, Ashley
1972   Statement on Race. 3d edition. New York: Oxford University Press.

Moore, Joan
1973   "Social constraints on sociological knowledge: academics and research concerning minorities." Social Problems 21 (1): 65–76.

Morgan, Leslie A., and Vern L. Bengtson
1976   "Measuring perceptions of aging across social strata." Paper presented at the 29th Annual Meeting of the Gerontological Society, New York, New York.

Mostwin, Danuta
1979   "Emotional needs of elderly Americans of Central and Eastern European background." In Donald Gelfand and Alfred Kutzik (eds.), Ethnicity and Aging: Theory, Research, and Policy. New York: Springer Publishing Company.

Mueller, Daniel
1980   "Social networks: a promising direction for research on the relationship of the social environment to psychiatric disorder." Social Science and Medicine 14A (1): 147–161.

Mulaik, S. A.
1972   The Foundations of Factor Analysis. New York: McGraw-Hill.

Murray, Albert
1973   "White norms, black deviation." In Joyce A. Ladner (ed.), The Death of White Sociology. New York: Vintage Books.

Myers, Lena M.
1978   "Elderly black women and stress resolution: exploratory study." Black Sociologist 8 (Fall): 29–37.
1980   Black Women: Do They Cope Better? Englewood Cliffs, New Jersey: Prentice-Hall.

Nam, Charles B., and Kathleen A. Ockay
1977   "Factors contributing to the mortality crossover pattern." Paper read at the 18th General Conference of the International Union for Scientific Study of Population, Mexico City.

National Center for Health Statistics (NCHS)
1972   Cohort Mortality and Survivorship: United States Death Registration Statistics, 1900–1968. Washington, D.C.: U.S. Government Printing Office.
1973a   Vital Statistics of the United States: Natality (volume 1). Washington, D.C.: U.S. Government Printing Office.
1973b   United States Vital and Health Statistics: Infant Mortality Rates: Relationships with Mother's Reproductive History (series 22, no. 15). Washington, D.C.: U.S. Government Printing Office.

1973c Monthly Vital Statistics Report, Supplement: Infant Mortality Rates by Legitimacy Status, United States, 1964–1966 (volume 20, no. 5). Washington, D.C.: U.S. Government Printing Office.

1973d Vital Natality Health Statistics: Infant Mortality Rates: Socioeconomic Factors, United States (series 22, no. 14). Washington, D.C.: U.S. Government Printing Office.

1973e Mortality Trends: Age, Color and Sex, United States, 1950–1969 (series 20, no. 15). Washington, D.C.: U.S. Government Printing Office.

1975 United States Life Tables: 1969–1971. Washington, D.C.: U.S. Government Printing Office.

1978a Advance Report, Monthly Vital Statistics: Final Mortality Statistics, 1976 (volume 27). Washington, D.C.: U.S. Government Printing Office.

1978b Vital Statistics of the United States: Mortality, part A, 1960, 1969, 1975 (volume 2). Washington, D.C.: U.S. Government Printing Office.

1980a Advance Report, Monthly Vital Statistics: Final Mortality Statistics, 1978 (volume 29). Washington, D.C.: U.S. Government Printing Office.

1980b Health United States, 1980. Washington, D.C.: United States Government Printing Office.

1980c Vital Statistics of the United States, 1978: Life Tables (volume 2, section 5). Washington, D.C.: United States Government Printing Office.

National Council on the Aging
1971 Triple Jeopardy: Myth or Reality. Washington, D.C.: National Council on Aging.

National Institute of Mental Health
1976 Issues in Mental Health and Aging: Proceedings of the Conference on Service Issues in Mental Health and Aging. Washington, D.C.: U.S. Government Printing Office.

National Institute on Aging
1980 "Minorities and how they grow old." Age Page (August). Washington, D.C.: U.S. Government Printing Office.

National Opinion Research Center
1977 Codebook for the Spring General Society Survey. Chicago: University of Chicago.

National Urban League
1964 Double Jeopardy: The Older Negro in America Today. New York: National Urban League.

Neugarten, Bernice
1979 "Time, age and the life cycle." American Journal of Psychiatry 136 (July): 887–894.

Neugarten, Bernice, and Robert Havighurst
1977 Social Policy, Social Ethics and the Aging Society. Washington, D.C.: U.S. Government Printing Office.

Neugarten, Bernice L.; Robert Havighurst; and Sheldon S. Tobin
1961 "The measurement of life satisfaction." Journal of Gerontology 16 (Summer): 134–143.

Nobles, Wade W.
1980 "African philosophy: foundations for black psychology." In Reginald A. Jones (ed.), Black Psychology. New York: Harper & Row.

Nowlin, John B.
1979 "Geriatric health status: influence of race and socioeconomic status." Journal of Minority Aging 4 (4): 93–98.

Nye, F. Ivan
1978 "Is choice and exchange theory the key?" Journal of Marriage and the Family 40:219–235.

Olsen, Marvin
 1970   "Social and political participation of blacks." American Sociological Review 35 (August): 682–696.

Orchowsky, Stan J., and Iris A. Parham
 1979   "Life satisfaction of blacks and whites: a life-span approach." Paper presented during the 32d Annual Meeting of the Gerontological Society, Washington, D.C.

Orcutt, Guy H., and associates
 1976   Policy Exploration Through Microanalytic Simulation. Washington, D.C.: Urban Institute.

Orshansky, Mollie
 1964   "The aged Negro and his income." Social Security Bulletin 27 (February): 3–13.

Owens, Yolanda; Fernando Torres-Gil; and Rosalie Wolf
 1973   "The 1971 White House Conference on Aging: An Overview of the Conference Activities." Unpublished paper. Heller Graduate School, Brandeis University, Waltham, Massachusetts.

Palmore, Erdman
 1969   "Sociological aspects of aging." In Ewald Busse and Eric Pfeiffer (eds.), Behavior and Adaptation in Late Life. Boston: Little, Brown and Company.

Palmore, Erdman, and Vira Kivett
 1977   "Changes in life satisfaction: a longitudinal study of persons aged 46–70." Journal of Gerontology 32 (May): 311–316.

Palmore, Erdman, and Clark Luikart
 1972   "Health and social factors related to life satisfaction." Journal of Health and Social Behavior 13: 68–80.

Paringer, Lynn, and associates
 1979   Health Status and Use of Medical Services: Evidence on the Poor, the Blacks and the Rural Elderly. Washington, D.C.: Urban Institute.

Paterson, James
 1964   "Marketing and the working class family." In Arthur Shostak and William Gomberg (eds.), Blue Collar World: Studies of the American Worker. Englewood Cliffs, New Jersey: Prentice-Hall.

Patterson, R.
 1976   "Community mental health centers: a survey of services for the elderly." In Issues in Mental Health and Aging: Proceedings of the Conference on Service Issues in Mental Health and Aging. Washington, D.C.,: National Institute of Public Health.

Paz, O.
 1959   El Laberinto de la Soledad. Mexico: Fondo de Cultura Econominca.

Petersen, William
 1971   Japanese Americans: Oppression and Success. New York: Random House.

Peterson, John
 1977   "The social psychology of black aging: the effects of self-esteem and perceived control on the adjustment of older black adults." In Wilbur H. Watson and associates (eds.), Health and the Black Aged. Washington, D.C.: National Center on Black Aged.

Pitts, James P.
 1974   "The study of race consciousness: comments on new directions." American Journal of Sociology 80 (3): 665–683.

Pratt, Henry J.
   1974   "Old age associates in national politics." Annals of the American Academy of Political
          and Social Science 415 (September): 106–119.

Putnam, Jackson K.
   1970   Old Age Politics in California. Stanford, California: Stanford University Press.

Raab, Earl, and Seymour M. Lipset
   1962   "The prejudiced society." In Earl Raab (ed.), American Race Relations Today. New
          York: Doubleday & Company.

Ragan, Pauline
   1973   "Aging among blacks, Mexican-Americans, and Anglos: problems and possibilities of
          research as reflected in the literature." Unpublished paper. Andrus Gerontology
          Center, University of Southern California, Los Angeles, California.

Ragan, Pauline, and José Cuellar
   1975   "Response acquiescence in surveys: a study of yeasaying among Chicanos and Anglos."
          Paper presented at the Annual Meeting of the American Association for Public
          Opinion Research, Los Angeles, California.

Ragan, Pauline, and Mary Simonin
   1977   Social and Cultural Contexts of Aging: Aging Among Blacks and Mexican Americans
          in the United States: A Selected Bibliography. Los Angeles: Andrus Gerontology
          Center, University of Southern California.

Ravetz, Jerome R.
   1973   Scientific Knowledge and its Social Problems. New York: Oxford University Press.

Reynolds, D. K., and Richard Kalish
   1974   "Anticipation of futurity as a function of ethnicity and age." Journal of Gerontology 29
          (March): 224–236.

Riley, Matilda
   1973   "Aging and cohort succession: interpretations and misinterpretations." Public Opinion
          Quarterly 37 (Spring): 35–49.

Riley, Matilda W.; Marilyn Johnson; and Anne Foner
   1972   Aging and Society, volume 3: A Sociology of Age Stratification. New York: Basic
          Books.

Rose, Peter I.
   1981   They and We: Racial and Ethnic Relations in the United States. 3d edition. New York:
          Random House.

Rosenberg, George S.
   1968   "Age, poverty and isolation from friends in the urban working class." Journal of
          Gerontology 23 (4): 533–538.

Rosenmayr, Leopold, and Eva Kockeis
   1963   "Propositions for a sociological theory of action and the family." International Social
          Science Journal 15 (4): 410–426.

Rubenstein, Daniel J.
   1971   "An examination of social participation among a national sample of black and white
          elderly." Aging and Human Development 2 (3): 172–182.

Rummel, Rudolph J.
   1970   Applied Factor Analysis. Evanston: Northwestern University Press.

Rushforth, Norman, and associates
    1977   "Violent death in a metropolitan country." New England Journal of Medicine 297
            (10): 531–538.

Ruther, Martin, and Allen Dobson
    1981   "Equal treatment and unequal benefits: a re-examination of the use of medicare
            services by race: 1967–1976." Health Care Financing Review 3 (Winter): 55–83.

Ryan, William
    1971   Blaming the Victim. New York: Vintage Books.

Safier, Ellen, and Jane Pfouts
    1979   "Social network analysis: a new tool for understanding individual and family functioning."
            Paper presented during the Annual Program Meeting of the Council on Social Work
            Education, Boston, Massachusetts.

Sage, Wayne
    1978   "Choosing the good death." In Harold Cox (ed.), Focus: Aging. Guilford, Connecti-
            cut: Dushkin Publishing Group.

Sainer, Janet; Louise L. Schwartz; and Theodore G. Jackson
    1973   "Steps in the development of a comprehensive service delivery system for the elderly."
            Gerontologist 13 (3): 98.

Sandberg, Neil C.
    1972   Ethnic Identity and Assimilation: The Polish American Community: Case Study of
            Metropolitan Los Angeles. New York: Praeger Publishers.

Sarason, Seymour, and associates
    1977   Human Services and Resource Network. San Francisco: Jossey Bass.

Sauer, William
    1977   "Morale of the urban aged: a regression analysis by race." Journal of Gerontology 32
            (September): 600–608.

Saunders, C.
    1967   The Management of Terminal Illness. London: Hospital Medicine Publications.

Scanlon, William, and associates
    1979   Long Term Care: Current Experience and a Framework for Analysis. Washington,
            D.C.: Urban Institute.

Scanzoni, John H.
    1971   The Black Family in Modern Society. Boston: Allyn and Bacon.

Schaie, K. Warner
    1979   "The primary mental abilities in adulthood: an exploration in the development of
            psychometric intelligence." In Paul B. Baltes and Orville G. Brin (eds.), Life-span
            Development and Behavior, vol. 2. New York: Academic Press.

Schaie, K. Warner, and Christopher K. Hertzog
    1982   "Longitudinal methods." In B. B. Wolman (ed.), Handbook of Developmental Psy-
            chology. Englewood Cliffs, New Jersey: Prentice-Hall.

Schaie, K. Warner, and Iris A. Parham
    1974   "Social responsibility in adulthood: ontogenetic and sociocultural change." Journal of
            Personality and Social Psychology 30: 438–492.
    1976   "Stability of adult personality traits: fact or fable?" Journal of Personality and Social
            Psychology 34: 146–158.

Schermerhorn, R. A.
  1970   Comparative Ethnic Relations: A Framework for Theory and Research. New York: Random House.

Schiller, Bradley R.
  1980   Poverty and Discrimination. Englewood Cliffs, New Jersey: Prentice-Hall.

Schneider, Robert L.
  1979   "Barriers to effective outreach in Title VIII Nutrition Programs." Gerontologist 19 (2): 163–168.

Schonfield, David
  1973   "Future commitments and successful aging: the random sample." Journal of Gerontology 28 (2): 189–196.

Sears, David O., and John B. McConalay
  1973   The Politics of Violence. Boston: Houghton-Mifflin.

Secord, Paul F., and Carl W. Backman
  1974   Social Psychology. 2d edition. New York: McGraw-Hill.

Selye, Hans
  1974   Stress Without Distress. New York: New American Library.

Sherman, George A.
  1978   Research and Training in Minority Aging. Washington, D.C.: National Center on the Black Aged.
  1980   Curriculum Guidelines in Minority Aging. Washington, D.C.: National Center on the Black Aged.
  1983   Curriculum Modules and the Black Aged. Washington, D.C.: National Caucus and Center on the Black Aged.

Shibutani, Tamotsu, and Kwan M. Kawn
  1965   Ethnic Stratification. New York: Macmillan.

Simpson, R. L.
  1972   Theories of Social Exchange. Morristown, New Jersey: General Learning Press.

Slater, Philip
  1976   The Pursuit of Loneliness: American Culture at the Breaking Point. Boston: Beacon Press.

Smith, Stanley H.
  1967   "The older rural Negro." In E. Grant Youmans (ed.), Older Rural Americans: A Sociological Analysis. Lexington: University of Kentucky Press.

Smith, T. Lynn
  1957   "The changing number and distribution of the aged Negro population of the United States." Phylon 18 (4): 339–354.

Smith, Tom W.
  1980   "Ethnic measurement and identification." Ethnicity 7 (1): 78–95.

Snyder, Donald C.
  1979   "Future pension status of the black elderly." In Donald Gelfand and Alfred Kutzik (eds.), Ethnicity and Aging. New York: Springer Publishing Company.

Solomon, Barbara
  1970   "Ethnicity, mental health and the older black aged." Proceedings of the Workshop on Ethnicity, Mental Health and Aging, Andrus Gerontology Center, University of Southern California, Los Angeles, California.

1977   "Better planning through research." In E. Percil Stanford (ed.), Comprehensive Service Delivery Systems for the Minority Aged. San Diego, California: University Center on Aging, San Diego State University.

Sotomayer, Frank
1973   "An explosion of Chicano literary consciousness." Los Angeles Times (January 28).

Spiegel, John
1971   Transactions: The Interplay Between Individual, Family and Society. New York: Science-House/Aronson.

Spiegelman, Mortimer
1968   "The curve of human mortality." Proceedings of seminars (1965-1969) of the Duke University Council on Aging and Human Development, Durham, North Carolina.

Spreitzer, Elmer, and Eldon E. Snyder
1974   "Correlates of life satisfaction among the aged." Journal of Gerontology 29 (July): 454-458.

Stack, Carol B.
1974   All Our Kin: Strategies for Survival in a Black Community. New York: Harper & Row.

Stagner, Ross
1981   "Stress, strain, coping and defense." Research on Aging 3 (1): 3-32.

Stanford, E. Percil
1977   Comprehensive Service Delivery Systems for the Minority Aged. San Diego, California: University Center on Aging, San Diego State University.
1978   The Elder Black. San Diego, California: University Center on Aging, San Diego State University.
1981   Minority Aging: Policy Issues for the '80s. Proceedings of the 7th National Institute on Minority Aging. San Diego, California: University Center on Aging, San Diego State University.

Stanford, E. Percil, and Clifford Alexander
1981   "Elderly in transition." In Gari Lesnoff-Caravaglia (ed.), Aging and the Human Condition. New York: Human Sciences Press.

Staples, Robert
1976   Introduction to Black Sociology. New York: McGraw-Hill.
1978   The Black Family: Essays and Studies. Belmont, California: Wadsworth Publishing Company.

Staples, Robert, and Alfredo Mirandé
1980   "Racial and cultural variations among American families: a decennial review of the literature on minority families." Journal of Marriage and the Family 42 (November): 887-903.

Stones, M. J., and A. Kozma
1980   "Issues relating to the usage and conceptualization of mental health constructs by gerontologists." International Journal of Aging and Human Development 11 (4): 269-281.

Streib, Gordon F.
1965   "Are the aged a minority group?" In Alvin W. Gouldner and S. M. Miller (eds.), Applied Sociology. New York: Free Press of Glencoe.

Sue, Stanley, and Nathaniel N. Wagner
1973   Asian Americans: Psychological Perspectives. Ben Lomond, California: Science and Behavior Books.

Sumner, William G.
1906   Folkways. Boston: Ginn and Company.

Sussman, Marvin
1959   "The isolated nuclear families: fact or fiction." Social Problems 6 (Spring): 333–340.

Suzuki, Peter T.
1975   Minority Group Aged in America: A Comprehensive Bibliography of Recent Publi-
        cations on Blacks, Mexican Americans, Native Americans, Chinese and Japanese.
        Omaha, Nebraska: Council of Planning Librarians.

Talley, Thomas A., and Jerome Kaplan
1956   "The Negro aged." Gerontological Society Newsletter 3 (4).

Thernstron, Steven
1980   The Harvard Encyclopedia of American Ethnic Groups. Cambridge, Massachusetts:
        Harvard University Press.

Thibaut, John, and Harold Kelley
1959   The Social Psychology of Groups. New York: John Wiley and Sons.

Thompson, Gayle B.
1978   "Pension coverage and benefits, 1972: findings from the retirement history study."
        Social Security Bulletin 41 (2): 3–17.
1979   "Black-white differences in private pensions: findings from the retirement history
        study." Social Security Bulletin 42 (2): 15–22.

Trela, James E., and Jay H. Sokolovsky
1979   "Culture, ethnicity and policy for the aged." In Donald Gelfand and Alfred Kutzik
        (eds.), Ethnicity and Aging. New York: Springer Publishing Company.

Turner, Jonathan H.
1978   The Structure of Sociological Theory. Homewood, Illinois: Dorsey Press.

United States Bureau of the Census
1970   "Characteristics of the population." 1970 Census of the Population, volume 1.
        Washington, D.C.: U.S. Government Printing Office.
1975   Historical Statistics of the United States, Colonial Times to 1970: Bicentennial Edi-
        tion, part 1. Washington, D.C.: U.S. Government Printing Office.
1977   "Projections of the Population of the U.S.: 1977–2050." Current Population Reports
        (series P-25, no. 704). Washington, D.C.: U.S. Government Printing Office.
1980a   "Marital status and living arrangements: March 1979." Current Population Reports
        (series P-20, no. 349). Washington, D.C.: U.S. Government Printing Office.
1980b   "Population profile of the United States: 1979." Current Population Reports (series
        P-20, no. 350). Washington, D.C.: U.S. Government Printing Office.
1980c   "Money income and poverty status of families and persons in the United States, 1979:
        Advanced Report." Current Population Reports (series P-60, no. 125). Washington,
        D.C.: U.S. Government Printing Office.
1981   "Age, sex, race, and Spanish origin of the population.," 1980 Census of Population
        Supplementary Reports: May 1981. Washington, D.C.: U.S. Government Printing
        Office.

United States Commission on Civil Rights
1978   Social Indicators of Equality for Minorities and Women. Washington, D.C.: U.S.
        Government Printing Office.

United States Department of Health and Human Services
1980   Health of the Disadvantaged: Chartbook-II. Washington, D.C.: U.S. Government
        Printing Office.

United States Department of Health, Education and Welfare
    1977   "Program and demographic characteristics of Supplemental Security Beneficiaries."
            Annual Report, Social Security Administration. Washington, D.C.: U.S. Government
            Printing Office.
    1978   "National summary of program operation under Older Americans Act, FY 1978."
            Administration on Aging. Washington, D.C.: U.S. Government Printing Office.

United States Department of Housing and Urban Development
    1979   Housing for the Elderly and Handicapped. Office of Policy Development and Re-
            search. Washington, D.C.: U.S. Government Printing Office.

United States Department of Labor
    1979   "Employment and Training Report to the President." Washington, D.C.: U.S.
            Government Printing Office.

United States Health Care Financing Administration
    n.d.   Medicare: Health Insurance for the Aged and Disabled, 1978: Utilization and
            Reimbursement Summary. Washington, D.C.: U.S. Government Printing Office.
            (Forthcoming)

Uzoka, Azubike
    1979   "The myth of the nuclear family: historical background and clinical implications."
            American Psychologist 34 (November): 1095–1106.

Valentine, Charles
    1972   Black Studies and Anthropology: Scholarly and Political Interests in Afro-American
            Culture. A McCaleb Module in Anthropology. Reading, Massachusetts: Addison-
            Wesley.

Valle, Ramon, and Lydia Mendoza
    1978   The Elder Latino. San Diego, California: University Center on Aging, San Diego State
            University.

Villemez, Wayne J., and H. Wiswell
    1978   "The impact of diminishing discrimination on the internal size distribution of black
            income: 1954–74." Social Forces 56 (3): 1019–1034.

Vroman, Wayne
    1977   "Worker upgrading and the business cycle." Brookings Papers on Economic Activity
            1: 229–250.

Wagley, Charles, and Marvin Harris
    1964   Minorities in the New World. New York: Columbia University Press.

Waldron, Ingrid, and Joseph Eyer
    1975   "Socioeconomic causes of the recent rise in death rates for 15–24 year olds." Social
            Sciences and Medicine 9: 383–396.

Waldron, Ingrid, and Susan Johnston
    1976   "Why do women live longer than men." Journal of Human Stress 2 (2): 19–30.

Walker, Kenneth; Arlene McBride; and Mary Vachon
    1977   "Social support networks in the crisis of bereavement." Social Science and Medicine 11
            (1): 34–41.

Wallace, Helen
    1979   "Selected aspects of perinatal casualties." Clinical Pediatrics 18 (4): 213–223.

Walther, Robin
    1976   "Economics and the older population." In Donna S. Woodruff and James E. Birren

(eds.), Aging: Scientific Perspectives and Social Issues. New York: D. Van Nostrand Company.

Watson, Wilbur H.
1980a Stress and Old Age: A Case Study of Black Aging and Transplantation Shock. New Brunswick, New Jersey: Transaction Books.
1980b "Older frail rural blacks: a conceptualization and analysis." National Center on the Black Aged/Quarterly Contact 3 (4): 1–2.
1982   Aging and Social Behavior: An Introduction to Social Gerontology. Boston: Wadsworth Health Science Publishers.

Watson, Wilbur H., and associates
1977   Health and the Black Aged: Proceedings of a Research Symposium. Washington, D.C.: National Center on the Black Aged.

Watson, Wilbur H., and Robert J. Maxwell
1977   Human Aging and Dying: A Study in Sociocultural Gerontology. New York: St. Martin's Press.

Wax, Murray L.
1971   Indian Americans: Unity and Diversity. Englewood Cliffs, New Jersey: Prentice-Hall.

Wax, Rosalie H., and Robert K. Thomas
1961   "American Indians and white people." Phylon 22 (4): 305–317.

Weinstock, Camilda, and Ruth Bennett
1968   "Problems in communication to nurses among residents of a racially heterogeneous nursing home." Gerontologist 8 (1): 72–75.

Weiss, Carol
1977   "Survey researchers and minority communities." Journal of Social Issues 33 (4): 20–35.

Weiss, Noel
1976   "Recent trends in violent deaths among young adults in the United States." American Journal of Epidemiology 103 (4): 416–422.

White House Conference on Aging (WHCOA)
1971   Special Concerns Sessions Reports: Asian American Elderly; Aging and Aged Blacks; the Elderly Indian; Spanish Speaking Elderly. Washington, D.C.: U.S. Government Printing Office.

Wilson, William J.
1978   The Declining Significance of Race: Blacks and Changing American Institutions. Chicago: University of Chicago Press.

Wirth, Louis
1945   "The problem of minority groups." In Ralph Linton (ed.), The Science of Man in the World Crisis. New York: Columbia University Press.

World Health Organization
1959   The Public Health Aspects of the Aging of the Population. Copenhagen: World Health Organization (Regional Office for Europe).

Wright, Erik O., and Luca Perrone
1977   "Marxist class categories and income inequality." American Sociological Review 42 (1): 32–55.

Wylie, Floyd M.
1971   "Attitudes toward aging and the aged among black Americans: some historical perspectives." Aging and Human Development 2 (1): 66–70.

Yetman, Norman R., and C. Hoy Steele
    1971   Majority and Minority: The Dynamics of Racial and Ethnic Relations. Boston: Allyn
            and Bacon.

Young, Donald
    1932   American Minority Peoples. New York: Harper and Brothers Publishers.

Zackler, Jack; S. L. Andelman; and F. Bauer
    1969   "The young adolescent as an obstetric risk." American Journal of Obstetrics and
            Gynecology 103 (3): 305–311.

Zak, Itai
    1973   "Dimensions of Jewish-American identity." Psychological Reports 33 (3): 891–900.

INDEX

Abbott, Julian, 151, 206

Achenbaum, W. Andrew, 11

Activity Model: and gerontology, 192; and the middle-class view, 193–94; policy and the, 191; research on, 191

Adam, June, 227

Adams, David L., 86

Administration on Aging (AoA), 11, 144–45

Advocacy, 137, 143–50; area agencies and, 145; consequences of, 150; government policies and, 143–44; history of, 146; and McLain movement, 144; and minority issues, 150; of minority and nonminority decision makers, 148; organizations, 144–45; and sociopolitical developments, 137; strategies of, 147; and Townsend movement, 144; values, 137, 149, 150. *See also* Minority aging professionals

Aged, 3, 51, 71; homogeneity of, 4, 5, 13, 89, 134, 144, 204. *See also* Asian elderly; Black elderly; Chinese elderly; Hispanic elderly; Native American elderly

Aging and Human Development, 8

Aging effects; and cohort or generation, 212, 223–34, 227–30; measuring, 212–13, 223–30; sequential strategies for determining, 224–25; and time or period, 212, 223–24, 228. *See also* Sequential strategies

Alexander, Clifford, 110

Allport, Gordon, 25

Almquist, Elizabeth M., 192

Althauser, R. P., 52

American Psychiatric Association, 90

Andelman, S. L., 56, 60

Anderson, Ronald, 177

Area agencies on aging, 145

Arensberg, Conrad, 117

Asian elderly: age and sex composition of, 36–37; literature on, 25; as a minority, 14, 23–24, 50–51, 232; Pacific, 10, 24, 145; population size, 33; and the White House Conference on Aging (1971), 9. *See also* Ethnic minority elderly

Babushka: as a care-giving role, 109–14; and employment, 111; as influenced by Soviet culture, 110, 113; and retirement, 111. *See also* Family; Grandmother

Backman, Carl W., 18

Bacon, John, 225–26

Bahr, Howard M., 15

Barron, Robert A., 19

Batey, Mignon O., 138

Bauer, F., 56, 60

Beard, Virginia H., 84, 86

Beatty, Walter M., 6

Bechill, William, 144–45

Bell, Duran, 77, 170, 181, 206

Bengtson, Vern L., 10, 79, 191, 204, 207, 218–22

Bennett, Ruth, 19

Bernard, Viola, 89

Berreman, Gerald D., 15

Bianco, Carla, 117

Biculturation, 96

Bild, Bernice, 86

Billingsley, Andrew, 109, 219

Binstock, Robert H., 14, 149

Black consciousness, 246

Black elderly: African origins, 104–06; age

CONTRIBUTING AUTHORS

Mignon O. Batey
Chief, Geropsychiatry Department, Kedren Community Mental Health Center, Los Angeles, California.

Vern L. Bengtson, Ph.D.
Professor of Sociology, Department of Sociology, and Laboratory Chief in the Gerontology Research Institute of the Andrus Gerontology Center, University of Southern California, Los Angeles, California.

David M. Brodsky, Ph.D.
Associate Professor and Chairperson, Department of Political Science, University of Tennessee at Chattanooga, Chattanooga, Tennessee.

Linda Burton
Doctoral candidate in the Department of Sociology, University of Southern California, Los Angeles, California.

Allen C. Carter, Ph.D.
Clinical psychologist in private practice; also member of the staffs of the Kirkwood Mental Health Center and the Department of Psychology at Morehouse College, Atlanta, Georgia.

James H. Carter, M.D.
Associate Professor of Psychiatry, Division of Community and Social Psychiatry, Duke University Medical Center, and Chief Consulting Psychiatrist, Lincoln Community Health Center, Durham, North Carolina.

Bertram J. Cohler, Ph.D.
William Rainey Harper Associate Professor of Social Sciences in the College and Associate Professor, Department of Behavioral Sciences (Committee on Human Development), University of Chicago, Chicago, Illinois.

John N. Colen, Ph.D.
Dean, School of Social Work, California State University at Sacramento, Sacramento, California.

Helen Foster Giles
Assistant Professor of Biology, Cheyney State College, Cheyney, Pennsylvania.

Bernice Catherine Harper
Medical Care Advisor, Office of Professional and Scientific Affairs, Health Care Financing Administration, United States Department of Health and Human Services.

Maurice Jackson, Ph.D.
Professor of Sociology, Department of Sociology, University of California at Riverside, Riverside, California.

Solomon G. Jacobson, Ph.D.
Vice President for Research, Morgan Management Systems, Inc., Columbia, Maryland.

Bohdan Kolody, Ph.D.
Associate Professor of Sociology, Department of Sociology, San Diego State University, San Diego, California.

Gari Lesnoff-Caravaglia, Ph.D.
Associate Professor of Gerontology, Gerontology Program, Sangamon State University, Springfield, Illinois.

Aaron Lipman, Ph.D.
Professor of Sociology, Department of Sociology and the Institute on Aging, University of Miami, Coral Gables, Florida.

Kenneth G. Manton, Ph.D.
Assistant Medical Research Professor, Department of Family and Community Medicine; Assistant Director of the Center for Demographic Studies; Adjunct Assistant Professor of Sociology, Duke University, Durham, North Carolina.

Ron C. Manuel, Ph.D.
Associate Professor of Sociology, Department of Sociology, Howard University, Washington, D.C.

Stan Orchowsky
Doctoral candidate in the Department of Psychology, Virginia Commonwealth University, Richmond, Virginia.

Iris Parham, Ph.D.
Chairperson of the Gerontology Department, Virginia Commonwealth University, Richmond, Virginia.

John Reid, Ph.D.
Associate Professor of Sociology, Department of Sociology, Howard University, Washington, D.C.

Antonio B. Rey, Ph.D.
Research scientist, Center for Studies in Aging, North Texas State University, Denton, Texas.

Lodis Rhodes, Ph.D.
Associate Professor of Public Administration, Lyndon B. Johnson School of Public Affairs, University of Texas at Austin, Austin, Texas.

K. Warner Schaie, Ph.D.
Professor of Psychology and Director of the Gerontology Research Institute, Andrus Gerontology Center, University of Southern California, Los Angeles, California.

Oliver W. Slaughter, Ph.D.
Clinical psychologist and Executive Director of Counseling and Psychological Associates, Inc., Inglewood, California.

Donald C. Snyder, Ph.D.
Assistant Professor of Economics, Department of Economics, Goucher College, Towson, Maryland.

Sue Perkins Taylor, Ph.D.
Assistant Professor of Anthropology and Director of Minority Aging Program, Institute of Gerontology, Wayne State University, Detroit, Michigan.

Fernando Torres-Gil, Ph.D.
Assistant Professor of Gerontology and Public Administration, Leonard Davis School of Gerontology, University of Southern California, Los Angeles, California.

Wilbur H. Watson, Ph.D.
Ware Professor of Sociology and Chairperson, Department of Sociology and Anthropology, Atlanta University, Atlanta, Georgia.

James L. Wood, Ph.D.
Associate Professor of Sociology, Department of Sociology, San Diego State University, San Diego, California.

About the Editor

RON C. MANUEL is Associate Professor of Sociology at Howard University in Washington, D.C. His earlier writings have appeared in journals such as the *Journal of Minority Aging* and the *International Review of Modern Sociology*. He is co-author, with Vern Bengtson of "The Sociology of Aging: Implications for the Helping Professions" in *Aging: Prospects and Issues* by R. H. Davis. He is also author of a major forthcoming publication, tentatively entitled "The Aged Black in America," which will update the Urban League's 1964 study on "Double Jeopardy and the Black Aged."